WEST-COUNTRY HISTORICAL STUDIES

WEST-COUNTRY
HISTORICAL
STUDIES

by

H. P. R. FINBERG

M.A., D.LITT., F.S.A., F.R.HIST.S.

Professor Emeritus of English Local History
University of Leicester

DAVID & CHARLES

NEWTON ABBOT

1969

7153 4348 3

Printed in Great Britain by
Latimer Trend & Company Limited
for David & Charles (Publishers) Ltd
South Devon House   Railway Station
Newton Abbot   Devon

TO
THE PRESIDENT AND FELLOWS
OF CLARE HALL
CAMBRIDGE

CONTENTS

BIBLIOGRAPHICAL NOTE

'Fact and Fiction from Crediton' was originally published under another title in *The Antiquaries Journal*, XLVIII, 1968, pp. 59–86. 'St Patrick at Glastonbury' is based on the author's O'Donnell Lecture delivered (10 May 1966) in the University of Oxford. First printed by Messrs Browne and Nolan in *The Irish Ecclesiastical Record*, it is re-issued here with corrections and additions. 'Church and State in Twelfth-Century Devon' appeared originally in the *Transactions of the Devonshire Association*, LXXV, 1943, pp. 245–57. The remaining items are reprinted, with corrections, from *Devonshire Studies*, 1952, a book now out of print and very scarce.

ABBREVIATIONS

AD   = *Adami de Domerham Historia de Rebus Gestis Glastoniensibus*, ed. T. Hearne, Oxford, 1727.

BM   = British Museum.

CCR   = *Calendar of Close Rolls.*

CPR   = *Calendar of Patent Rolls.*

CS   = *Cartularium Saxonicum*, ed. W. de G. Birch. 3 vols. London, 1885–93.

DA   = Devonshire Association (*Transactions*).

DB   = Domesday Book.

DCNQ = *Devon & Cornwall Notes & Queries.*

EHR   = *English Historical Review.*

ETC   = 'Some Early Tavistock Charters' (EHR LXII).

HMC   = Historical Manuscripts Commission.

JG   = *Johannis . . . Glastoniensis Chronica sive Historia de Rebus Glastoniensibus*, ed. T. Hearne, Oxford, 1726.

K   = Kemble, J. M. (ed.), *Codex Diplomaticus Aevi Saxonici*. 6 vols. London, 1839–48.

PND   = *The Place-Names of Devon*, Cambridge, 1931–2.

PRO   = Public Record Office.

VCH   = (followed by the name of a county) Victoria County History.

W   = Woburn Abbey muniments (now in the Devon County Record Office).

TWO ACTS OF STATE

AMONG the treasures which that omnivorous and none too scrupulous antiquary Sir Robert Cotton gathered into his collection was a royal charter dating from near the middle of the ninth century. He seems to have purchased or perhaps just 'borrowed' it from the dean and chapter of Winchester, for the parchment is endorsed in a handwriting which has been identified as that of John Chase, a conscientious archivist who was appointed clerk to the chapter in 1622, nine years before Cotton's death.[1] Fortunately it escaped the fire which damaged part of Cotton's library in 1731, and since 1753 it has been in the British Museum.[2] It remained unpublished until 1840, when J. M. Kemble printed it as No. CCLX in the second volume of his *Codex Diplomaticus*. It has since been widely recognized as a document of unique historical, topographical, and linguistic interest.

The charter may well have been housed at Winchester from the time when it was written, for Winchester, then the chief city of Wessex, was an obvious place of deposit for the royal archives. But the act of state which it embodies was carried out at Dorchester on the second day of Christmas in the year 847. Professor Dorothy Whitelock points out that since the year was then probably reckoned as beginning at Christmas—or, according to other authorities, on the 24th of September—we should read this as 26 December 846.[3]

The document leads off with a solemn preamble, quoting scripture on the duty of giving alms and helping one's neighbours in their need. Then Æthelwulf, king of the West Saxons, goes on to say that with the consent and leave of his bishops and chief men he has ordered twenty hides of land to be

[1] P. Chaplais, 'The Origin and Authenticity of the Royal Anglo-Saxon Diploma', *Journal of the Society of Archivists*, III, 1965, p. 57. On Cotton's depredations, see *A Guide to a select Exhibition of Cottonian Manuscripts*, 6 May 1931, pp. 5, 6.
[2] BM Cotton Ch. VIII, 36, reproduced in *Facsimiles of Ancient Charters in the British Museum*, II, 30.
[3] *English Historical Documents*, I, 1955, p. 482.

assigned to himself in hereditary ownership. The occupants are to be exempt from every kind of secular obligation except military service and the building of bridges. The Latin text does not say where the twenty hides are, but a vernacular survey of the boundary which follows places them in "Homme." The charter is attested by the king's second son Æthelbald and by Ealhstan, bishop of Sherborne, with two abbots, two ealdormen, and seven thegns.

Scholars are agreed in recognizing the charter as an authentic record of a politically important if somewhat enigmatic act. Kemble remarked that Æthelwulf would not have needed a charter had the land been already his own. "And if not land of his own, whose could it be, that he and his council had thus a right to dispose of it? It was clearly the public land or *Folcscearu*, which, in his capacity of king on the one part, with the assent of his nobles, he conveyed to himself, in his private capacity, on the other."[1]

Kemble is attempting here to define the status of the twenty hides before 846. He does not discuss Æthelwulf's reasons for appropriating them, nor does he ask what use was in fact made of the appropriation. In W. H. Stevenson's opinion, on the other hand, the twenty hides were already Æthelwulf's own property, and the charter was really a disguised form of benefaction to the Church. Stevenson calls it "a famous case" of land being dedicated by charter to religious uses. "The exemption from royal services is meaningless if Æthelwulf intended to keep the land in his own possession. That he did not so intend is proved by the proem, in which the duty of almsgiving is inculcated."[2]

To this interpretation Stenton has added the weight of his authority. "The king," he says, "is, in fact, removing every kind of secular burden from a portion of his demesne in order that it may be devoted without encumbrance to the service of religion." And he adds: "The fact that he could only do this by making a charter granting the estate to himself is a curious illustration of the limited range of conceptions which governed Old English land law in the ninth century."[3]

[1] J. M. Kemble, *Codex Diplomaticus Ævi Saxonici*, 1839–48, II, p. ix.
[2] W. H. Stevenson, *Asser's Life of King Alfred*, Oxford, 1904, p. 189.
[3] F. M. Stenton, *Anglo-Saxon England*, Oxford, 1943, p. 305.

Curious indeed! The criticism prompts us to ask whether the ideas of King Æthelwulf and his counsellors were really so limited as to dictate such a roundabout method of going to work. Kemble, Stevenson, and Stenton are three of the greatest names in Anglo-Saxon scholarship, but all three discussed the charter of 846 without knowing exactly where the land lay. Kemble did not attempt to solve this problem. Birch, when he re-edited the charter, placed "Homme" tentatively in Dorset.[1] Then a private correspondent, G. H. Wheeler, wrote to Haverfield suggesting that it should be sought in Devon, "at the neck of the peninsula which has Start Point at its s.e. extremity."[2] Since then it has been accepted that the charter is concerned with the part of Devon commonly known as the South Hams. In 1929 the late Frances Rose-Troup tried to elucidate the boundary, but her aptitude for the work was not equal to her zeal. Of thirty-three landmarks she identified only three correctly, which is as much as could be expected seeing that she took as her point of departure a wholly imaginary stone on Dartmoor.[3] The compilers of *The Place-Names of Devon* made a brief note of her findings but were plainly not impressed by them, and her attempt could safely be ignored had it not been cited in the authoritative context of Professor Whitelock's translation of the charter.[4]

To interpret the bounds has been a formidable task, but it will be well worth while to set them out in detail, for besides helping us to a right understanding of Æthelwulf's act of state they throw a gleam of new light on the early history of Devon. With the help of references to the National Grid, which are supplied, they can be followed on sheets SX 64, 74, 75, and 85 of the 2½-inch Ordnance Survey.

1. First into *Mercecumb*,
    A combe which serves as a *mearc* or boundary. The name Kingston, although apparently not recorded until the thirteenth century (PND p. 279), solves the difficulty created by the omission of any point of

[1] CS 451.
[2] F. Haverfield, *The Romanization of Roman Britain*, 4th ed., 1923, p. 26 *n*.
[3] DA LXI, 1929, pp. 266–76.
[4] *English Historical Documents*, 1, p. 482; PND p. lix. With some necessary emendations Professor Whitelock's version has been followed in this study.

departure for the survey. This royal *tun* is bounded on the west by the River Erme. From a creek between Orcheton Wood and Tor Wood the boundary enters the *mercecumb* at 628490.

2. then to the green pit,

The flat ground where Clyng Mill stands, at the foot of the steep combe.

3. then to the tor at the source of *Mercecumb*.

A towering rock-pile, now known as Tor Rock (636488), pierces the sky-line near the head of the combe, down which a rivulet flows into the Erme.

4. Then to Denewald's stone.

A longstone which is not now to be seen; the Devonians have shown a propensity to remove these antiquities and use them as gate-posts. It has, however, left traces of its former presence in the name *Langstone* (PND p. 279). The tithe apportionment of Kingston, dated 1839, shows a field—one of four since thrown into one—named Great Stone Park, near Seven Stones Cross. From the highest ground in this field (659493) Tor Rock is clearly visible.

5. Then to the ditch where Esne dug across the road.

? at 667495, where there is a curious kink in the road (B3392) and a lane leading down to Cumery.

6. Thence down to the source of the spring.

Either the spring by Upper Cumery (669491) or the one at Titwell (682491), which is on the parish boundary between Aveton Gifford and Bigbury.

7. Then down from there by the brook as far as *Tiddesford*.

A ford over the Titwell brook at 679478. There is no ford now; the brook is carried through a culvert under the road.

8. Then up the brook as far as Heott's ditch to the water-hole (*flodan*).

The boundary now turns up another brook, one which flows down between Challon's Combe Wood and Easton Wood. It is not possible to distinguish Heott's ditch with certainty from the other ditches hereabouts, but probably it was the water-course that takes its rise at Holwell (665474) from a spring (later known as a Holy Well) which gushes out of the hillside.

9. From the water-hole down where the vixen's ditch meets the brook,

I am told that foxes still come down from Easton Wood to drink at the rivulet which "meets the brook" near Foxhole (676473). The brook here is the united waters of the three streams that have met at *Tiddesford*.

10. and then down the brook to the sea.

The brook flows into the Avon at 684468, after which the boundary runs downstream to Avon Mouth. This portion of the 20 hides takes in some 6,000 acres, comprising the greater part of three parishes: Kingston, Ringmore, and Bigbury.

11. Then from Thurlestone

A thurlstone is a stone with a hole pierced through it. Here it is a large free-standing rock on the coast, pierced by the action of the sea (675414). It is not in the parish to which it has given its name, but is partly in South Milton, partly in South Huish.

12. up the brook as far as the narrow combe.

It is not clear what led the compilers of PND to identify this *smalan cumb* with a *Smalacombe* recorded in 1619, and the latter tentatively with a "Mollycombe" which appeared briefly on the 6-inch Ordnance map (1907 edition) as the name of a house in Thurlestone. The identification is tacitly adopted by Professor Whitelock, but it is topographically as well as etymologically untenable.

From the middle of Thurlestone Rock the boundary between South Milton and South Huish runs for more than a mile up a brook to the narrow combe at 697413, where it meets the boundary of West Alvington. The South Milton tithe apportionment (1839) gives "Smallacombe Orchard" as the name of No. 59 on the map drawn up at that time, and a house at the top of the combe is called Smallacombe today.

13. From the head of the narrow combe to the grey stone.

Probably at 701419, on a hill-crest commanding wide views in all directions.

14. Then up above the source of the spring to *odencolc*.

Kemble misread the last word as *odencole*. No Anglo-Saxon dictionary gives any clue to its meaning, but H. Meurig Evans and W. O. Thomas, in *Y Geiriadur Mawr* (Welsh-English Dictionary, p. 343, English-Welsh, p. 161), Aberystwyth, 1958, give *odyn-calch* or *odyn-galch* as Welsh for lime-kiln. Professor Kenneth Jackson informs me that *oden* would be the Primitive Cornish form of the word for kiln. The second element is derived ultimately from the classical Latin *calx*=lime. Outcrops of limestone occur in several parts of the South Hams.

All the rest of the boundary is written in the early West Saxon form of Old English. It is indeed the earliest authentic West Saxon writing that survives.[1] The occurrence of this purely Welsh or rather Cornish word in the middle of it is remarkable. Taken in conjunction with other evidence to which we shall come shortly, it suggests that in 846 the

[1] C. L. Wrenn in *Transactions of the Philological Society*, 1931–32, p. 69. On this see further R. Vleeskruyer, *The Life of St Chad*, Amsterdam, 1953, pp. 42, 43.

Anglo-Saxon settlement of the South Hams had not yet entirely displaced the indigenous Cornu-Britons and their language.

The spring of this landmark is on the hill above Sutton (705422), and Sutton may well have been the site of the kiln.

15. **Thence on the old way towards the white stone.**

The farm named Oldaway (712424) identifies the "old way" of this landmark with A381, a ridgeway coming up from the coast below Salcombe and crossing the estuary at Kingsbridge. The white stone may have been at Preston Cross (717434).

16. **Thence to the hill which is called "at the holly."**

The West Alvington parish boundary passes between Huxton Wood and Bowringsleigh Wood (707446). There is holly in both, and it may once have been more widely diffused over this hill-top.

17. **Thence to the hoar stone.**

A likely place for this boundary stone would be the high ground above Huxton Cross.

18. **Thence to the source at Sedge-well.**

The position of this well at 707449 is determined by the tithe apportionment of Churchstow (1841), the map of which gives No. 289 as an arable field of 7 a. 2 r. 29 p. called Sedgewell, belonging to Elston. It was quite dry when I found it, but must originally have been the source of Buckland Stream.

19. **Thence to the east of the earthwork.**

This *burg* has given its name to Stadbury (685459), which is a compound of *stod*=stud, herd of horses, and *burh*=earthwork (PND p. 266). A. H. Smith remarks that the Anglo-Saxons often used ancient enclosures for horse-folds.—*English Place-Name Elements*, 1956, II, p. 157, s.v. *stodfald*.

20. **Thence to the west of the little earthwork.**

No trace of this earthwork has been found, but it may well have been at the sharp turn in the parish boundary near Merrifield (698459).

21. **Thence to the street.**

A379.

22. **Thence below the wood straight out to the reed-pool.**

A rushy pool, now largely embanked and drained, at 692469, by Aveton Gifford Bridge.

23. **Then up the Avon until the old swine-enclosure runs out to the Avon.**

This enclosure will have been on the river-bank below Rake (720473).

24. **Then by that enclosure on to a hill.**

A ring of beech-trees at Sorley Green Cross (728464), plainly visible from the corner of the Avon we have just left, distinguishes the hill of this landmark.

25. **Then to Sorley Well.**

At 735468, on the parish boundary between Churchstow and Buckland-Tout-Saints. Sorley is *suordleage*, a lea shaped like a sword-blade (cf. A. H. Smith, *op. cit.*, II, p. 172). The description fits the terrain very well.

Landmarks 25, 26, 28, and 29 will recur as Landmarks 17, 16, 15, and 12 in the Sorley charter, to be examined later in this study.

26. **Thence to the head of Wolf-well.**

The name Woolcombe (758502), meaning wolves' valley (PND p. 313), identifies Wolf-well with what is now called Torr Brook.

27. **Thence along the Welsh Way to the stone at the water-hole (*flodan*).**

The Ordnance map records at 772515 the site of a former standing stone, described in 1819 as "a huge pyramidal stone, erect, of great height and breadth."[1] In a field which the road passes a little further on is a patch of wet ground (769518) which now represents the *flode* of this landmark.

The stone was called the "Old Man." This contains the Welsh word *maen*, Cornish *mên*, for a stone or rock.

Professor Whitelock translates *wealweg* here as "wall-way," but Welsh Way seems a likelier and more intelligible name for A381, the ridgeway which has already taken us past *odencolc* (where it was known as "the old way") and will soon reach the Harbourne near a manor named Englebourne, the bourne or stream of the English (PND p. 326). This last name must have been given by Anglo-Saxon settlers in a still predominantly Celtic-speaking district. The landmarks discussed here provide additional indications of pre-English influence on the toponymy of Devon.

28. **From the stone on along the highway to the ditch.**

But for its recurrence in the Sorley charter it might have been impossible to identify this ditch, especially as the words *forth on thone herepath* (on along the highway) could be taken to imply that the boundary continues to follow the Welsh Way. But the latter, shortly after passing "the stone," meets B3207, which is the highway along which we now turn. From Moreleigh Mount (754526) a bank and deep ditch run southward over Place Moor, forming the parish boundary between Woodleigh and Moreleigh.

---

[1] R. Southwood, *Kingsbridge and Salcombe*, Kingsbridge, 1819, p. 113.

29. Thence down as far as Woodland Ford.

> *Wealdenes ford*, the *Wealding forda* of the Sorley charter, is now represented by Gara Bridge (729534). The country hereabouts is well wooded even today.

30. Thence to the hollow way.

> From Gara Bridge a lane sunken between high hedgebanks runs past Curtisknowle to Crabadon (758551).

31. Thence down the brook

> From Crabadon the Ashwell Brook flows into the Harbourne (771563).

32. to *Hunburgefleot*,

> Since there are only three landmarks between Gara Bridge and the sea, a distance of at least eight miles, it must be understood that the boundary, having now reached one recognizable water-course flowing into another, continues downstream until it runs into a *fleot* or creek. *Hunburgefleot* will then be Bow Creek on the Dart (819562).

33. and there to the sea.

> At Dartmouth.

These bounds provide the earliest authentic description of a Devonshire landscape that has come down to us. They record a notable feat of surveying, one which must have involved days of riding along the ridgeways, clambering up and down steep valleys, and anxiously interrogating the inhabitants. (Even with the facilities of modern transport and the help of excellent maps it took me three weeks to go over the ground.) Presumably some local priest was ordered to write down the landmarks, and his notes would be sent to Dorchester or Winchester, there to be copied into the formal charter.

The first thing to be noticed in this remarkable survey is that after reaching the Avon the boundary does not go straight across the river but runs out to sea and then makes a fresh start from Thurlestone Rock, thus excluding what are now the parishes of Thurlestone and South Milton. Any explanation of this fact can only be conjectural, but the excluded area may have been left out because it was already bookland: that is, it had been granted out before 846 by 'book' or charter to another beneficiary. There is in fact a Buckland in Thurlestone, the Domesday *Bochelanda*, now divided into East and West Buckland; but there is no certain means of knowing how far back its history goes.

A more important point is that the boundary as now understood seems hardly compatible with the construction put
upon the act of 846 by Stevenson and Stenton. An area nine
miles wide, comprising some 65,000 acres of the best land in
the kingdom of Wessex, can scarcely have been intended as a
gift to the Church. This enormous territory would have been
a handsome endowment even for a bishopric, and there is no
evidence that any bishop ever got it. Nor is it likely that the
Church would acquire and subsequently lose an estate of these
dimensions without leaving some trace of the fact in record or
tradition. The circumstance, mentioned by Professor Whitelock, that by 904 the bishop of Sherborne possessed an estate
at Plympton is not relevant here, for Plympton is half a dozen
miles beyond the nearest point in Æthelwulf's bookland.

Æthelwulf was no simpleton or weakling. Stenton remarks
that his reign is one to which historians have sometimes done
less than justice. The annexation of Kent, Sussex, Surrey, and
Essex to the West Saxon kingdom, which had been the work
of his father, Egbert, was never challenged in his time, and he
himself recovered Berkshire from the Mercian kings.[1] In 851
he gained a decisive victory over the Vikings, inflicting, says
the chronicler, "the greatest slaughter on a heathen army that
we have ever heard of until this present day." His pre-eminence
among the English kings of the time is attested by his dealings
with the Frankish realm and the papacy.

Recent work has drawn attention to other aspects of his
policy. Mr Eric John, in particular, has argued convincingly
that Æthelwulf gave a new extension to the implications of
royal authority, with a skill which contributed not a little to
the success of his descendants in establishing their rule over the
whole of England. Æthelwulf is shown to have laid the foundations of a permanent royal demesne, not automatically divisible
among coheirs. By this means he ensured that future kings
should begin their reigns a good deal richer than his predecessors had ever been.[2]

Besides enriching himself and his successors Æthelwulf
brought about a notable change in the conditions of land
tenure. In his day land might be held either as bookland or as

[1] Stenton, *op. cit.*, p. 242.
[2] E. John, *Orbis Britanniae*, Leicester, 1966, pp. 37-44.

loan-land. Estates held by 'book' or charter were originally confined to the Church, or when granted to a layman were understood to be given for the purpose of building and endowing a minster, the ownership of which would be inheritable by the founder's kin. Even this most privileged form of tenure was subject to numerous burdens. A charter of 904 reveals that the ecclesiastical bookland of Taunton had until then been liable to provide one night's hospitality for the king and nine nights' for his falconers, to maintain eight hounds and their keeper, to escort travellers on their way to the nearest royal residence, and to supply horses and carts for transporting anything the king needed either to Curry or to Williton.[1] Elsewhere there might be a duty to supply additional post-horses for travellers, and labour for royal building. On some estates an archaic system of food-rents survived down to and beyond the Norman Conquest; it took the form of a liability to supply one, two, or three nights' provisions for the king and his court. For the discharge of all these obligations the unit of assessment was the hide.

In Æthelwulf's charters we can discern a process of freeing holders of bookland from all but two public burdens. They were still required to supply labour for the construction and repair of bridges and to send a certain number of armed men whenever the king or the ealdorman called out the host. These two obligations, it will be remembered, were imposed on the twenty hides in the South Hams which Æthelwulf booked to himself. But four years earlier the king had begun to exact a third charge, namely, labour for the construction and repair of fortifications. Viking inroads no doubt made this very necessary. Before long the practice became standard, and Æthelwulf and his successors, when granting bookland, habitually reserved the right to exact bridge-work, fortress-work, and military service.

In 844 Æthelwulf devised a plan for giving all holders of booklands, whether churchmen or laymen, a reduction of assessment. In calculating the incidence of public charges other than the inevitable three, every ten hides were in future to be reckoned as nine. But the plan, although embodied in a formal charter, seems to have miscarried; the time was not propitious,

[1] CS 612.

with the Vikings on the warpath, for any such relaxation. Ten years later the position had so far improved that by a new charter, drawn up at Wilton on the 22nd of April 854, Æthelwulf took power to grant one tenth of the entire royal demesne piecemeal to the churches, and at the same time to change the tenure of laymen established on the land so granted from loan-land into bookland.[1]

Loan-land was a precarious tenure, in the sense clearly expressed by Æthelwulf's great son. "Every man," wrote King Alfred, "when he has built himself a home on land lent to him by his lord, with his help, likes to stay in it sometimes, and to go hunting and fowling and fishing, and to support himself in every way on that loan-land, both by sea and land, until the time when through his lord's mercy he may acquire bookland and a perpetual inheritance."[2] In other words, the thegn, though he has the full beneficial enjoyment of the estate so long as he lives, cannot alienate it or leave it to his children without the king's permission, and if he dies without issue it will revert to the king. Only a 'book', a royal charter, can give him full power to sell, exchange, or bequeath it as he may think fit.

Read in the light of Alfred's remarks, Æthelwulf's charters begin to stand out as having a significant place in the history of English land-law. In particular, the charter of 854 must have stimulated the already keen appetite of laymen for a secure hereditary tenure. Any discussion of the step taken at Dorchester on the 26th of December 846 will miss the mark if it fails to take account of the notions expressed in these other documents.

In booking to himself twenty hides of land between the Erme and the Dart, Æthelwulf, I suggest, was taking power to enlarge his own demesne in the first instance, but also to grant away portions of the area as bookland. Much of it may be supposed to have been in what we should call an undeveloped condition. This was perhaps less true of the portion between the Erme and the Avon, where out of ten landmarks four con-

[1] For a full discussion, based on a new edition of Æthelwulf's two 'decimation' charters, see H. P. R. Finberg, *The Early Charters of Wessex*, Leicester, 1964, pp. 187–213.

[2] J. M. Kemble, *The Saxons in England*, 1849, I, p. 312.

tain Anglo-Saxon personal names (Denewald, Esne, Tidi, Heott), than of the much larger portion between the Avon and the Dart, where the landmarks are combes, brooks, wells, stones, hills, and ditches. It looks as if this part of the South Hams was but sparsely settled at the time, with a population perhaps mainly of Cornu-Britons. Its natural fertility, however, clearly invited exploitation. Behind the grandeur of the coast, where ravens, buzzards, and birds of even rarer species find sanctuary in the inaccessible cliffs, lies an upland region, almost bare of trees on the hill-tops, but broken by numerous warm and sheltered valleys, rich in pasture and cornland. Marshall, writing at the close of the eighteenth century, observed: "This district, with respect to soil, ranks high among the fertile districts of the island. There are very few, of equal extent, to place in competition with it."[1]

With the expansion of settlement and agriculture the initial assessment of twenty hides could gradually be increased. Churches too would be built and endowed, each with a suitable allotment of glebe. This policy of development was one in which Æthelwulf would have little difficulty in securing the concurrence of his magnates.

With the single exception of the Sorley charter, to be examined presently, no surviving document throws any further light on the history of the South Hams until we come to Domesday Book. But when we look ahead to Domesday, we find that by 1086 the king has two important manors at West Alvington and Chillington, linked by the bridge which has given its name to Kingsbridge. And by that time the South Hams stand well above the average for Devon both in population and the number of plough-teams.[2] The original assessment of twenty hides has been left far behind. In the relatively small part of the area between Kingsbridge and Stokenham we find eighteen Domesday manors assessed altogether at 25 hides.[3]

[1] W. Marshall, *The Rural Economy of the West of England*, 2nd ed., 1805, I, p. 275.
[2] H. C. Darby and R. Welldon Finn, *The Domesday Geography of South-West England*, Cambridge, 1967, p. 293.
[3] Charleton (Cheletona) 5 h.; South Pool (Pola) three manors, 2 h., ½ h., ½ h.; Combe (Comba) ½ h.; Chivelstone (Cheveletona) 1 h.; Ford (Forda) 1 h.; Prawle (Prenla) 1 h.; South Allington (Alintona) 1 h.; Sherford (Sireford) 2 h.; Keynedon (Chenighedona) ½ h.; Malston (Mellestona) 1 h.;

Place-names add their testimony. Attention has already been drawn to the significance of the name Kingston. Buckland-Tout-Saints is a Domesday bookland; North and South Huish each represent a distinct *hiwisc* or hide.

In creating new booklands within the area Æthelwulf and his successors doubtless reserved bridge-work and military service in accordance with the act of 846, and they were free to add fortress-work if they thought fit. To Stevenson's argument that the exemption from other royal services is meaningless if Æthelwulf intended to keep the land in his own possession, the answer is now clear. He intended to keep only a portion for himself; and why should he not call upon the inhabitants even of that portion, when occasion arose, to discharge the three common dues? As for the duty of almsgiving inculcated in the preamble to the charter, the king practised what he preached by making a will bidding his successors provide from every tenth hide of his demesne, so long as the land should be occupied and under cultivation—a significant proviso, this—food, drink, and clothing for one poor man.

The other charter which calls for notice here was granted by King Edgar in 962.[1] It survives in what appears to be the original form, but the parchment has been damaged in places, and the name of the beneficiary is only in part legible. He was certainly a layman, a thegn with some such name as Æthelwine. The document, unknown until about fifty years ago, was first printed by Frances Rose-Troup, with a commentary in which she identified six of the twenty landmarks correctly.[2] Recent fieldwork has made it possible to complete this necessary task and in so doing to place the charter where it belongs in the perspective of local history.

The boundary can be followed on sheets SX 74, 64, and 75.

Stancombe (Stancoma) ½ h.; Coleridge (Colriga) 2 manors, ¼ h., ¼ h.; Widdecombe (Wodiacomma) ¼ h.; Chillington (Cedelintona) 7 h.; Dunstone (Dunestantona) ½ h.

[1] Essex County Record Office, Chelmsford, D/DP T209.

[2] *Chimes* (the Buckfast Abbey periodical), I, 1928, pp. 169–79; DA LXI, 1929, pp. 249–66.

1. First from Kingsbridge
   The bridge which gave its name to the town. It has now disappeared under a car-park.

2. out to the Avon.
   "Out" here might be taken to imply that the boundary goes down the Kingsbridge estuary and out to sea, then turns westward past Bolt Head and Bolt Tail, thus including the parishes of Malborough, South Huish, South Milton, and Thurlestone. But this seems far too extensive a territory to be tacitly comprised in the grant. It is far more likely that the boundary follows the Kingsbridge stream up to its source in Bow-ringsleigh Wood (713447), then goes down the other side of the ridge and reaches the Avon by Aveton Gifford Bridge (692469).

3. Upstream to the outfall of the brooklet.
   The Alleron Brook, which forms the eastern boundary of Aveton Gifford. It falls into the Avon near Knap Mill (708473).

4. Up the brooklet to Black Pool.
   The names Blackwell and Blackdown Camp indicate that the pool lay in what is now the marshy ground near Stanton (706510).

5. From Black Pool to Stone Hurst.
   Hyrst means a wooded bank or hill. In this instance it is the patch of wood near Churchland Green (705520).

6. From Stone Hurst to the bend in the road which leads to Beocca's bridge.
   The boundary goes up to California Cross (704530), then turns north-eastward along the road which passes Lupridge and Penson on its way to Bickham Bridge. Bickham is Beocca's combe (PND p. 304). The bend is reached at 713547.

7. Up by the old way
   The "old way" climbs up the ridge which has given its name to Lupridge, then crosses the valley to Coarsewell (708547).

8. to Penta's mead.
   Tempting as it may seem to connect Penta with the Penson men-tioned under Landmark 6, the idea must be dismissed, for the earliest recorded form of this name is Payneston 1334 (PND p. 303). The mead of this landmark must have been at the bottom of the deep valley (710542) between Lupridge and Coarsewell.

9. Then west by the way
   The direction is really north-westward via Coarsewell Cross to Fowelscombe Gate.

10. to the grey stone.
    The "way" of Landmark 9 goes past a farm named Stone. A likely

spot for the boundary stone which gave it this name would be the high ground (697556) near Fowelscombe Gate.

11. Then to the hedgerow where the brooks meet.
    Wyrtrum, here translated as hedgerow, is a compound of *wyrt*=root and *truma*=troop, array. It seems to mean a row or circle of trees or stumps left standing in the process of deforestation to mark a boundary line. The brooks meet at 696563, where the parish boundary of North Huish turns eastward.

12. Downstream to Woodland Ford.
    Gara Bridge: see Landmark 29 of Æthelwulf's charter. To reach it, the boundary goes down the brook which flows through North Huish to join the Avon below Bickham Bridge, and then down the Avon.

13. Then to Manning Ford.
    A ford over Cock's Brook at 732532.

14. By the lane as far as the earthwork.
    From the ford last mentioned a lane climbs up the valley, and after passing High Marks Barn (737527) becomes the parish boundary between Woodleigh and Moreleigh. We follow it to Moreleigh Mount (754526).

15. Then by the ditch
    See Landmark 28 of Æthelwulf's charter, then 26 and 25.

16. to the source of Wolf Well.
    Now Torr Brook.

17. To Sorley Well.
    At 735468.

18. From Sorley Well to *Wagu fen.*
    This name, which could now be Warne, means 'quaking marsh' (PND p. 201). There may have been some marshy ground in the vicinity of Combe Cross (736452).

19. Then to Willerd's hill.
    Probably the steep hill on which the thirteenth-century market town of Kingsbridge is built.

20. Then back to Kingsbridge.
    The royal bridge which formed the starting-point.

The charter describes this as a grant of land at Sorley (*Swurd leage*). In fact the bounds take in the whole of what are now the parishes of Churchstow, Loddiswell, Kingsbridge, and Woodleigh, with part of North Huish, an aggregate of something between 9,000 and 10,000 acres. The parish of North Huish consists of four Domesday manors: Huish, Butterford, Lupridge, and, on the other side of the Avon, Broadley; but of these only Butterford and Lupridge are comprised within the bounds. They and Loddiswell lay outside the territory Æthelwulf had 'booked' to himself in 846; the rest of "Sorley" lay within it. Had the Sorley estate been assessed proportionately to Æthelwulf's "Homme," it would have been rated at about three hides.

In the charter the Anglo-Saxon survey is placed before the dating clause and the witness-list. It is introduced with the statement: "This is the boundary of the hide, less one-eighth part, at Sorley."[1] In other words, the property is assessed at seven-eighths of a hide, equivalent to three and a half yardlands. This is a highly beneficial rating. It looks as if King Edgar had used his prerogative to let an exceptionally favoured subject have the land on easy terms.[2] In Latin the yardland is commonly expressed as *virgata*, but in south-western charters it is often called *pertica*. When we turn back from the vernacular bounds to the Latin text, we find that the original assessment has been erased, and in its place *tres perticas* is written. These two words are very widely spaced out to fill the erasure, so far as possible, with an assessment thus reduced from three and a half yardlands to three. The man who took it upon himself to attempt this clumsy piece of 'editing' either failed to notice or was not worried by the discrepancy he was perpetrating between the Latin and Old English texts. The discrepancy gives him away, but leaves us wondering. Why did he do it?

We turn to Domesday Book for light. It tells us that in the course of a century the estate King Edgar gave to his thegn has disintegrated. At its core is the manor of Notona, assessed at two hides. This now belongs to Buckfast, an abbey founded in 1018.[3] Sorley (*Surlei*) appears as a distinct manor which by

---

[1] "This is thæs hiwisces land gemære buton anon eahtothan dæle æt swurd lege." Mrs Rose-Troup completely misunderstood this sentence, and failed to notice the discrepancy between it and the Latin text.

[2] Cf. the charter of 976, pp. 57, 61 below, granting "Hyple's old land" as one yardland.

[3] H. P. R. Finberg, Supplement to *The Early Charters of Devon and Cornwall* (printed with W. G. Hoskins, *The Westward Expansion of Wessex*, Leicester, Department of English Local History, Occasional Paper No. 13, 1960), p. 29.

1066 had passed into lay hands, with an assessment of half a hide, or two yardlands. So had Loddiswell, Butterford, Lupridge, Woodley, Combe Royal, and Leigh, with a total assessment of 6 hides 1 yardland.[1] Thus in the process of expanding settlement between 962 and 1066 new holdings have been created, and the assessment has been greatly increased to keep pace with the growth of the economy.

The process may well have begun during the half-century which elapsed between King Edgar's grant to a lay thegn and the foundation of Buckfast Abbey. But if so, it had not yet damaged the integrity of the estate, which seems to have passed to the abbey as an undivided whole, with Edgar's charter as its title-deed. Between 1018 and 1066 considerable portions were alienated, probably by grants from the abbey to lay tenants; and it was perhaps at an early stage of this development, when the estate had been reduced by only half a yardland, that somebody at Buckfast thought it advisable to bring the original figure of assessment imposed by Edgar into accord with the new situation. Since 1012 the formidable annual levy known as Danegeld had become the first charge on the taxable resources of the country. This naturally caused every landowner to look carefully at his assessment.

Subdivision entailed further changes not only of assessment but also of local nomenclature. As Sorley itself was alienated before 1066, the Buckfast manor came to be called Notona. This name, which is thought to mean 'sheep-farm' (from Old English *hnoc*=wether), figures on the map today as Norton. During the thirteenth century somebody at Buckfast endorsed Edgar's charter with a note that it dealt with Norton near Sorley before the foundation of the abbey.[2] But by that time the monks had built a church of St Mary on the summit of the ridge between Norton and the Avon, and this conspicuous landmark caused the manor and parish to become known as Churchstow. At about the same time, on the southern edge of the manor, the abbot created the new market town of Kingsbridge.

In 1558 the manor of Churchstow and borough of Kings-

---

[1] Lodeswella 2 h.; Botreforda, two manors, $\frac{1}{2}$ h., $\frac{1}{2}$h.; Rluperiga $1\frac{1}{2}$ y.; Luperiga $\frac{1}{2}$ h.; Odelea $1\frac{1}{4}$ h.; Comba $\frac{1}{4}$ h.; Lega $3\frac{1}{2}$ y.
[2] "De Surdleg juxta Norton ante fundacionem."

bridge were purchased by Sir William Petre, and the title-deeds passed into his ownership. It was among the archives of the Petre family that the Sorley charter came to light some fifty years ago. The credit for its rediscovery is due to the late Canon Kuypers, but the first scholar to identify it as a Devonshire charter was Dom John Stéphan, o.s.b., of modern Buckfast, happily still with us, and well known as the historian of the abbey.

The surviving charters of the Anglo-Saxon period are the documentary foundations of English local history. They are also a source of primary value for the national historian; but, as will be seen, they do not readily yield up their secrets. When they can be made to do so, they sometimes take light from each other. This has been the case with the "Homme" and Sorley charters. Taken together, they tell us a little more than was known before about the process by which the politic rulers of Wessex contrived to turn a sparsely populated but potentially fertile district in the old Celtic-speaking Dumnonia into a flourishing portion of the English realm.

FACT AND FICTION FROM CREDITON

THE FIRST SANDFORD CHARTER

ON THE 3rd of April 930 King Athelstan was holding court at Lyminster in Sussex. There, in the presence of the two archbishops, ten bishops, as many ealdormen, and twenty thegns, he issued a solemn diploma granting four hides of land to the bishop of Selsey.[1] The text has been preserved only in a fourteenth-century copy, but the formulas are those of Athelstan's reign, and there is no reason to doubt its authenticity.

In the course of the next three weeks Athelstan moved into Wessex. By the 29th of April he was at Chippenham in Wiltshire. The same prelates were in attendance, with the addition of Frithestan, bishop of Winchester, but five of the ealdormen and six thegns had dropped out, and their places were taken by equal numbers in each rank. In their presence Athelstan issued another solemn diploma. This was a grant of three hides at Sandford to Eadulf, bishop of Crediton, and to his *familia*, the clergy of the minster. It is the oldest extant document which makes any reference to Sandford by name.

The Chippenham diploma was first printed by Napier and Stevenson in their edition of the Crawford charters. The Crawford collection had been acquired by the Bodleian Library in 1891, and this parchment is now Bodleian MS. Eng. hist. a.2, no. iii.[2] Stevenson declared it to be "the original charter . . . an addition to the very brief list of charters of Æþelstan that have come down to us in their original form."[3] No one knew better than Stevenson that in granting away their royal rights over a piece of land the Anglo-Saxon kings nearly always reserved the right to call upon the inhabitants for military service and

---

[1] *Cartularium Saxonicum* (hereafter cited as CS), ed. W. de G. Birch, 1885–93, no. 669.

[2] *Crawford Charters*, IV.

[3] *ibid.*, p. 65.

for the repair of bridges and fortifications; and one of the most striking features of the Chippenham diploma is that it frees the three hides at Sandford from these obligations. This, however, did not shake Stevenson's faith in its authenticity. In his classic article on the three common dues he pointed to it as the exception that proved the rule, the "one clear and indisputable case" of land granted with an exemption even from the inevitable three.[1]

More recent critics have shown themselves less confident. In 1935 Drögereit listed the parchment in the Bodleian as a copy, not an original. Mr T. A. M. Bishop limits himself to describing the charter as "probably" authentic.[2] Dr Chaplais goes much further. So far from being an original contemporary charter, he says, it is a forgery. The handwriting "has the artificial appearance of an imitative script." In an otherwise 'insular' alphabet it uses a half-uncial *d*; the forms of long *s*, with ascender and descender in final position, are curious; and in certain words *i* is an ascender.[3] In the light of these palaeo-graphical observations the clause of total exemption can hardly fail to excite suspicion.

One feature which Dr Chaplais does not take into account is a detailed survey, with twenty-seven landmarks, of the boundary of the three hides at Sandford. I have argued elsewhere that topography is a vital element in all these land-grants, and that criticism cannot approach finality until the landmarks have been securely plotted. Stevenson would probably not have disputed this principle. He identified seven of the Sandford boundary points which are recognizable on modern maps, but said they were "not sufficient to enable us to lay down the boundaries accurately."[4] In the light of recent field-work an attempt can now be made to complete this necessary task. The bounds can be followed on sheets SS70 and 80 of the 2½-inch Ordnance Survey.

---

[1] *English Historical Review*, XXIX, 1914, p. 702.

[2] R. Drögereit, 'Gab es eine angelsachsische Königskanzlei?', *Archiv für Urkundenforschung*, XIII, 1935, p. 434; T. A. M. Bishop, 'Notes on Cambridge Manuscripts', *Transactions of the Cambridge Bibliographical Society*, II, 1954–58, p. 195.

[3] *Bulletin of the Institute of Historical Research*, XXXIX, 1966, p. 11.

[4] *Crawford Charters*, p. 67.

1. First from Fint's lea
    An open glade or clearing between Poundshill Cross (838008) and the East Lodge of Creedy Park. The National Grid reference is 839011. "Fint's ridge" occurs in the bounds of Tisbury, Wilts. (K641), but the name seems not to be recorded elsewhere.

2. west on the highway to the head of Hollacombe.
    Near Barnstaple Cross (805014). The 6-inch O.S. map of 1889 (sheet LXVII N.W.) shows that the parish boundary of Sandford formerly ran from East Lodge across the park and joined the road to Coleford, which is the present boundary, on George Hill. It probably takes this course in the charter.

3. Thence north to the ditch.
    This and the next three landmarks are on or close to the present parish boundary. The ditch is a little s. of Cross (805022).

4. Straight to the east of Cudda's knoll.
    Near *Knowle* Quarry (791024).

5. There west on the highway to the thorny way.
    The present boundary continues westward for about 200 metres, then turns up a footpath leading N. and W. to Beacon Post (782031). According to Napier and Stevenson (*Crawford Ch.*, p. 68), the word *thornisc* is not found elsewhere; but the names *Thorn* Cottage and Kna*thorn* hereabouts would seem to justify the interpretation given here. In any case, the "thorny way" must be the lane from Higher Elston to Ash Bullayne.

6. On the thorny way; thence north to the Sheep-brook.
    This *scipbroc* gives its name to the Domesday *Eschipabroca*, now Shobrooke in Morchard Bishop. The united waters of the Ash Brook and the Knathorn Brook form a tributary of the Yeo now called the Knighty Brook. Today the parish boundary touches the Ash Brook at 779037, follows it down to its junction with the Knathorn Brook, and goes up the latter to Spirelake (782054). Of these streams the Knathorn Brook is the one nearest to Shobrooke, and the ensuing landmarks imply that it is the Sheep-brook of the Sandford boundary, reached at or near Woodparks (773049).

7. Upstream to the highway.
    The road from Crediton to Morchard Bishop. From Woodparks the boundary apparently goes up a feeder of the Knathorn Brook called the Oldborough Brook, reaching the "highway" at Oldborough Quarry (775060).

8. Thence straight to Lil's ford.
    Where the road crosses the Spirelake (782053).

9. Thence to the west of the cold linch.
    The linch is the hill N. of Linscombe, a name in which Napier and

Stevenson discerned a possible relationship with the *hlinc* of this boundary. "Cold" because it faces N. and N.E. (786050).

10. **Thence along the hedgerow to the east of the cold linch.**
    To 795054 or thereabouts. The word *wyrtrum*, here and later rendered by "hedgerow," has given rise to much discussion (cf. *Crawford Ch.*, p. 68). It is a compound of *wyrt* = root and *truma* = troop, array, and seems to mean a row of trees or stumps left standing in the process of deforestation to mark a boundary line.

11. **Thence along the hedgerow further north to Broxham.**
    "Broxham Copse" appears on the old 6-in. O.S. map. The parish boundary goes N. of this copse (799055).

12. **Thence from the down to the enclosure below Bromley.**
    805056, where the boundary makes a sharp turn. Bromley is called Brimley on the 1889 map.

13. **Thence straight to Pidsley.**
    A path from Brimley leads to West Pidsley (811051).

14. **Thence straight down to Loseley.**
    The name means swine-pasture. We have left the modern boundary to go down Pidsley Hill.

15. **Thence on the stream to the hay-lea.**
    The stream is probably the one that flows past Doggetsbeer (819045).

16. **North on the highway to Thelbridge.**
    Thelbridge means 'plank bridge'. It was where the road to Kennerleigh crosses two tributaries of the Creedy (819048).

17. **Thence upstream to Æsculf's intake.**
    Up the Creedy. *Weorthig* means a piece of land taken in from forest or moor and cleared to make a farm. Usually, as here, it is compounded with a personal name. *Æsc(w)ulf's weorthig* would today be Ashelworthy or something like it, but no such name is recorded anywhere near Sandford. Yelland(=old land) may represent the original intake (821055). It is just possible, however, that the first element survives in *Ash*ridge (824062).
    The charter is endorsed in a hand of the early fourteenth century "Carta . . . de Est Sandford." Hitherto the landmarks have all been w. of the Creedy; they now take us over to the other side of the parish.

18. **Thence north straight to the edge of the wood.**
    ? 821059 or 832066.

19. **Thence along the hedgerow to Luca's intake.**
    There is a Luca's *weorthig* in Molland, now Luckworthy, but again the name is missing in the Sandford district.

20. North to the enclosure as far as Cyneferth's brook.
   This enclosure (*haga*) is probably to be identified with Downhayne (838063). Near this farm the Sandford parish boundary crosses a brook flowing down from Stockleigh English.

21. Thence on the stream from the down to the Creedy
   "On the stream" here is an interlinear addition. At 841045 the brook of the previous landmark flows into the Holly Water, which in the great Crediton boundary, to be considered later, is called "the eastern Creedy."

22. as far as the brook that flows out from the hay-lea.
   A brook which joined the Creedy at or near 834039. The construction of mill-leats has interfered with the natural water-courses here.

23. Upstream to the stone ford.
   Probably at Dowrich Bridge (827046).

24. Thence south along the hedgerow to the east of Henstill.
   The direction is really south-westward, along the road between Bussels and West Sandford, to a point near 818041.

25. Thence straight to Ruxford.
   The ford, now a footbridge, is at 818022.

26. Thence south to the look-out post.
   At 825010, on the summit of George Hill, whence there is a fine view of the surrounding country.

27. Thence along the hedgerow to Fint's lea.
   Through Creedy Park back to the starting-point.

Anyone who takes the trouble to follow this perambulation on the map will see that it takes in a large area of Sandford parish east of the Creedy and another area in the west, but carefully excludes the central core of the parish where Sandford itself lies. This is a salient and quite unexpected feature. If we bear it in mind while examining the document more closely it will help us to a solution of some other puzzles.

In the charter Athelstan speaks of the three hides as a portion of land which has been under the bishop's control, "but payment for wrongdoings was formerly made to myself" (telluris particulam . . . que sub episcopali dicione fuit, sed tamen mihi census iniquorum actuum prius reddebatur). Stevenson wished to read *censu* here in place of *census*. This alteration would change the meaning: we should have to understand that the property had been under the bishop's control but had been forfeited to the king as a penalty for misdeeds, committed presumably by the bishop's tenant or tenants. Stevenson quotes other instances of church lands confiscated by the secular power because of some offence committed by the lay occupier, and this interpretation gains some colour from a later passage in the diploma which expressly guards the estate against judicial forfeiture. Morever, Stevenson believed that Sandford was part of the original Crediton endowment. In view of its close proximity to Crediton, this is not unlikely; and if so, it would have been covered by the terms of the foundation charter, granted in 739, which exempted the lands of the minster from all secular dues except military service.[1] But it will appear in the course of this study that we have no solid information concerning the original extent of the Crediton endowment. Between 739 and 909 Crediton lay in the diocese of Sherborne, and its lands had only to support a staff of canons—how large or small a staff we have no means of knowing. But in 909 it was made an episcopal see with jurisdiction over all Devon and Cornwall. The bishop took over a number of estates in those two shires which had belonged to his colleague at Sherborne, and the existing endowment of the minster, now his cathedral, may well have been enlarged for his benefit at the same time. In 926 Athelstan provided him with an auxiliary to look after Cornwall, and seems to have assigned three of the former Sherborne estates in Cornwall for the maintenance of this deputy bishop.[2] He may then have granted Sandford to the bishop of Crediton in compensation, but without giving him full regalian rights. There is at any rate no reason to doubt the statement in the Chippenham diploma that already before 930 Sandford had been an episcopal estate. Now that the topography has been elucidated, we know that the diploma dealt only with three hides on the periphery of the estate, leaving the bishop in control of Sandford itself. We have no ground whatever for supposing that the estate had been partitioned before, and that the three peripheral hides had been forfeited to the king. The purpose of the diploma, as we shall see in a moment, is something quite other

[1] *Crawford Charters*, p. 2.
[2] H. P. R. Finberg, *Lucerna*, 1964, pp. 110–13.

than a restitution of confiscated property. It is an axiom of criticism that a text should only be emended if there is good reason to suspect it of being corrupt. In the Chippenham diploma this part of the text makes perfectly good sense as it stands.

The diploma is granted to the bishop in the first instance, but his name is brought in almost perfunctorily, to introduce the statement about his earlier tenure that has just been discussed. When we read on, we find that the three hides are in fact being granted to the canons, the bishop's *familia*, as a source of provisions for their table ("ad mensam"), and incidentally as a source of revenue, since the king is relinquishing the profits of justice in their favour. They are to hold the three hides freely and in perpetuity, with complete exemption from secular dues. If any of them commit some dreadful crime, punishment is to be inflicted by due process of law, but the land is to remain secure and inalienable, firmly and for ever appointed to supply the table of the brethren of the aforesaid minster who will humbly and loyally render obedience to God, to the Church, and to the bishop. (Here we seem to hear the episcopal voice telling the canons just how they are expected to behave.) The brethren are not to alienate their three hides to king, bishop, or any other man, unless in exchange for some larger and better estate also held, like this one, under a charter of perpetual tenure.[1]

The purpose of the diploma is now clear. What the bishop is doing is to carry out a division of the *mensa*, and to secure for it the backing of a royal charter. Keeping in his own hands the central portion of Sandford from which the estate takes its name, he is making over the three hides of what we may call

---

[1] ". . . ut illa [*sc.* familia] eam sine expeditionis profectione. arcis pontis constructione. omnique regalium vel secularium tributorum seruitutis exactione. liberaliter ac eternaliter in perpetuum habeat. si autem . . . aliqui ex familia. quod libet iniquitatis facinus commiserint, hoc in eis iudicialiter atque regulariter uindicetur. predictus agellus in sua stabilitate. semper fratribus ad mensam. qui in antefato ergasterio, Deo. eclesie. domno prelato. humiliter fideliterque obtemperare uoluerint. firmus etinauferabilis perduret. nec habeant fratres licentiam. illum foras dandi. regi. episcopo. uel cuilibet homini. nisi alium maiorem atque meliorem. pro eius uicissitudinis commutatione. alia similiter cum cartula. perpetualiter hereditaria recipiant."

outer Sandford to his canons as a separate and distinct endowment for their refectory. There were precedents for such an
act. Mr Eric John has marshalled a convincing array of evidence
to prove that the endowment of cathedral clergy with lands of
their own, distinct from their bishop's property, was far from
rare in the Old English period.[1] Of the documents he cites,
perhaps the one nearest in spirit to the Sandford charter is the
will of a lady named Ceolwin who leaves fifteen hides at Alton
Priors to the clergy of Winchester cathedral for their refectory, and "commands, in the name of God and of St Peter,
that the community shall never give it away from their refectory for money unless in return for another estate which is
nearer and more convenient for them."[2]

The preamble to the Sandford charter, a piece of turgid
prose more than a hundred and fifty words long, is identical
with that of the charter drawn up at Lyminster twenty-six
days earlier. The anathemas are virtually identical. The close
but not too perfectly exact correspondence of the two witness-
lists has already been noted. It is just conceivable that Eadulf of
Crediton, one of the bishops who was present at Lyminster,
took a copy of the diploma drawn up on that occasion, and
brought it home with him intending to use it as a model in
concocting another diploma for his own ends. It is conceivable,
but is it likely? His object, as we now know, was to give away
some four or five thousand acres; why should he go about it
in that surreptitious way? Scholars nowadays recognize that
under Athelstan diplomas were normally drawn up by clerks
of the royal household who used set formulas over and over
again.[3] It is therefore in all respects probable that the clerk in
attendance at Lyminster was still in attendance three weeks
later when the king had moved to Chippenham, and that both
diplomas were drawn up by one and the same hand.

Is there anything, then, to prevent us from accepting the
parchment now in the Bodleian as a true or very nearly true

[1] *Journal of Ecclesiastical History*, VI, 1955, pp. 143–55.
[2] *Anglo-Saxon Charters*, ed. A. J. Robertson, 1956, p. 31.
[3] R. Drögereit, *op. cit.*, pp. 335–436; F. M. Stenton, *The Latin Charters of the Anglo-Saxon Period*, 1955, p. 54. Dr Chaplais suggests that clerks of the Winchester scriptorium were employed for this purpose.—*Journal of the Society of Archivists*, III, 1965, p. 59.

copy of an authentic charter, made some time after the date of issue? Dr Chaplais pronounces the script to be artificial and imitative. If the copyist took the trouble to imitate the original script, this suggests that his intention may not have been entirely straightforward. He certainly had the opportunity to 'improve' the text if he chose to do so. Before we accord his work an unqualified acceptance it will be well to take one more look at it.

The clause of immunity provides that the *familia* shall hold the three hides "without" (*sine*) military service, fortress-work, bridge-work, or any other form of service to the secular power. Dr Chaplais demonstrates with abundant citations that in other charters this phrase occurs at the end of the clause, not at the beginning as here, and that "sine" is there used in the sense of "except": the land is to be held free of all secular obligations *except* military service and the other two. So it is here, if anywhere, that the copyist may have taken liberties with his text.

Now the year of issue, 930, falls within the period of about six years during which Athelstan habitually granted land "without the yoke of unpopular service" (sine jugo exosae servitutis).[1] The Lyminster diploma has "sine jugo detestandae servitutis," a variant of the same phrase. No reservations are stated; on the face of it the immunity granted is one of total exemption. Modern scholars find it difficult to take this at its face value, and are inclined to hold that the three common dues were still reserved, though tacitly. We have no means of deciding one way or the other, but it is at least possible that the charters mean exactly what they say.[2] The years from 928 to 934 were years of peace and glory for Athelstan. He had established his supremacy over all the other monarchs in the island and absorbed Northumbria into his own kingdom.[3] His mood may well have been expansive enough to prompt more bountiful measures than had been customary in the past.

[1] H. P. R.Finberg, *The Early Charters of Wessex*, 1964, p. 205, n. 3.

[2] The draftsman of CS 1074 was evidently convinced that they did so. This is a charter given by Edgar in 961, which reproduces *verbatim* the formulas of Athelstan's reign, including "sine jugo exosae servitutis." But since this could be taken to imply complete exemption, a clause was added expressly reserving the three common dues.

[3] *Anglo-Saxon Chronicle*, s.a. 927.

If the Lyminster and Chippenham diplomas were both drawn up by the same clerk, as the verbal resemblances forcibly suggest, we may take it that he used the same phrase ("sine jugo detestandae servitutis") to express the immunity in both. And if so, it follows that the Crediton copyist took out the last three words and put in their place a full specification of the public burdens to which the estate was not to be liable. This would explain the anomaly of the preposition "sine." He may have honestly believed that the charter was intended to confer total exemption, and that by substituting a more explicit phrase he was merely expressing that intention more precisely. If he thought so, there is no evidence to prove that he was mistaken. But it certainly looks as if he 'edited' the original at this point. Whether or not we give him the benefit of the doubt, it is clear that we cannot follow Stevenson in accepting the Sandford diploma as the "one clear and indisputable case" of exemption from even the three common dues.

Dr Chaplais has discussed this charter in terms of purely diplomatic and palaeographical criticism, without reference to the topography or the historical background. He concludes that "the charter may have been forged early in the eleventh century." I submit that a judgement expressed in such terms is likely to leave the student under a highly misleading impression. The clause of immunity is admittedly suspect, but at every other point the text stands up well to critical scrutiny, and the fact cannot be too clearly stated.

THE SECOND SANDFORD CHARTER

NOTHING more is heard of Sandford until the reign of Ethelred II. In 997, when Alfwold was bishop of Crediton, King Ethelred granted him by charter two hides at Sandford, free of all but the three common dues.[1] The preamble is identical with that of at least one charter issued in the previous reign.[2] The blessing and anathema contain some verbal errors which can be corrected from a charter of

[1] British Museum, Stowe charter 34; *Ordnance Survey Facsimiles of Anglo-Saxon Manuscripts*, 1878–84, III, no. 35.
[2] CS 1285, a Wilton charter.

Cnut where the same formulas are used again.[1] The eight bishops who attest are identifiable from a Winchester diploma of the same year, where their sees are given as Canterbury, York, Winchester, London, Crediton, Selsey, Sherborne, and Elmham.[2] Besides an abbot named Godwine, whose monastery cannot be identified, the abbots of Glastonbury, Abingdon, Muchelney, Bath, New Minster, St Augustine's, Malmesbury, and Athelney attest in that order. In the same contemporary Winchester diploma the four ealdormen and nine of the sixteen thegns reappear. Of the remaining seven witnesses at least five are vouched for by other charters of the period.[3]

It is generally agreed that by the end of the tenth century diplomas for churchmen were drafted not by royal clerks as in Athelstan's day, but by the beneficiaries. That being so, the fact, noted by Dr Chaplais, that Ethelred's diploma as we have it is written in a contemporary Crediton hand, is not disturbing.[4] The clause of immunity from all but the three common dues should have read: "omni terrenae servitutis liberum,[5] nisi tantum expeditione, si necessitas exigat, et pontis instructione arcisve," but the scribe has carelessly omitted the first four words, leaving the rest as a pendent clause. This and the verbal errors in the blessing and anathema may indicate that what we have is not the original but a contemporary copy.

However that may be, the document satisfies every test of authenticity so far; and it may be said at once that further enquiry will not reveal anything to shake our faith in it. But the existence of this second charter for Sandford prompts the question whether it casts a retrospective shadow over the first. Experience has warned us not to expect an answer to such questions until the bounds have been perambulated. Fortunately the survey, unlike the one in Athelstan's charter, is

[1] J. M. Kemble, *Codex Diplomaticus Ævi Saxonici*, 1839–48 (hereafter cited as K), no. 744, dated 1031.

[2] K 698.

[3] Ælfmaer, K 629, dated 981; Ælfwine, K 641 (984); Æthelsige, K 687 (994) and a Hyde charter of 988 (*Liber de Hyda*, pp. 238–42; I have to thank Dr C. R. Hart for this reference.); Eadric and Osulf, K 705 (1001).

[4] *Journal of the Society of Archivists*, III, 1965, p. 60.

[5] cf. K 622, 632, 633.

brief and comparatively easy to elucidate. It can be followed on the same maps.

1. First, on the highway from Creedy Bridge;
   From 846011 along B3214.

2. Thence to the northern way.
   To the East Lodge of Creedy Park (839011).

3. Along the highway above the cold spring.
   Following the line of the old parish boundary: see the note on the second landmark in Athelstan's charter. The spring is just inside the park (839012). Originally the scribe wrote "to the cold spring," but he erased "to" and inserted *bufan* (=above) over the erasure.

4. From the cold spring west along the old ditch
   There is a deep ditch, now full of nettles, beside the pathway through the park (834013).

5. again to a highway.
   The road from Crediton to Sandford (830012).

6. Thence west along the ditch by the way to the look-out post.
   At 825010. This and the next three landmarks occur in Athelstan's charter (24–26), but in the reverse direction.

7. From the look-out post north to Ruxford.
   818022.

8. From Ruxford due north to Henstill.
   818041 or thereabouts.

9. From Henstill north to the hedgerow.
   On the line of the road between Bussels and West Sandford.

10. From the hedgerow north to the enclosure
    ? Bussels (820044).

11. and on the brook to Thelbridge.
    819048. The brook is the "stream" in Landmark 15 of Athelstan's charter.

12. From Thelbridge down along the stream to the Creedy.
    The waters meet at 821048.

13. Thence downstream to Creedy Bridge.
    Back to the starting-point.

It is not always possible to be sure that an Anglo-Saxon charter boundary comprises the whole of the territory covered by the grant. Sometimes we find hints, or even explicit statements, that beyond it lies an indeterminate area of waste or woodland over which the recipient will have certain rights. For instance, in a charter of 958 the bounds of Ayshford and Boehill in east Devon are followed by the statement that "beyond the common lea here is an old paved road. Farther on there are many hills that may be put under plough."[1] A charter of Ethelred II *c*. 987 gives the bounds of two and a half yardlands by the Dart, then adds: "and appurtenant woodland rights ["wudu rædene"] of two and a half yardlands."[2] It seems that the two hides of Sandford enjoyed similar rights over adjoining woodland, for on the back of the charter, in an Exeter handwriting of perhaps the third quarter of the eleventh century,[3] is another boundary, prefaced by the statement: "This is the *wude rædenn*."

14. First, from White Way to the snake-pit.
    The White Way is Pidsley Hill (813047). Here the soil ceases to be the red earth of the Crediton district. *Wurmstealle* might mean either a place where snakes abounded or a dragon's lair. It was probably near the Broxham of Athelstan's charter (11).

15. From the snake-pit to the gate of the enclosure.
    The "enclosure below Bromley," Landmark 12 in Athelstan's charter.

16. From the gate of the enclosure to a point south of the road-fork.
    806068. The parish boundary here makes a sudden turn eastward.

17. Along the rivulet to the water.
    Along the rivulet (810066) that flows down to the head-water of the Creedy.

18. Down the water to the White Way rivulet.
    The Thelbridge brook (821047).

---

[1] CS 1027.
[2] W. G. Hoskins, *The Westward Expansion of Wessex*, Leicester Univ. Press, 1960, p. 33. The original belongs to the Marquess of Anglesey. When editing it (*ibid.*, pp. 33–35), I remarked that no explanation could be offered of its presence among Lord Anglesey's muniments, most of which relate to the lands of Burton Abbey in Staffordshire. A highly probable explanation is that he inherited it from his ancestor William Paget, the first baron (1505–63), who is named by John Bale, in a letter dated 30 July 1560, as one of those who had collected many documents after the dissolution of the monasteries.— *Trans. Cambridge Antiquarian Soc.*, III, 1865–78, p. 173.
[3] According to Mr Bishop, *Trans. Cambridge Bibliographical Soc.*, II, pp. 195, 196.

19. Up the rivulet back to the White Way.
Back to the starting-point on Pidsley Hill.

There is nothing here that conflicts with Athelstan's charter of 930. On the contrary, the bounds fit beautifully together like the two halves of an indenture. The two hides of 997 consist of inner Sandford, the smaller and perhaps more profitable central area which the bishop had kept to himself in 930. We may suppose that the canons were still in undisturbed possession of the three outer hides. There is no indication that the bishop had lost control of inner Sandford in the interval. Why, then, did he need a royal charter to put him in control of what he already possessed?

The answer is that the charter gives Bishop Alfwold the land for his own use during his lifetime, with liberty to bequeath it to any one he pleases.[1] This is a relatively unusual feature. The right of testamentary disposal is a normal accompaniment of grants to laymen, but when a churchman is the recipient the grant is usually made to him and to his successors in perpetuity, or for as long as Christianity shall flourish in England. Between Ethelred's accession and the date of the Sandford charter I have noted only four departures from this practice, and the four are exceptional in other ways.[2] The sequel shows that it was precisely this right to leave the land by will that Bishop Alfwold wanted. It was the *raison d'être* of the charter.

Some time before 1012, when his successor begins to attest diplomas,[3] Alfwold made his will and died. The will begins by leaving "the land at Sandford" to the clergy of the minster, but goes on to give one hide thereof to Godric, with a plough-team of oxen. A later passage in the will refers to Godric as

[1] "ea condicione ut ipse habeat utensque feliciter fruendo possideat quamdiu vivat, et se de hoc migrante saeculo cuicumque illi placabile sit liberam . . . in perpetuum in eadem libertate relinquendi licentiam habeat."

[2] K 635 (A.D. 983), a meadow outside Winchester for Æthelgar, bishop of Selsey; K 640 (also 983), a fishery on the Darent for Ethelwold of Winchester. In both cases the property is outside the bishop's own diocese. K 647 (985) is a grant to the king's "faithful priest" Wulfric, probably a royal clerk or chaplain. K 689, 690 deal with an estate pledged to Æscwig, bishop of Dorchester, by Archbishop Sigeric in return for a loan of ready money, and now 'booked' to him in order that he may restore it to Sigeric's successor.

[3] K 719.

the testator's brother-in-law. Since there were only two hides in all, Godric is really being given half the estate.[1]

This, then, is why the bishop thought it advisable to obtain a royal charter. He intended to make provision for a relative out of land belonging to his bishopric. The next bishop might well dispute the transaction and try to recover the land, unless the bequest were legalized beforehand by the king. The charter is really a licence to alienate part of the episcopal domain. As for the canons of Crediton, any possible objection from that quarter is forestalled by adding another hide in Sandford to the three which had become theirs by grant of Athelstan and Bishop Eadulf.

When the two charters have been subjected to the full battery of historical, topographical, diplomatic, palaeographical, and textual analysis which alone enables them to be correctly understood, they begin to bear fruit for the historian, who until then has been wary of using them, if indeed he has not dismissed them as worthless.

In the first place, the ecclesiastical historian can add the charter of 930 to the list of evidences for the division of endowments between a bishop and his cathedral clergy. The second charter, coupled with the will of Alfwold, shows how a prudent bishop went to work when he intended to make provision for a relative at the expense of his successors: a form of nepotism for which there are many parallels, and which naturally often led to friction.

The agrarian historian, too, can glean something from these documents. The central portion of Sandford, covered by the rich red earth of the Crediton district, was naturally the earliest to be exploited. But to the north the red sandstones and marls fade out into the carboniferous series known as the Culm Measures. In the early Saxon period the valleys here must have been thickly wooded. Kennerleigh, the parish adjoining Sandford on the north, makes no appearance in the records until the thirteenth century, and its very name imports a *leah* or woodland clearing. Morchard Bishop, another ad-

[1] *Crawford Charters*, x, p. 23. It would be particularly interesting if we could agree with Dr Chaplais that both the will and Ethelred's charter were written by the same scribe (*Bulletin of the Inst. of Historical Research*, xxxix, 1966, p. 21).

joining parish, derives its name from two British words, *mawr coed*, the 'great wood'. The deforestation of Sandford had evidently begun well before 930, but it was a laborious process, and there were setbacks, as when two of the farms named in Athelstan's charter vanished, one of them, perhaps, to be reclaimed at a later date and called Yelland, the 'old land'. The charter speaks of a *hlosleah*, or swine-pasture, and we can be sure that pig-keeping played an important part in the economy of the estate. The Domesday account of Crediton, in which Sandford is tacitly included, speaks of thirty swineherds who render yearly one hundred and fifty swine.[1] It is hardly fanciful to think of Swannaton (*Swāna-tūn*, the farm of the swineherds), on the western edge of Sandford, as the home of one of these *porcarii*. But it would be idle to look for the dwellings of the slaves on whom the lord mainly depended for the cultivation of his demesne. They may have been housed, not in huts of their own, but in the outbuildings round his courtyard. Bishop Alfwold directed in his will that several slaves he himself had purchased, and others who had fallen into servitude as a penalty for crime, should be set free on each of the episcopal estates. The resulting loss of man-power must have been made good by his successors, for in 1086 there were still forty slaves at Crediton.

THE BOUNDS OF CREEDY-LAND

AT SOME DATE not far removed from that of the second Sandford charter a scribe, working—it is reasonable to suppose—in the Crediton scriptorium, took a piece of parchment, drew a cross on it near the top left corner, and proceeded to write: "✠ This sint þa landgemæro cridian landes" (These are the bounds of Creedy-land). After this preface he wrote out a survey describing in great detail—there are no fewer than seventy-eight landmarks—the boundary of a large territory in the heart of Devon.

The parchment, one of the Crawford collection, is now in

---

[1] *The Devonshire Domesday and Geld Inquest*, Plymouth, 1884–92, p. 98.

the Bodleian Library.[1] Napier and Stevenson, who published it in their edition of the Crawford charters, made the serious mistake of printing the boundary as *Crawford* II, under a heading which ties it to a document written the best part of a century later and printed as *Crawford* I.[2] The result is that *Crawford* II has not been discussed on its merits as an independent text fraught with problems of its own.

Stevenson successfully identified thirty-four of the landmarks. Since then, local scholars have contributed spasmodically to the discussion, but the boundary has not yet been elucidated as a whole. The next step, therefore, must be to complete the task so well begun by Stevenson. When that has been accomplished, we can go on to ask when and why the survey was made in the first instance.

The bounds can be followed on Sheets SS80, SX89, 99, 89, 79, 78, 79, 69, 79, SS70, 80 of the $2\frac{1}{2}$-inch Ordnance Survey, in that order. They follow a clockwise direction.

1. First from Creedy Bridge
   The National Grid reference for the starting-point is SS80·846011.

2. on to the highway,
   The road which forms the eastern boundary of Crediton, skirting Shobrooke Park (848012).

3. along the highway to *sulhford* to the Exe;
   The *sulforda* of the Stoke Canon charter (CS723), i.e. the ford on the Exe just below Fortescue (SX99·931995).

4. then along the Exe as far as Focga's eyots.
   The islets at the junction of the Exe and the Creedy. The first part of the name survives at Voghay (now Foxhayes), a quarter of a mile lower down the Exe (*The Place-Names of Devon*, hereafter cited as PND, p. 458).

5. From Focga's eyots along the boundary ridge.
   The ridge N. of Exwick Barton (SX899·00951).

6. From the boundary ridge to Luha's tree.
   Perhaps at 895951.

7. From Luha's tree to the gate of the messuage.
   Probably at East Rowhorne (884947).

[1] MS. Eng. Hist. a. 2, no. 11a.
[2] The mistake is unfortunately repeated in Mr P. H. Sawyer's *Annotated List and Bibliography* of Anglo-Saxon charters (Royal Historical Soc. Guides and Handbooks, No. 8), p. 135, no. 255.

8. From the gate of the messuage to Dodda's ridge.
The ridgeway passes West Rowhorne (879949).

9. From Dodda's ridge to Grendel's pit.
The natural feature which gives its name to Pitt Farm (870947).

10. From Grendel's pit to the ivy-grove.
The southern boundary of Newton St Cyres, which we are now following, runs down between Whitestone Wood and Newton Wood (868955).

11. From the ivy-grove to the ford of *Hrugan*-combe.
Ashford (867964), by Venny Cleave. The first element in the name of the combe, according to Ekwall, *Oxford Dictionary of English Place-Names*, 1960, s.v. Rugley, is an Old English word *hrugce* meaning woodcock.

12. From the ford of *Hrugan*-combe to Fern Hill.
The summit of this hill is reached at 852955.

13. From Fern Hill to Eagle's Ridge.
The ridge which gives its name to Oldridge Road (846968).

14. From Eagle's Ridge to the ford in Wealda's combe.
Wealda has given his name to Oldridge, which in Domesday Book is *Walderige* (PND p. 457). At the bottom of the combe is a ford over the Kelland Brook (833966).

15. From Wealda's combe to Tetta's burn.
The stream which gives its name to Venny Tedburn and Tedburn St Mary. It is here known as the Culvery (822973).

16. From Tetta's burn upstream to the Lilly Brook.
818964.

17. From the Lilly Brook to the middle ridge.
The high ground between the two streams (817958).

18. From the middle ridge to the ford on the highway.
Herepath, here translated 'highway', is literally 'army-path'. The ford is at 814959, and its path, now Harford Lane, leads up to Posbury, the hill-fort which Professor Hoskins has convincingly identified with the *Posentesbyrig* of the Anglo-Saxon Chronicle, where in 661 the king of Wessex, Cenwealh, fought the Britons.[1]

19. From the ford on the highway to Cyrtla's gate.
Perhaps at Fivegate Cross (810969). Cyrtla has left his name to a rivulet not far away (SX79. 792961) that flows by *Curt*lake Cottage (PND p. 405).

[1] W. G. Hoskins, *op. cit.*, p. 14.

20. From Cyrtla's gate to the crab-apple tree.
    Somewhere midway between Fivegate Cross and the next landmark.

21. From the crab-apple tree to the Green Way.
    Crediton Lane, which forms the parish boundary between Tedburn
    St Mary and Cheriton Bishop.

22. From Green Way to Wolf-pit.
    From Crediton Lane westward and down through Colihole (a natural
    and perfect lair for a wolf) to the bottom of the valley. Colihole has
    now changed its name to the less appropriate form Collihill.

23. From Wolf-pit upstream to where the brooks meet.
    Near East Ford (789955).

24. Then up the middle of the ridge.
    Probably up Ford Hill (780959).

25. Along the ridge to the path.
    The road from Yeoford, which is reached perhaps midway between
    Three Gate Cross and Caddiford Cross (773959).

26. From the path straight to the alder.
    Apparently moving a short distance from the path, which may not
    then have taken exactly the same course as now.

27. Southward over to the precipice.
    Just above Lewdon (769950).

28. From the precipice to the head of Birch-combe.
    Near Cross Farm (765944).

29. From the head of Birch-combe to Hana's ford.
    Westward down Crosshill Lane to the ford just north of Staddon
    Plantation (760947).

30. Thence to Broad Ash.
    ? near Wilson, originally Wulfgar's *tun*, and lately rechristened
    Wulfgar's Farm (756953).

31. From Broad Ash to the head of Fox-combe.
    Where the parish boundary starts going downhill to the Yeo (749952).

32. Thence to Stanford (the stone ford) on the Yeo.
    Where the road from Hittisleigh Cross passes over the Yeo (741946).

33. From Stanford to the alder-thicket.
    ? near Easton Cross (723942).

34. From the alder-thicket to the landslip.
    A steep declivity north of the road, halfway between Fursham Cross
    and Chapple (710938). Greenwood's map of Devon, published in 1827,

47

shows that the parish boundary of Drewsteignton formerly turned aside from the Hittisleigh road just before Fursham Cross and passed straight across the head of the "landslip."

35. **Thence to Green Down.**
Following the line of the old Drewsteignton boundary as shown by Greenwood, who however had transposed Flood (which he calls "Blowder"!) and Chapple. Returning to the Hittisleigh road near Chapple, the boundary turns southward past Flood, and reaches the main road at a point slightly east of Grendon (710928), which is the Green Down of the charter.

36. **From Green Down on the highway**
A30, the main road from Exeter to Okehampton.

37. **to Putta's post.**
Probably at Harepath Cross (718924), where a side-track leads off to *Puddi*combe. The earliest recorded form of this name is *Pode*combe, and the authors of PND therefore question its association with the Putta of this boundary (p. 403 *n.*), but cf. the analogous development of Puddington (*ibid.*, p. 389).

38. **Thence to Beornwynn's tree.**

39. **From Beornwynn's tree to Stanford on the Yeo.**
This ford is omitted in a later copy of the bounds. If correctly inserted, it should probably be identified with the ford at Vete (736915). Yeo, a common stream-name in Devon, means simply 'water'.

40. **Thence to Bucga's ford.**
By Greystone, where the road crosses another brook (749916), an affluent of the one which now forms the boundary between Cheriton Bishop and Drewsteignton. This boundary stream, like the ford over its tributary, appears to have been named after Bucga, for in 1285 it was known as Boggebrok (PND p. 431). Between the two streams is a farm now called Lower *Budbrook*.

41. **From Bucga's ford to Brunwold's tree.**
? at Narracott (757915).

42. **Thence to Ash-combe.**
The site of Coombe Hall (761912).

43. **From Ash-combe to Wonbrook.**
Greenwood's map takes the parish boundary of Drewsteignton over the Budbrook at Coombe Hall and across the ridge to the next valley. Here it touches a stream which rises near Cheriton Cross. This must be the Wonbrook (777916). It flows down past a farm called Woodbrook, which is probably not a corruption of the older name, but an alternative introduced some time before 1244, when it makes its first recorded appearance.

44. **Along the stream to the Teign.**
   Down the Woodbrook *alias* Wonbrook to its junction with the Bud-brook, and thence to the Teign (SX78·778900).

45. **Upstream on the Teign to Path-ford.**
   Where A382 crosses the Teign (713893). This is now called Dogmarsh Bridge, but the original name survives on both sides of the river in the corrupt forms Parford and (Great) Pafford.

46. **Thence to Franca's combe.**
   A footpath along the north bank leads gently uphill. Franca has been forgotten, but the path runs up past a farm which may have been his; it is now known as Coombe (720897).

47. **From Franca's combe to the head of Drascombe.**
   Via Bowden Farm, and going westward, either along the road from Drewsteignton or by the field-path, now disused, which led from Bowden to Stone Farm. The head of the combe is reached just above Under-down (SX79 ·707910).

48. **Thence to Deormere.**
   The lake now known as Bradford or Bradmere Pool (700910).

49. **From Deormere to the Longstone.**
   There are still a number of longstones in the vicinity of Spinsters' Rock (see the illustrations in *Trans. Devon Assoc.*, LXII, 1930, plates XXV–XXVII), and there may formerly have been others nearer to Whiddon Down.

50. **Thence to the head of Hurra's combe.**
   The spelling Hurracombe survived until the seventeenth century (PND p. 446); it is now Hollycombe. Greenwood's map shows the Drewsteignton boundary crossing the main road about 500 yards west of Whiddon Down and returning to it from the head of the combe, which is near Martin, i.e. *mære tun*, the 'boundary farm' (SX69 ·690925).

51. **From the head of Hurra's combe to Rush-ford on the Nymet.**
   Going down the combe to Hollycombe Ford on the River Troney (SX79 ·723970), which in this boundary is called the Nymet (cf. *Crawford Charters*, p. 58; PND p. 348). The boundary runs down that stream. Rush-ford is probably the ford at Quince Cross, near the meeting of the Bow, Hittisleigh (formerly Drewsteignton), and Spreyton parish boundaries.

52. **Thence to Hillerton.**
   Hillerton Cross (720981). Hillerton, the *healre dune* of this boundary, is *Helleredun* in 1238 (PND p. 360).

53. **From Hillerton to Wærna's fastness.**
   Somewhere in the vicinity of Lockgate Cottage (731979).

54. Thence to Cidda's ford.
    At 741975, where the parish boundaries of Clannaborough and
    Colebrook meet.

55. From Cidda's ford to Cæfca's grove.
    Walson Wood (739982).

56. Thence to Cain's acre.
    At 738990 the parish boundaries of Bow and Colebrooke are separated
    only by the width of a single field. Cain's acre may have been here.

57. From Cain's acre to the head of Wolf-combe.
    At 734994, near Hilldown Cross.

58. Thence to the stone hill.
    The hill east of Walson Barton (SS70 ·739007).

59. From the stone hill to the cress well.
    St Mary's Well (745007). The cress is much in evidence.

60. From the cress well to Tinder (?) ford.
    At 746018, where the road from Bow to Coleford crosses a tributary
    of the western Yeo.

61. Thence to the ditch-gate.
    Now Aller Gate (738027).

62. From the ditch-gate to Unna's hill.
    733038. The tithe map of Down St Mary (1842) shows two fields
    named Firebeacon on the summit of this hill.

63. Thence to swine-combe.
    735044.

64. From swine-combe to Egesa's tree.
    At Thorne (740047). (On the latest map this is called North Thorne.)

65. Thence on Rush-brook
    The stream which rises above Ellicombe (744048). Since the draining
    of the marshy ground between Ellicombe and A377 the stream has
    been diverted into field-ditches. In midsummer, when I saw them, they
    were partly dry, but the rushes were there in plenty.

66. downstream to Sheep-brook.
    This is the Domesday *Eschipabroca*, now Shobrooke in Morchard
    Bishop (PND p. 409). Its modern name is Knighty Brook. The outflow
    of the Rush-brook is obscured by the highway, A377, and a railway
    embankment.

67. On Sheep-brook downstream to the Nymet.
    The western Yeo (737067).

68. On the Nymet downstream to the Dalch.
    736074.

69. From the Dalch upstream to the willow slade.
    750088. Tatepath Lake, the brook which runs down this slade, almost bisects the parish of Morchard Bishop, in which only three tithings belonged to the Hundred of Crediton (DA LIV, 1922, p. 154).

70. From the willow slade to eight oaks.
    On or near Beech Hill (782083).

71. Thence to Hawk-combe.
    The combe below Emlett Hill (SS80 ·809078).

72. From Hawk-combe to the gate of the messuage.
    ? near Higher Upton.

73. Thence out to the precipice.
    824083, on the boundary between Kennerleigh and Woolfardisworthy.

74. Thence to Binneford on the Creedy.
    831080.

75. Thence on the stream as far as Hawk-combe.
    Ashridge Wood (825067).

76. Thence to the gate of the enclosure.
    Downhayne (838063); this is the *haga* of the first Sandford charter (Landmark 20).

77. Thence on the old highway
    Downhayne Hill (837062).

78. as far as the eastern Creedy.
    Now called Holly Water (844045).

79. Thence along the stream to Creedy Bridge.
    Back to the starting-point.

Stevenson saw that the nucleus of "Creedy-land" consisted of the Hundred of Crediton. In the fourteenth century, when the lordship of this hundred was recorded as being vested in the bishop of the diocese, it comprised the parishes of Crediton (with Crediton Hamlets), Colebrooke, Sandford, Kennerleigh, Newton St Cyres, and the tithings of Rolstone, Southcott, and Ridge Arundel in Morchard Bishop.[1] But this is not

[1] *Feudal Aids*, I, p. 373; *Trans. Devon Assoc.*, (hereafter cited as DA) LIV, 1922, p. 153; *An Old Exeter Manuscript*, ed. O. J. Reichel and W. E. Mugford (supplement to *Devon Notes and Queries*, IV), Exeter, 1907, p. 26.

all. The boundary also takes in Upton Pyne, Brampford Speke, Oldridge, Hittisleigh, and Drewsteignton, all in the Hundred of Wonford; and parts of Clannaborough and Down St Mary in the Hundred of North Tawton: in all, an area of about 50,000 acres.

Nothing whatever is known about the history of the Devonshire hundreds before the Norman Conquest. The geld accounts in the Exeter Domesday are the oldest documents which give any clue to their constituents. Our first, and negative, conclusion must be that the territory comprised within the boundary of *Crawford* II coincides with no known administrative unit of any date.

Surveys of this character are usually, but not invariably, found inserted in, or appended to, land-grants. In the earliest land-charters they are written in Latin and confine themselves to specifying landmarks at some or all of the four cardinal points.[1] But after a time English place-names assume more and more importance in the determination of boundaries. Vernacular begins to appear in combination with Latin in 778, and by itself in a not entirely trustworthy charter of 785.[2] The two earliest contemporary or near-contemporary diplomas giving elaborately detailed perambulations in Old English are CS 346, dated 814, and CS 451, a Devon charter of 846. There is thus a well-marked line of evolution in the development of these surveys; and if we ask whereabouts in that line the Crediton bounds naturally fall, the answer must be: hardly before the ninth century, and most probably in the tenth, for after 900 detailed surveys in Old English are a well-established convention.

Stevenson, of course, was well aware of these facts. Nevertheless he opined that despite their length the Crediton bounds

[1] CS 111 (dated A.D. 704), 154 (736), 214 (774), 230 (779), 326 (808), 339 (811), 341 (812), 370 (822), 373 (823), 380 (c. 830), 381 (824), 411 (833), 442 (843), 496 (858), 497 (859), 507 (863). All of these are parchments which either are or appear to be contemporary with the transactions they record. Their consensus creates a reasonable presumption that where the text is preserved only in a later copy, as in CS 143 (725), 166 (718 × 745), 207 (772), the Old English bounds are an interpolation. In this respect the contrast between CS 229 and 230, both dated 779, the one from a twelfth-century cartulary, the other an original, is instructive.

[2] CS 225, 245. Earlier examples are found only in late copies.

might have originated as far back as the second quarter of the eighth century, "for the original charters of this period are sadly too few to justify our drawing hard and fast conclusions from them upon such points as this . . . Possibly a few additional features may have been introduced into the boundaries" when *Crawford* II was written. On the strength of this judgement Stevenson, and later scholars in his wake, have used the Crediton bounds as a key to the early topography of Anglo-Saxon Devon.[1] Some years ago, bowing down before the authority of Stevenson, the great pioneer of modern charter criticism, I developed an argument which presupposed that these bounds illustrate a very early phase of English settlement in the south-west.[2] In the light of the fieldwork now completed this supposition must be discarded as untenable. The boundary cannot be as old as that. It would certainly not be possible to summarize its complex topography by a bare reference to the four cardinal points.

Was the boundary transcribed from an ancient land-grant? We have no means of answering that question. All that can be said with confidence is that the parchment in the Bodleian looks like a complete and independent document. There is nothing in its shape or aspect to suggest that it had, or was intended to have, any context.

THE IMMUNITY OF CREDITON

IN LOOKING for a diploma to which these bounds might be relevant, we cannot avoid glancing at one which purports to have been granted by King Athelstan in 933. In return for a payment of sixty pounds of silver by Eadulf, bishop of Crediton, Athelstan frees the bishopric from the ancient customary taxes ("ab antiquo ritu vectigalium") which his predecessors have usurped the right to levy. To do so, he repeats almost *verbatim* the clause of immunity by which King Æthelwulf in 844 had exempted a tenth of every chartered estate from all secular dues except bridge-work,

[1] *Crawford Charters*, pp. 41, 44.
[2] H. P. R. Finberg, *The Early Charters of Devon and Cornwall*, Leicester, 1953, pp. 21–32, reprinted in *Lucerna*, pp. 116–30.

fortress-work, and military service.[1] I have discussed this and Æthelwulf's later 'decimation' in detail elsewhere, and have given reasons for doubting whether the act of 844 ever took effect. A copy of it was however kept at Sherborne, and as Crediton lay in the diocese of Sherborne until 909, the text was easibly accessible to the Crediton clergy.[2]

A shadow has rested over the diploma of immunity since Chadwick pointed out that the date 933 cannot be reconciled with the witness-list.[3] The witnesses would present no difficulty if the date were given as 939 and the indiction as 12, but by that time Eadulf was no longer bishop of Crediton, having been succeeded by Æthelgar. Morever, the text ascribes to Athelstan a general intention to free the minsters of his kingdom from secular dues, and there is no trace of any such intention in his authentic charters.

In considering this doubtful text, it is well to bear in mind a pregnant remark of Maitland, that "kings and sheriffs did not permit themselves to be cheated wholesale out of valuable rights."[4] That a bishop should pay the king a substantial sum

[1] CS 694. The phrase in Æthelwulf's charter "sive taxationibus quod nos dicimus *witeræden*" is clumsily altered to "atque expeditionalibus videlicet taxationibus," and bridge-work, which Æthelwulf had reserved, is not reserved by Athelstan.

[2] H. P. R. Finberg, *The Early Charters of Wessex*, Leicester, 1964, pp. 187–213. In her review of this book Professor Dorothy Whitelock argues at some length that both of Æthelwulf's 'decimation' charters are spurious. She seems to think the first one was probably concocted at Sherborne and Malmesbury after the Norman Conquest, when these monasteries were in contact (not before?), and she cites Athelstan's diploma of 933 as suggesting that Sherborne borrowed the immunity clause from Crediton instead of *vice versa*. She does not explain why the two decimation charters, if spurious, were dated ten years apart and provided with different preambles, *verba dispositiva*, anathemas, and witness-lists. Much of her argument runs counter to her own earlier observation that "from time to time formulae are revived after apparetnly being discontinued for a long period" (*English Historical Documents*, I, 1955, p. 341). She concludes with the remark that before accepting any views based on the assumption that Æthelwulf's decimation charters are reliable, "one would like to see the diplomatic evidence set out" (*English Historical Review*, LXXXI, 1966, p. 102). It is in fact set out on pp. 206–13 of the book she is reviewing, where the texts in question are printed in full, with an *apparatus criticus* of variant readings from the oldest manuscripts.

[3] H. M. Chadwick, *Studies on Anglo-Saxon Institutions*, Cambridge, 1905, p. 183 n.

[4] F. W. Maitland, *Domesday Book and Beyond*, Cambridge, 1907, p. 269.

to procure a local immunity and the secular jurisdiction that went with it is not in the least unlikely. We know that Ethelwold of Winchester did just that in the reign of Edgar, when he paid 150 mancuses of gold to obtain regalian rights over Taunton.[1] His example may well have prompted a contemporary bishop of Crediton to make a similar bargain. The contemporary in this case would probably be Sidemann, a prelate who was eminently well placed to secure favours from the king. Edgar made him abbot of Exeter in 968, and bishop of Crediton five years later. Sidemann combined his episcopal duties with the office of tutor to the king's eldest son, Edward the future Martyr. In 977, when attending on Edward at Kirtlington in Oxfordshire, he died suddenly, and was buried at Abingdon, although with his last breath he had expressed a wish to be buried at Crediton.[2]

Several indications point to the decade 970–80 as the period when an immunity granted, on this hypothesis, by Edgar or Edward at Sidemann's instance was antedated by putting it into a diploma ostensibly issued by Athelstan more than forty years earlier. Dr Chaplais states that the script of the false diploma resembles that of the genuine Nymed charter issued by Edgar in 974. It shares with that and with other Devonshire charters of the same decade the peculiarity of omitting the letter 'g' in certain words: eli[g]ens, fi[g]ens.[3] During Edward's brief reign (975–8) the country was in a state bordering on civil war, with the new claims of the churches forming a principal subject of contention. His murder enabled the party which had been in opposition under him to regain power and to effect an abrupt reversal of policy. At such a time it might well seem prudent to disguise the Crediton immunity as a long-established right.

The spurious diploma, however, even if a real transaction lies at its core, does not help us with the Crediton boundary.

---

[1] H. P. R. Finberg, op. cit., p. 229.

[2] Monumenta Historica Britannica, ed. Petrie, 1848, p. 577; English Historical Documents, I, pp. 210, 842.

[3] Dr Chaplais compares this with Ælfsi[g]e and Wulfsi[g]e in CS 1195, dated 967, e[g]o in CS 1303 (974), and fu[g]itivis and ru[r]i[g]enis in the Treable charter of 976.—Bulletin of the Institute of Historical Research, XXXIX, 1966, pp. 11, 12.

The immunity is granted to the whole bishopric, and the bishop of Crediton owned estates in Devon which are not comprised within the bounds: Ashburton, for example, the *Æscburnan land* of Bishop Alfwold's will. At the same time, the bounds include some estates which did not belong to the bishop in the period when *Crawford* II was written: Brampford Speke, for instance, which in 944 was sold by King Edmund for eighty gold mancuses to a nobleman named Athelstan, who afterwards became a monk at Glastonbury.[1]

So far we are still very much in the dark; but a glimmer of light begins to dawn when we consult two other charters of the period. In 974 King Edgar granted three hides at "Nymed" to his faithful thegn Ælfhere.[2] The bounds are described, and have been worked out in detail by Professor Hoskins. They comprise all that part of Zeal Monachorum which lies south of the stream now called Gissage Lake, together with most of Down St Mary, the adjoining parish.[3] An endorsement on the charter tells us that this three-hide estate of Nymed descended to a priest named Brihtric, who gave it to the minster at Crediton for the support of the canons there. But the canons, it seems, did not keep it, nor did it continue to form a single unit of tenure. By 1066 we find in its place a one-hide manor called "Limet," corresponding to Zeal Monachorum, and another of two hides called Dona, or Down St Mary. Both belonged in 1086 to the abbot of Buckfast,[4] but if the abbot had

[1] CS 799; cf. CS 728.
[2] CS 1303.
[3] W. G. Hoskins, *op. cit.*, pp. 26–29. I venture to propose a different interpretation of the eighth landmark, "where Rush-brook strikes on Nymet." Stevenson, I think, was right in taking "Nymet" here to mean the River Yeo, and the Rush-brook will then be the brook which joins the Yeo near Stopgate Cross (733055). From that point the boundary goes "east along Rush-brook to Sheep-brook," which are identical with landmarks 65 and 66 of the Crediton boundary (above, p. 50). This interpretation implies that there were two Rush-brooks less than a mile apart, but such poverty of local nomenclature is no more surprising than the occurrence of two "Nymets" in the Crediton bounds, one signifying the Troney, the other the western Yeo. My interpretation has the effect of excluding Bradiford from the grant to Ælfhere, and it is supported by Reichel's identification of Bradiford with the separate Domesday manor of *Oluardesdona* (DA LIV, 1922, p. 153 n. 2).
[4] *The Devonshire Domesday and Geld Inquest*, p. 252.

acquired them simultaneously they would surely have continued to form a single manor as in Edgar's reign. Buckfast was founded in 1018, early in the reign of Cnut, and in later times claimed to have received Zeal Monachorum as a gift from that king.[1] It follows that the original estate must have been divided before the end of his reign: that is, before 1035, and that the two hides of Down St Mary were acquired by a separate gift or purchase.

Now if the Crediton boundary had been drawn up in or before 974, or later while the original "Nymed" still belonged to the canons, it would surely have taken in the whole territory of the three-hide estate. But in fact it includes no part of Zeal Monachorum, only the two hides of Down St Mary. Therefore the boundary as we have it must have been determined after Zeal was detached from the original estate, but probably before Down St Mary passed out of Crediton hands.

This conclusion is reinforced by a charter of the following reign. In 976 King Edward granted one yardland called "Hyple's old land" to his "faithful vassal" Ælfsige. I have elsewhere identified the landmarks of this property, and shown that it included the parish of Cheriton Bishop and part of Drewsteignton.[2] In discussing the topography I called attention to a remarkable détour in the boundary of "Creedy-land." That boundary goes nearly ten miles out of its way to exclude Cheriton Bishop but to take in the portion of Drewsteignton which had formed part of "Hyple's old land." This is highly significant, though not in the sense postulated in my earlier discussion. It can only mean that the Crediton boundary was drawn some time after 976, but not until Drewsteignton had been detached from the property granted to Ælfsige in that year.

Palaeographers are of opinion that *Crawford* II was written towards the end of the tenth century or early in the eleventh.[3]

---

[1] *The Early Charters of Devon and Cornwall*, 2nd ed., 1963, p. 14, no. 53; W. G. Hoskins, *op. cit.*, p. 29, no. 52a.

[2] H. P. R. Finberg, *Lucerna*, pp. 116–30. One rectification should be made. The modern name of "Lamford" is "Lambert," and old maps show a Lambert Cottage at 774945. The ford of landmark 5 (p. 126) is therefore in all probability East Ford (789955).

[3] I have to thank Professor F. Wormald, Mr N. R. Ker, and Mr T. A. M. Bishop for giving me their opinions on the script.

Topographical study confirms this finding; it proves by dint of comparison with two other charter boundaries that "the bounds of Creedy-land" were drawn little if at all before they were committed to writing on the parchment now in the Bodleian.

Modern maps include the whole of Down St Mary in the Hundred of North Tawton. But the geld accounts show that as late as Domesday the Buckfast estate of *Dona* lay in the Hundred of Crediton. The only tenants-in-chief in that hundred to possess geld-free demesne were the bishop of Exeter and the abbot of Buckfast. The abbot was not liable for geld on half a hide, and the Domesday entry shows that this half-hide of demesne lay within the three hides of *Dona*.[1] Furthermore, the bishop was reported to have taken possession of Chaffcombe in Down St Mary and to have settled it on his canons. In 1066 Chaffcombe had been occupied by a thegn who held it *pariter*. This term is usually held to reflect a division between co-heirs. If so, the thegn in question may have been co-heir with another "free man," Alward Merta, who at the same date held a yardland in "Nimet," called "Merdesnymeth" in 1242 and "Wolvysnymet" in 1359, now Woolfin, a property adjoining Chaffcombe.[2] It looks as if these two thegns inherited the land from a lay tenant originally settled in "Nymet" by the canons of Crediton. Chaffcombe was valued at 10s. in 1086, and in 1598 was still paying a high rent of 10s. to Crediton, long after it had been transferred to another hundred.[3] Again, in 1066 a priest appropriately named Godman held one hide in Brampford Speke and three yardlands in Clannaborough, both of which lie within the Crediton boundary.[4] Was he himself a canon, or a tenant of the minster? There seem here to be hints—and in the case of Down St Mary something more than a hint—that the Hundred of Crediton was once of larger extent than it is known to have been after the Norman Conquest. If so, the bounds in *Crawford* II may give a truthful delineation of it at the beginning of the eleventh century.

[1] *Devonshire Domesday*, pp. xxi, 252.
[2] VCH *Devon*, I, p. 540; PND p. 368.
[3] DA LIV, 1922, p. 159.
[4] *Devonshire Domesday*, pp. 430, 512.

Can we now make a guess at the purpose for which the bounds were drawn?

A possible clue may be found in the statement of the *Leges Henrici Primi* that "shires are divided into hundreds and ship-sokes." Under a system which is thought to have been introduced in Edgar's reign, hundreds were organized in groups of three to provide the crew for a warship. Liebermann suggests that they did so by sending or hiring one man from every five hides to man a ship of sixty oars. These triple hundreds, of which Oswaldslow in Worcestershire is the best-known example, were called ship-sokes. The bishop of Worcester was not the only prelate to be put in charge of one. A letter written between 1001 and 1012 by Æthelric, bishop of Sherborne, refers to "the three hundred hides that other bishops had." Æthelric complains that ship-money is no longer being paid from thirty-three of his hides, and he asks the ealdorman of the western shires to help him retrieve the situation. His ship-soke lay mainly in Dorset, but it also included Holcombe Rogus in Devon.[1] At about the same date Bishop Alfwold of Crediton made a will which suggests that he too was involved in the system, for he leaves the king a ship of sixty oars. The *Anglo-Saxon Chronicle* states that in 1008 the system was imposed on the whole country. This probably had the effect of making local magnates responsible for collecting ship-money from estates other than their own. The bishop of Crediton was by far the greatest landowner in the district where his cathedral stood. Whether or not this part of his ship-soke extended over adjacent manors belonging to lesser men, it would be useful to have a careful record made, showing the exact extent of the area for which he was accountable, *Crawford* II may be the only survivor of a group including similar surveys of "Ashburn-land" and other blocks of territory which made up the episcopal ship-soke. It was certainly written at a time when Ethelred II and his counsellors were straining every resource to build up an effective naval defence against the Vikings.

[1] H. M. Cam, 'Early Groups of Hundreds' in *Historical Essays in honour of James Tait*, Manchester, 1933, pp. 13–25, esp. pp. 14, 15; F. E. Harmer, *Anglo-Saxon Writs*, Manchester, 1952, pp. 266–70, 482–6; E. John, *Land Tenure in Early England*, Leicester, 1960, pp. 119–22.

It would be unjustifiable to claim anything more for this hypothesis than that it fits in plausibly with the known circumstances of the time. With rather more confidence we can allow these Crediton documents to tell us something of the political and agrarian history of Devon.

The men of Wessex had established their military superiority over the once powerful British kingdom of Dumnonia as far back as the reign of Cenwalh (643–72), and probably began to settle in Devon soon afterwards. The Britons, however, were still giving trouble at the beginning of the ninth century, and a British dynasty survived in Cornwall until the early years of the tenth. Britons continued to live side by side with Saxons in the city of Exeter, and some British landowners remained undisturbed in Devon until the reign of Athelstan (924–39), who imposed drastic administrative and demographic changes.[1] As late as 944 King Edmund, in a charter disposing of land in Devon, styles himself "king of the English and ruler of this British province" (hujusque provincie Britonum ruris gubernator)—clear proof that Dumnonia was still thought of as an appendage not fully integrated into the English realm.[2]

Such being the political background, Anglo-Saxon settlement could not but be a long-drawn-out process. With the unerring judgement of good farmers, the English established themselves from the first on the red soils. From their British neighbours they took over the names of streams and other natural features, and used them freely in the delimitation of boundaries. In 846 King Æthelwulf secured to himself and to his heirs by charter a large area in the South Hams. Its boundary, the earliest on record from this county, is full of springs, brooks, combes, downs, tors, and woods, but yields relatively little evidence of human settlement.[3] We have to wait nearly a century for another Devon boundary, that of the first Sandford charter, and by this time English personal names are prominent. Two generations later still the bishop's estates at Crediton and Ashburton are still named simply "Creedy-

[1] H. P. R. Finberg, *Lucerna*, pp. 99–112, 121–4; W. G. Hoskins, *op. cit.*, pp. 7–22.

[2] CS 799, the Brampford Speke charter.

[3] CS 451; see above, pp. 21–7.

land" and "Ashburn-land." Each is clearly a lordship of scattered hamlets, identified by the name of its principal stream, though Crediton by this time has the central *tun* which gives it its modern name.

It is clear that we cannot now take the Crediton boundary to reflect a pattern much older than the tenth century, but we can agree with Stevenson that it presupposes a considerable English settlement.[1] The other documents examined in this study bear witness to an energetic process of expansion in the last century of the Old English state. The three hides of Nymet, a single tenure in 974, have split up by 1066 into four holdings (Limet, Dona, Nimet, Chefecoma), only two of which still bear the original name. In 976 some ten thousand acres called "Hyple's old land," from a former British owner whose true name, Ebell, is perpetuated in the thirteenth-century Tryf-ebel, now Treable, passed by royal grant to one Ælfsige, under the remarkably favourable assessment of only one yardland. Ælfsige may have been an exceptionally favoured personage,[2] but when we find that by 1066 Drewsteignton has become detached from the area appurtenant to Ebell's old *tref* to form a manor of two hides, while the rest of the area has been divided between two holders, with a rating of 2 hides 2½ yardlands,[3] it begins to look as if there has been a rapid expansion of the rural economy, accompanied, perhaps, by an equally rapid growth in the number of mouths to be fed.

KING ÆTHELHEARD'S CHARTER

THE last of the Crediton documents to be considered here is that printed as *Crawford* 1 from Bodleian MS. Eng. hist. a.2, no. 1. This is written, Dr Chaplais tells us,

---

[1] *Crawford Charters*, p. 44.

[2] Ordgar, ealdorman of Devon, who died in 971, left two sons, one of whom was buried at Tavistock before 981. He may have been the Ælfsige of the Treable charter, for the ealdorman's other son, Ordulf, is recorded as freeing a serf at Bodmin "for the soul of Ælfsige."—*Lucerna*, pp. 190–93.

[3] Eighebera (Eggbeer), 2½ yardlands, with Lanforda (Lambert), 1 y., both held by Leofgar; Lantford (Great Lambert), 1 y.; Ceritona (Cheriton), 1 y.; Midelanda (Medland), 1 hide; Cuma (Coombe), 1 y.—all four held by Ælfstan. By 1086 Leofgar's portion has been divided between two holders.—*Devonshire Domesday*, pp. 514, 1088, 1158, 1160.

in the same hand as an authentic original of 1069.[1] It gives the text of a charter apparently issued in 739 by Æthelheard, king of Wessex, granting twenty hides in "Creedy" to Forthhere, bishop of Sherborne, for the founding of a minster. The land is granted free of all secular dues except military service. This is just the immunity we should expect to find in a Wessex charter of the eighth century; though expressed in different terms, it is identical in substance with one conferred by King Beorhtric in 794.[2] A description of the bounds is introduced with the words "Territoria autem hec sunt," which may be compared with the corresponding clause "Et haec sunt territoria" in CS 143, a charter of Ine dated 725. Then follows the text of the great boundary of "Creedy-land." The scribe omitted three or four landmarks and occasionally 'modernized' the spelling as he went along, but substantially it is the same boundary as in *Crawford* II, an anachronism, as we have seen, in a charter of 739. Stevenson made light of the anachronism; Professor Whitelock, more prudently, and, as the foregoing discussion will have shown, rightly, suggests that the bounds have been added to a genuine early text.[3]

The latest commentator, Dr Chaplais, does not go so far as to reject the charter in so many words, but all the features to which other scholars have pointed as authenticating it serve only to inspire him with dark suspicions. The preamble "is so common that it could have been adapted from a genuine charter by any competent forger." The dispositive words "suggest a Wessex model." The subscriptions "seem to have

---

[1] P. Chaplais, *Bulletin of the Institute of Historical Research*, XXXIX, 1966, pp. 10, 32; but cf. T. A. M. Bishop, *op. cit.*, p. 196: the date 1069 "may be no better than an earlier limit to the true date of writing."

[2] H. P. R. Finberg, *The Early Charters of Wessex*, pp. 120, 188. Two years later Beorhtric reserves bridge-work (CS 282; see also CS 389, dated 825). Fortress-work is not reserved in any Wessex charter of unimpeachable authenticity until 842 (CS 438).

[3] *English Historical Documents*, I, p. 455. The scribe breaks off in the middle of a line with landmark 64, then begins a new line with a large initial and starts off again with a compressed version of 68 and 69. This suggests that he was not working from *Crawford* II, in which the missing landmarks 65–67 are continuous and perfectly legible, but from some other manuscript which he was unable to decipher here. The same mistakes recur in the late fifteenth-century version printed as *Crawford* III; evidently this is based on *Crawford* I, not II.

been borrowed from a genuine text," and one of the formulas "also suggests a genuine model of the first half of the eighth century." Dr Chaplais has nothing to say about *Crawford* II, but concludes his remarks by calling attention to a very significant circumstance which Stevenson and Professor Whitelock overlooked: namely, that both in the text and in the contemporary endorsement the figure xx for the hidation of the estate is written over an erasure, having been substituted for another numeral which occupied less space in the line.[1]

It is a great service to have brought this fact to light. Taken in conjunction with the palaeographical finding that the document was written after the Norman Conquest, it provides a clue which it will be well worth while to follow up when *Crawford* I and II come to be definitively re-edited in the correct sequence. For we know from the geld-roll that in the Conqueror's reign the Hundred of Crediton was rated at exactly twenty hides.

The church at Crediton was not exposed to Viking attacks to anything like the same extent as Exeter, where the monastery of SS. Mary and Peter is said to have had all its ancient charters destroyed by fire in the course of an attack by heathens.[2] It is therefore not at all improbable that the original or a true copy of the foundation charter should have been preserved at Crediton until the eleventh century. It seems to have included some description of the bounds ("Territoria autem hec sunt"), but we can be tolerably certain that they were not the elaborate bounds of *Crawford* II. We shall never know how many hides were really granted to Bishop Forthhere for the support of the new minster, for the original figure is irrecoverable even under ultra-violet light.[3]

The most reasonable inference to be drawn from these circumstances is that after the Norman Conquest Bishop Leofric or his successor Osbern had a copy made of Æthelheard's charter, the genuine foundation-deed of 739, but in so

---

[1] Chaplais, *op. cit.*, p. 10.

[2] K 729.

[3] It may be worth noting that Glastonbury preserved in its *Landbok* the text of a charter dated 729 by which King Æthelheard granted the abbey ten hides in the valley of the Torridge.—Finberg, *Early Charters of Devon and Cornwall*, p. 7.

doing 'edited' it for his own purposes. The 'editing' took the form of substituting for the original bounds the boundary of Crediton Hundred as recorded the best part of a century before his time, and, as an afterthought, altering the hidation to make it agree with that of the Domesday hundred. The results of this tampering lie before us in *Crawford* i.

It may be that the document thus 'improved' helped the bishop to recover Chaffcombe for his canons. A larger estate, Newton St Cyres, was also in dispute. Bishop Leofric recovered it "by means of his advocacy and his money,"[1] but this was only a temporary success. In the course of the Domesday inquest and ensuing litigation Bishop Osbern laid claim to three hides in Newton, at that time occupied by one Domnus, who had indeed paid geld on two of them. The bishop produced charters which showed that his church had been in possession before 1042. That settled the matter; judgement was given for the bishop; and the word "claims" in the Exeter Domesday was altered to "has."[2] What were the charters that produced this result, so eminently satisfactory for the bishop if not for Domnus?

In or about 1018 Bishop Eadnoth had borrowed thirty mancuses of gold to help him pay his portion of the Danegeld, and had mortgaged some land by the Creedy to the lender. A copy of the mortgage deed is written, in a hand of Bishop Leofric's time, on the dorse of the first Sandford charter. It contains a boundary which proves that the land lay in Newton St Cyres, but Newton is not named and the land is rated at only one yardland.[3] By itself this would scarcely have clinched Bishop Osbern's claim to an estate of three hides, equivalent to a dozen yardlands. Nor would *Crawford* ii, which is undated, be acceptable evidence of the state of things before good King Edward came to the throne. But a copy of a royal charter dated 739, with a boundary which included the whole of Newton, might well be expected to impress the royal commissioners. No other documents bearing on the early

[1] *Anglo-Saxon Charters*, ed. A. J. Robertson, Cambridge, 1939, p. 226.
[2] *Devonshire Domesday*, pp. xxi, 98. In this record the words "antequam rex Eduuardus regnaret" take the place of the usual "tempore regis Eduuardi."
[3] *Crawford Charters*, pp. 9, 76; on the script, see Bishop, *op. cit.*, pp. 195, 196.

history of Newton exist or are known to have existed in the
past.

PRINCIPLES OF CRITICISM

IN DISCUSSING these Crediton documents, it has
been necessary to cite and occasionally to controvert the
opinions of some eminent living scholars. The last few
years have seen the publication of a number of important books
and articles on the surviving charters of the Anglo-Saxon
period.[1] There is even talk of a new critical edition of
the entire corpus, which has long been one of the great
desiderata of English historical scholarship. It may be oppor-
tune, therefore, to conclude this study with a few remarks of
wider application.

Some documents proclaim themselves fictitious at a glance.
It is unlikely that any one nowadays will be deceived by the
charter said to have been granted by Athelstan to his burgesses
of Malmesbury.[2] But it is safe to say that all or nearly all such
gross fabrications have long been recognized as such. Between
them and the diplomas which have usually been accepted as
genuine lie the many which invite suspicion by one doubtful
feature or another, or have had suspicion cast upon them, not
always justly, by hypercritical scholars.

The criticism of charters is not an end in itself. Its object is
to provide the historian with trustworthy tools for reconstruct-
ing the past life of a community. The texts must be judged in
the light of history, to the end that they may help to increase
that light.

Some years ago Sir Frank Stenton warned us against the
pitfalls of criticizing Anglo-Saxon charters in terms of pure
Diplomatic.[3] Professor Whitelock, in the admirable introduc-

---

[1] The following should be added to those already cited: C. R. Hart, *The
Early Charters of Eastern England*, Leicester, 1966; P. Chaplais, 'The Origin
and Authenticity of the Royal Anglo-Saxon Diploma', *Journal of the Society
of Archivists*, III, 1965–6, pp. 48–61; id., 'The Anglo-Saxon Chancery: from
the Diploma to the Writ,' *ibid.*, III, pp. 160–76; Eric John, *Orbis Britanniae*,
Leicester, 1966.

[2] CS 720.

[3] F. M. Stenton, *The Latin Charters of the Anglo-Saxon Period*, Oxford,
1955, pp. v, 11–23.

tion to her anthology of charters, showed herself well aware of the pitfalls,[1] yet in her recent criticism she makes much play with diplomatic *minutiae*, as does also Dr Chaplais. The effect is to cast doubt on a number of charters without offering any hint of a motive for their fabrication. It may now be suggested that the time has come for critics and editors to take Stenton's teaching to heart, and to recognize as the first golden rule of criticism his dictum that the absence of any known motive for the fabrication of charters raises a presumption that they are basically authentic.[2]

The second golden rule has already been quoted from Maitland. Successful frauds were sometimes perpetrated, as when Robert de Limesey moved his see from Chester to Coventry in 1102 and obtained baronial rights over half the town by producing a series of forged charters.[3] But in general, Maitland warns us, "the diplomatist's scepticism should be held in check by the reflexion that kings and sheriffs did not permit themselves to be cheated wholesale out of valuable rights, when the true state of the facts must have been patent to hundreds of men."[4]

[1] *English Historical Documents*, I, pp. 337–49.

[2] Stenton, *op. cit.*, p. 20.

[3] Joan C. Lancaster, 'The Coventry Forged Charters', *Bulletin of the Institute of Historical Research*, XXVII, 1954, pp. 113–39.

[4] Domesday Book records that Chilcomb, a manor belonging to the church of Winchester, was rated at only one hide, though it had land for sixty-eight ploughs. Behind this unusually favourable assessment lie a series of spurious or interpolated charters. When these have been discarded, there remain (1) a charter, perhaps in English, of Alfred the Great, which was read out in the presence of Ethelred II early in the eleventh century and survived until 1643, but is now lost; and (2) a writ of Ethelred II confirming Alfred's charter and decreeing that Chilcomb shall continue to be assessed at one hide for all purposes. Dr Harmer, most judicious of editors, found no indications of falsity in this writ. She concluded that if it is a fabrication, the forger has succeeded remarkably well in giving it an appearance of authenticity. Concerning Alfred's charter Professor Whitelock remarks coldly that it "is not proved authentic by its survival until 1643," and Dr Chaplais declares—on what evidence?—that "it probably was no more reliable" than the recognized forgeries. Brushing aside Dr Harmer's suggestion that it could have been the source of certain textual similarities between Ethelred's writ and one of the forged charters, he declares them to be "so striking that they are likely to be the works of the same forger." This is surely a gratuitous assumption. It is quite as likely that a forger would be careful not to repeat

Many texts that would otherwise be lost survive because they were transcribed into cartularies. The palaeographical expert can sometimes throw much light on the structure of these compilations. For example, Mr N. R. Ker's masterly analysis of the Cottonian MS. Tiberius A XIII must be the point of departure for any modern study of the Worcester charters.[1] But when parchments are or profess to be contemporary with the transactions they record, palaeographical study becomes particularly important. If under expert scrutiny the script turns out to be an imitative one, this may indicate that the scribe or his employer meant to pass it off as an original. On the other hand, the intent need not have been fraudulent: we have seen that the first Sandford charter, denounced by Dr Chaplais as a forgery because written in an imitative script, is substantially a true copy of a perfectly genuine diploma. Again, a young scribe learning calligraphy may sometimes have been set to copy an old charter merely for practice in the art. Scripts, in any case, can seldom be dated with complete assurance. A latitude of ten or fifteen years each way is probably the least that should be allowed.

Our re-examination of the Crediton charters should have made one thing obvious. Where land is in question, criticism will remain blindfold until it is known where exactly the land lay. The place-names must be identified correctly, and if bounds are given, the landmarks must be pin-pointed wherever possible by means of references to the National Grid. The two Sandford charters cannot be understood until they are seen to deal with different tracts of land. Nor can the approximate date of the Crediton boundary be established and its historical implications drawn out until it is compared with the bounds of the Nymet and Treable charters. When the topography has

---

himself in so many words. Having thus done his best to undermine every one of the documents, Dr Chaplais leaves the reader to infer that the favourable hidation of Chilcomb was obtained by fraud. Maitland was inclined to think so too, in spite of his own salutary warning against such nihilistic criticism.— Finberg, *Early Charters of Wessex*, pp. 220–48; Harmer, *Anglo-Saxon Writs*, pp. 373–80, 395; Whitelock, *English Historical Review*, LXXXI, 1966, p. 103; Chaplais, *Journal of the Soc. of Archivists*, III, 1965–6, p. 171; Maitland, *op. cit.*, pp. 269, 497.

[1] N. R. Ker, 'Hemming's Cartulary', in *Studies in Medieval History presented to F. M. Powicke*, Oxford, 1948, pp. 48–75.

been securely based, the text can be studied in the context of local and national history. It is only in that context that possible incentives to fabrication will come to light. Outside that context the value of the charter as historical evidence cannot be assessed.

This is not work that can be left to await the chance interest of some local antiquary. It may involve visits to distant libraries and muniment-rooms where old estate maps, tithe maps, and terriers can be consulted. These are often more instructive than the Ordnance maps of the present day, which are of course indispensable, but can sometimes be misleading since the boundaries they show are those of civil parishes and do not always coincide with those of the older ecclesiastical parish. Above all, the investigator must visit the place and inspect the landmarks on the ground. He may have to scramble up and down some difficult places; he may even get his clothes torn and his feet wet. It is a laborious and expensive business, and this no doubt is why it is so often shirked: far more comfortable to sit in a library checking dates and comparing formulas. But it is work that brings its own abundant reward. Often it provides just the key to unlock the mystery of a puzzling charter. It takes the explorer into secret and lovely places, conjuring up a vision of the landscape as it appeared to English eyes a thousand years ago.

Finally, when texts appear to have been miscopied, textual criticism must be brought to bear in accordance with the recognized canons of such work. Confronted with such a blunder as that of the scribe who copied Edward the Elder's Hurstbourne charter into the cartulary of the Old Minster, and in place of "ab illo Repuno episcopo" wrote the meaningless "Apelred uno episcopo," a modern editor will not just reproduce the blunder, as Birch did. He will indicate the true reading and justify it in his *apparatus criticus*.[1]

The criticism of Anglo-Saxon charters, it will be seen, is a

---

[1] Finberg, *Lucerna*, p. 134. Professor Whitelock declares (*loc. cit.*) that the presence of Swithun in both witness-lists of CS 423, another Winchester charter, shows that it has been tampered with. She would perhaps have reconsidered this judgement had she noticed that the anachronism is pointed out on p. 30 and the obvious textual emendation supplied on p. 16 of the book she is reviewing.

multifarious task. It requires not only a competent knowledge of Latin and Old English, but also fieldwork, textual acumen, and familiarity with the historical background. The help of palaeography and diplomatic must also be invoked. It would be too much to expect all these varieties of *expertise* to be united in one person, and even if they were they would need to be tempered with a large admixture of common sense. But nothing short of total criticism will produce the definitive results that history demands.

ST PATRICK AT GLASTONBURY

WHEN Walter de Gray Birch began to publish a new edition of the surviving Anglo-Saxon charters, he led off inauspiciously by printing on the first page a document which is neither Anglo-Saxon nor a charter. He found it embedded in the tractate *On the Antiquity of Glastonbury* composed early in the twelfth century by William of Malmesbury, but this work is known to have been subsequently embellished with numerous imaginative additions by other hands. The so-called Charter of St Patrick is probably one of these interpolations. It is cast in the form of an autobiographical narrative by the apostle of Ireland. Patrick relates that after converting the Irish and establishing them solidly in the Catholic faith, he returned to his native land and was led by guidance from on high to Glastonbury. There he came upon certain holy men living the life of anchorites. Finding themselves all of one mind with Patrick, they decided to form a community and elected him as their superior. Some considerable time later he and one of the brethren made their way up, not without difficulty, to the summit of Glastonbury Tor. There they spent three months fasting and praying in the ruins of an old chapel, until Patrick was admonished in a vision to revisit the brethren down below. They decided that henceforth two members of the community should always reside on the Tor and serve its chapel. The first pair to do so were two Irish companions of Patrick, implausibly named Arnulf and Ogmar. To these two Patrick entrusted a written account of the proceedings, at the same time thoughtfully lodging a duplicate in the treasury of the main church.

Summarized in these terms, the Charter of St Patrick takes the beginnings of organized monastic life at Glastonbury back to the middle of the fifth century: that is to say, two hundred years before its authentic history begins. And in the first flush of invention its ingenious author may have been content to assert this comparatively modest claim. But if so, his original composition has been expanded; at any rate, in its finished form it supplies even more sensational details. The brethren show Patrick ancient writings from which he learns that twelve disciples of the apostles Philip and James built the church of St Mary at Glastonbury, prompted by the archangel Gabriel, that the Lord himself consecrated it, and that three pagan kings gave twelve portions of land for its endowment. More recent writings told of Saints Phagan and Deruvian, emissaries of Pope Eleutherius in the second century after Christ. It was these two who built the chapel on the Tor in honour of St Michael. They dwelt there for nine years, and obtained an indulgence of thirty years for all pilgrims to the spot. Their doings were recorded in a dilapidated volume which came to light while Patrick was rummaging in the ruins on the Tor.[1]

In this fantasy the only plausible feature is the statement or implication that there were solitaries living in hermitages amid the Somersetshire marshes before any monastery was founded at Glastonbury. This may well be true. At present there is no convincing evidence, either documentary or archaeological, for the existence of a monastic institution at Glastonbury before the third quarter of the seventh century.[2] As for the apostle of Ireland, we have his own word for it that he felt bound to stay in Ireland to the end of his days. In his authentic writings he insists on this repeatedly and with the most solemn emphasis. "Even if I wished to go to Britain," he writes in his *Confessio*, "... I am bound by the Spirit, who gives evidence against me if I do this, telling me that I shall be guilty; and I am afraid of losing the labour which I have begun—nay, not I, but Christ the Lord, who bade me come here and stay with them for the rest of my life."[3]

The so-called Charter deceives nobody today, and would scarcely have seemed plausible even in the twelfth century had there not been other grounds for associating Patrick with

[1] *Cartularium Saxonicum*, ed. W. de G. Birch, 1885–93, no. 1. The passages "qui successerunt ... Deruviani," "Et cum vitam monasticam ... acquisivi," and "Egredientes ... visitantibus" may be additions to the original text.

[2] CS 25, undated but *c.* 670, is the oldest extant Glastonbury charter. On the archaeological evidence see C. A. R. Radford in *Proc. Somerset Arch. & Nat. Hist. Soc.*, CVI, 1962, p. 32.

[3] *The Works of St Patrick*, trs. and annotated by L. Bieler, 1953, p. 35. See also the Letter to Coroticus, § 10, *ibid.*, p. 43; Confessio, § 13, p. 25, and § 37, p. 32.

Glastonbury Abbey. Belief in this association has indeed persisted through the centuries. Writing as recently as 1961 from
the Dublin Institute for Advanced Studies, Professor James
Carney says: "There seems to be at least a possibility that
Patrick, tired and ill at the end of his arduous mission, felt released from his vow not to leave Ireland, returned to Britain,
and died at the monastery from which he had come, which,
if this be so, may perhaps be identified as the monastery of
Glastonbury."[1] Professor Carney is a scholar who has made
some notable contributions to the study of Patrick's career,
and if he is prepared to entertain, however hesitantly, the
notion that Patrick ended his days at Glastonbury, there must
be more behind it than a flagrant literary imposture. How far
back in time can the idea be traced?

A catalogue of saintly relics and shrines begun, according to
Liebermann, before 995 and completed by 1030, states that
St Aidan and St Patrick, with many other saints, lie at rest in
Glastonbury.[2] The calendar of the Leofric Missal includes the
feast of St Patrick the bishop on the usual day, March 17th.
This calendar is contemporary with the catalogue already
cited, and in the judgement of liturgiologists it reflects the
liturgical practice of Glastonbury.[3] The first step in this enquiry
thus takes us back in one long stride to the end of the tenth
century. At that time the original church of Glastonbury, an
unpretentious little building formed of wattles, was still standing. On the south side of the high altar a stone monument,
described as a pyramid, marked the reputed burial-place of
Patrick. A pyramid in this context seems to mean any structure
tapering upwards from a broad base to a narrower summit,
like a coped tomb, or like the sculptured crosses of Northumbria and Ireland. The coped tomb is perhaps a likelier form for
a monument inside the church. Whatever its shape, the monument ascribed to St Patrick, originally plain, was nobly
adorned with gold and silver by the time William of Malmesbury saw it. There it stood until the old church was destroyed
by fire in 1184. In the course of rebuilding excavation took
place on the site; the bones of the saint were then recovered,

[1] J. Carney, *The Problem of St Patrick*, Dublin, 1961, p. 121.
[2] *Die Heiligen Englands*, ed. F. Liebermann, Hannover, 1889, p. 17.
[3] *The Leofric Missal*, ed. F. E. Warren, Oxford, 1883, pp. liii, liv, 25.

and placed in a casket, as were also those of another Irish saint, Indract, whose monument had stood on the other side of the altar.[1]

The tradition is thus of an antiquity which anywhere else might be called respectable. But the muniments of the abbey contained two charters which, if they could be trusted, would take it still farther back. One of them, dated 704, is a concession by Ine, king of Wessex, to the monks who serve God in the church of St Mary and St Patrick at Glastonbury, exempting them from all secular dues and charges.[2] Now the abbey possessed half a dozen or more charters from King Ine, but this is the only one that contains any reference to St Patrick, and on closer inspection it turns out to be merely a local adaptation and almost word-for-word copy of the instrument by which Ine, following the example set five years earlier by Wihtred, king of Kent, released all the churches and minsters of his kingdom from secular dues.[3] There was a copy of Ine's general concession in the *Liber Terrarum* or *Landbok* compiled at Glastonbury about the beginning of the eleventh century, but the particular concession to Glastonbury, with its reference to St Patrick, exists in no copy older than the thirteenth century.[4]

The other document which calls for a passing mention is dated 681. It is a charter by which King Baldred grants land at Pennard to the church of blessed Mary and St Patrick.[5] The grant itself may be substantially a genuine act, but the oldest extant copy is a pseudo-original written in a curiously imitative hand which, according to competent palaeographers, cannot be older than the tenth century and may well be later. As evi-

[1] *Adami de Domerham Historia de Rebus Gestis Glastoniensibus*, ed. T. Hearne, Oxford, 1727, pp. 23, 335. (In subsequent footnotes I refer to this work as AD.) The seventh-century Irish biographers of Patrick give conflicting accounts of his burial. Muirchú places it at Downpatrick; Tirechán says that no one knew where his bones were laid, but after a while the Holy Ghost revealed to St Columba that Patrick was buried at Saul.—*Liber Ardmachanus*, ed. J. Gwynn, 1913, pp. 16a, 30b.

[2] CS 109.

[3] CS 99, 106.

[4] *Johannis Glastoniensis Chronica sive Historia de Rebus Glastoniensibus*, ed. T. Hearne, Oxford, 1726, p. 370: "Carta Ynae de libertatibus concessis ecclesie in Westsaxonia," apparently identical with the "Privilegium Ynae concessum generaliter omnibus ecclesiis," *ibid.*, p. 375.

[5] CS 61.

dence for the cult of St Patrick at Glastonbury before the tenth century it may be dismissed, with Ine's charter, out of hand.

Now the tenth century, to which all our clues have led so far, was the century of St Dunstan. Born near Glastonbury in or about 910,[1] he was sent to school in the abbey, which at that time—so his biographers inform us—housed a colony of Irishmen. We shall obviously have to take a close look at this Irish colony; but first let us recall the outlines of Dunstan's career. Ordained priest in 939, he was appointed abbot of Glastonbury some five years later, became bishop successively of Worcester and London, and died in 988, having been archbishop of Canterbury for the last twenty-eight years of his life. His first biography was written about twelve years after his death by a Saxon priest of whom we know only the initial, B. It is a badly written composition, but the author had gathered much of his information from Dunstan's own mouth, and much else from Dunstan's pupils.

B makes it plain that Dunstan received an excellent education at Glastonbury. To account for this, he states that "pilgrims of Irish race, like many others of the faithful, frequented Glastonbury with great devotion, especially in honour of blessed Patrick, who is said to have ended his life happily there in the Lord. These men's books he diligently studied, finding in their wisdom the pathway of true faith."[2] It will be difficult, if not impossible, to make sense of this passage if by pilgrims, *peregrini*, we understand people who travel to some shrine or other and after paying their devotions there return home again. Such pilgrims do not leave a library of books behind them. But, as a leading historian of Celtic Christianity has remarked, *peregrini* is "a word which as a general rule we must beware of translating by 'pilgrims'."[3] The matter is more intelligibly and more correctly stated in the *Life of Dunstan*

[1] J. Armitage Robinson, *The Saxon Bishops of Wells*, British Academy, 1918, pp. 28–48; idem, *The Times of Saint Dunstan*, Oxford, 1923, pp. 92–4.

[2] "Porro Hibernensium peregrini locum, quem dixi, Glestoniae, sicut et ceterae fidelium turbae, magno colebant affectu, et maxime ob Beati Patricii junioris honorem, qui faustus ibidem in Domino quievisse narratur. Horum etiam libros rectae fidei tramitem phylosophantes, diligenter excoluit." —*Memorials of Saint Dunstan*, ed. Stubbs, Rolls ser. 63, p. 10. On the date of composition, see *ibid.*, p. xi.

[3] L. Gougaud, *Christianity in Celtic Lands*, London, 1932, p. 130.

written a hundred years later by Osbern, precentor of Canterbury.

"At that time," says Osbern, "Glastonbury belonged to the king's treasury and knew nothing of the monastic life. For Englishmen as yet felt no inclination to surrender their personal freedom in order to live in religious communities. The title of abbot was practically unheard of, and as for a monastic brotherhood, nobody had set eyes on one. But if a man had a mind to live a pilgrim life, he would leave his native country, either alone or with a few like-minded companions, and betake himself to foreign parts, wherever opportunity permitted, there to spend his life as an alien and exile. This well-intentioned and still prevalent custom is almost second nature with the Irish. Many distinguished scholars, eminent both in sacred and profane learning, who quitted Ireland to embrace a life of voluntary exile in England, chose Glastonbury for their habitation, as being a retired but convenient spot, and one famous for its cult—a point of special attraction, this, for the exiles— of Patrick, who is said to have come after a lifetime of miracle-working and preaching the gospel, and to have ended his days there in the Lord. Such considerations brought these notable Irishmen to Glastonbury, but as the place did not afford them a sufficient livelihood, they undertook to give the sons of the nobility a liberal education, so that the generosity of their pupils might supply what the natural resources of the place could not provide."[1]

[1] "Ea tempestate Glestonia regalibus stipendiis addicta, monasticae religionis penitus erat ignara. Nondum enim in Anglia communis vitae ratio colebatur, non usus deserendi proprias voluntates hominibus affectabatur. Abbatis nomen vix quisquam audierat. Conventus monachorum non satis quispiam viderat. Sed cui forte id voluntatis erat ut peregrinam vellet transigere vitam; is modo solus, modo paucos ejusdem propositi comitatus, patrios egrediebatur fines, et qua opportunitas vivendi licentiam dabat, illic alienigena vitam agebat. Hisque mos cum plerosque tum vehementer adhuc manet [? movet] Hibernos, quia quod aliis bona voluntas in consuetudinem hoc illis consuetudo vertit in naturam. Quorum multi atque illustres viri divinis ac saecularibus litteris nobiliter eruditi, dum relicta Hibernia in terram Anglorum peregrinaturi venissent, locumque habitationis suae Glestoniam delegissent; propterea quod esset et a civili multitudine sequestratus et humanis usibus accommodus, et, quod maxime affectabant peregrini, Patricii religiosa veneratione gloriosus, qui olim evangelizando regnum Dei illuc perveniens, vita, doctrina, signis, mirabilibus, multipliciter claruisse

This passage, which J. R. Green dismissed as "Osbern's fiction of an Irish school" at Glastonbury,[1] does not strike me as being either incredible or fictitious. Dunstan was still a living figure in Canterbury tradition when Osbern wrote. There were English books about him which had survived the great fire at Christ Church in 1067. Osbern had visited Glastonbury and inspected Dunstan's handiwork there.[2] His interpretation of the Irish *peregrinatio* is in perfect accord with known Celtic practice. The only feature of his account which ought to give us pause is the statement or implication that the cult of Patrick was already established at Glastonbury before the Irishmen arrived. As we have seen, the only two documents which give any support to this idea are quite untrustworthy. The suspicion arises that at this point in the narrative cause and effect have been, perhaps innocently, transposed.

But for the biographers of Dunstan we should probably never have heard of the Irish school at Glastonbury. They tell us that it was quite a large community—"multi atque illustres viri"—but not when it began and ended. Their statements about the cult of St Patrick seem to be derived from information handed on by Dunstan himself. If so, the cult must already have been established at Glastonbury when the future archbishop was sent to school there, in 919 or thereabouts. This was in the reign of Edward the Elder (899–924), a king whose preoccupation with his great campaign for the reconquest of the Danelaw can have left him little leisure for promoting educational enterprises. If a conjecture is permissible, it seems far more likely that the Irish school at Glastonbury was opened under Alfred the Great. Alfred's interest in learning, his desire for an educated laity and clergy, his readiness to welcome foreigners, and his gifts to Irish monasteries, are well-known

---

et post omnia haec ibidem in Domino quievisse perhibetur. Cum ergo hi tales viri talibus de causis Glestoniam venissent, nec tamen quicquid sibi necessarium erat sufficientissime in loco repperissent, suscipiunt filios nobilium liberalibus studiis imbuendos, ut quod minus ad usum loci ubertas exhiberet, eorum quos docebant liberalitate redundaret."—*Memorials*, p. 74.

[1] *Proceedings of the Somersetshire Archaeological and Natural History Society*, XI, 1861–2, p. 132 n.

[2] *Memorials*, pp. 70, 83, 84.

facts.[1] The Alfredian Chronicle relates that in 891 "three Scots came to King Alfred in a boat without any oars from Ireland, which they had left secretly, because they wished for the love of God to be in foreign lands, they cared not where. The boat in which they travelled was made of two and a half hides, and they took with them enough food for seven days. And after seven days they came to land in Cornwall and went immediately to King Alfred. Their names were as follows: Dubslane, Machbethu, and Maelinmum. And Swifneh, the best scholar among the Scots, died."[2] The chronicler Æthelweard adds that the three hardy mariners went on to Rome, and intended to continue their journey as far as Jerusalem,[3] so we have no warrant for connecting them with Glastonbury; but the annal is good evidence of contact between Irish scholars and Alfred's court. In view of all that is known about him, it seems not at all unlikely that he would have encouraged a band of learned Irishmen to settle at Glastonbury and there to open a school for the sons of the nobility. What better use could be found for a decayed monastery in the king's hand?[4] But in the reign of Athelstan (924–39) a lady named Æthelflaed installed a number of *clerici* or secular priests in the abbey and maintained them at her own expense.[5] Dunstan became her right-hand man and eventually her executor. A few years later King Edmund formally appointed him abbot of Glastonbury. The priest B says he was the first abbot of English birth.[6] There had of course been English abbots at Glastonbury two

---

[1] For his gifts to Irish monasteries, see *Asser's Life of King Alfred*, ed. W. H. Stevenson, Oxford, 1904, p. 89.

[2] *The Anglo-Saxon Chronicle*, trans. and ed. by Dorothy Whitelock, London, 1961, p. 53.

[3] *Monumenta Historica Britannica*, ed. H. Petrie and J. Sharpe, London, 1848, p. 517.

[4] The derelict monastery at Abingdon was also in the king's hand at this time: see F. M. Stenton, *The Early History of the Abbey of Abingdon*, Reading, 1913, p. 31. Similarly Ely, which lay derelict after the Danish invasions, "regio fisco serviebat" until the reign of Edgar.—*Liber Eliensis*, ed. E. O. Blake, Camden 3rd ser., XCII, 1962, p. 73.

[5] *Memorials*, pp. 16, 17–20, 85–9, 175–8. Osbern and Eadmer give the name of Dunstan's patroness as Ælfgifu.

[6] *Memorials*, p. 25. Before his appointment as abbot, Dunstan may have been a teacher in the abbey school; the biographers frequently refer to his "discipuli" and "scholastici," cf. *Memorials*, p. lxxxv.

hundred years before Dunstan's time, but the statement probably means that Dunstan's appointment marked the formal end of the Irish interlude, which on this showing will have lasted for not quite half a century, beginning perhaps between 887 and 892, when Alfred's kingdom was at peace, and ending with the refoundation of the abbey by Dunstan and Æthelflaed.

Whether this chronology is acceptable or not, it seems clear that from the first quarter of the tenth century onwards the denizens of Glastonbury were affirming, and quite possibly believing, that the bones of Patrick lay enshrined in St Mary's old church. But which Patrick? There was room for argument here. An Irish hymn composed in the eighth century says that "When Patrick departed this life, he went first to the other Patrick; together they ascended to Jesus the Son of Mary." This verse reflects an early and persistent Irish belief that there was an older Patrick—Sen-Phátric, Patricius Senex or Senior— who somewhat unconventionally postponed his entry into heaven until he could be accompanied by his junior namesake. Whether this older Patrick ever existed, and if so, when, are questions still debated, not without heat, among Patrician scholars.[1] In the ninth century the Irish were so sure of his existence that they provided him with a feast-day in their calendars. In order to do so, they turned to the Hieronymian Martyrology and lifted from it the feast of an unoffending Gaulish abbot and confessor, also named Patricius, who was commemorated in the Nièvre on the 24th of August.[2] From Ireland this liturgical misappropriation was imported into Somerset. The calendar of the Leofric Missal shows that the feast of "Patrick senior" was kept at Glastonbury on the 24th of August, as well as that of "St Patrick the bishop" and apostle of Ireland on the 17th of March.[3]

Given, then, in the minds of the Irish teachers at Glastonbury a belief that there had been an older and a younger Patrick, the

[1] See the valuable review of the whole question by D. A. Binchy, 'Patrick and his Biographers', in *Studia Hibernica*, II, 1962, pp. 7–173; also F. Shaw, 'Post-mortem on the Second Patrick', *Studies*, LI, 1962, pp. 237–67.

[2] P. Grosjean, 'S. Patrice d'Irlande et quelques homonymes dans les anciens martyrologes', *Journal of Ecclesiastical History*, I, 1950, p. 153.

[3] *The Leofric Missal*, pp. 25, 30. Cf. the calendar of the Bosworth Psalter, which also reflects Glastonbury practice.—*The Bosworth Psalter*, ed. Gasquet and Bishop, 1908, p. 100.

question arose: which of the two was enshrined in the abbey church? In its original form B's *Life of Dunstan* makes it Patrick junior; but the Life was revised at Canterbury some time before 1050, and the revised text has Patrick senior.[1] The Glastonbury chroniclers who wrote after the Norman Conquest admit quite frankly that it was often debated whether the apostle of Ireland had really been a monk and abbot there.[2] They add that the truth of the matter was finally revealed to one of the monks in a dream, when he heard somebody reading aloud a description of St Patrick's miracles, ending with the words: "And so he was adorned with the sanctity of a metropolitan's pallium. But afterwards he became a monk and abbot in this place." The reader added that if there was any doubt about the matter he would show the monk this passage written in letters of gold. That settled the question to the entire satisfaction of contemporaries: "omnem scrupulum absolvit."[3] We, who know what an anachronism it is to speak of a pallium in connection with the apostle of Ireland, are left with our misgivings unallayed.

Notwithstanding the visionary confirmation, there are traces in the Glastonbury chronicles of a confusion between St Patrick and St Petroc. The abbey claimed to possess one of Petroc's bones and some of his clothing.[4] He was a saint who enjoyed great popularity in the south-western shires and also in Brittany, although—or perhaps because—next to nothing was known about him. A Welshman by origin, he is said to have set sail for Britain after studying for some years in Ireland, and to have landed at "Hægelmuth" in Cornwall.[5] Hægelmouth is the old name of the Camel estuary. The town of Padstow is named after him; so too is Petrockstow in Devon. Petroc, the Welsh Pedrawg, is a different name from Patrick, but the history of these place-names shows that confusion might and sometimes did arise between them.[6] This perhaps

---

[1] *Memorials*, pp. xxvii, xxix, 10.

[2] AD p. 23; *Johannis Glastoniensis Chronica*, p. 67. (In subsequent footnotes I refer to this work as JG.)

[3] AD p. 23.

[4] JG pp. 28, 450.

[5] *Analecta Bollandiana*, LXXIV, 1956, p. 151; *Die Heiligen Englands*, p. 18.

[6] Padstow is *Padristowe* in 1351, and Petrockstow *Patricstowe* in 1268;

is why John of Glastonbury makes Patrick cross the sea from Ireland to "Hailemout."[1] It rather looks as if some of the brethren had identified their Patrick with the saint of Padstow.

Confusion, doubt, and controversy thus began to revolve around Patrick's monument in the old church, if not in Dunstan's lifetime, at any rate soon afterwards. Here were all the marks of an uncertain and insecurely founded tradition. The question that interests the modern critic, when he has noted it as such, is how it had arisen in the first place. It is a question which may never be completely answered; but at least we can see the direction in which the answer should be sought. Little as is known about Dunstan's Irish teachers, there are one or two significant indications of their way of thinking. We are assured that they were very learned men. In other sciences they may have been so, but they have a good claim to be numbered among the worst philologists Britain has ever known. The havoc they wrought upon the place-names and personal names of Somerset was deplorable, all the more so for the effect it has had upon the work of some eminent modern scholars.

Some two miles from Glastonbury, on the east side of the road from Wells, is a farm called Southway. This is really the name of the road, which on Anglo-Saxon lips was originally *Suggaweg*, meaning a marshy way. The initial move in the direction of a false etymology was to confuse the first element of the name, *sugga*=marsh, with *sugu*=a sow.[2] The next was to imagine a swineherd who one day, while driving his pigs along the road from Wells, came upon a sow distinguished from other sows by having eight feet instead of the customary four. This interesting creature was found suckling her litter under an apple-tree near the site of the future abbey: a circumstance which, coupled with the other attractions of the place, induced the swineherd to settle there with his wife and children.[3] As the earliest known inhabitant of Glastonbury he had

---

cf. Ekwall, *The Concise Oxford Dictionary of English Place-Names*, 1960, p. 356; J. E. B. Gover, A. Mawer, and F. M. Stenton, *The Place-Names of Devon*, p. 105.

[1] JG p. 62 ("Hailemont").
[2] A. H. Smith, *English Place-Name Elements*, Cambridge, 1956, II, p. 166.
[3] AD p. 16.

to have a name, and here no one familiar with St Patrick and his doings could be at a loss. The Book of Armagh, a manuscript dating from c. 800, contains a tale about a swineherd who after being dead a hundred and twenty years was brought back to life by the saint. His name was Cas, son of Glas. It was a simple matter to bring him over to Somerset, invert his family tree by calling him Glas, son of Cas, and identify him with the finder of the Glastonbury octoped.[1] Unnecessary, after this, to ask why the place is so named: Glastonbury is obviously the *bury* of the swineherd Glas, and of his descendants, the Glastings.

On the western edge of Glastonbury is a place named Beckery. It makes its first recorded appearance in the third quarter of the seventh century, when Cenwalh, king of Wessex, by a charter now lost, gave Beckery ("Beokerie"), Godney, Marchey, and "Andreyesie" to the abbey.[2] There is no reason to doubt that the last element in all four names is the Old English *ig* or *ieg*, meaning an island or an area at least partly surrounded by water. Another Old English word, *bēocere*, is now recognized as entering into a number of place-names, such as Bickershaw, Bickerton, and Bickley.[3] It means bee-keeper; and when we recall the importance of honey and of the liquor brewed from honey in the economy of Anglo-Saxon households—it needed a miracle to ensure a sufficient flow of mead when King Athelstan visited the lady Æthelflaed at Glastonbury[4]—we can hardly doubt that Beckery is a purely English place-name meaning bee-keeper's island. But

---

[1] *Liber Ardmachanus*, p. 27 *b*; F. Lot, 'Glastonbury et Avalon', *Romania*, XXVII, 1898, pp. 531–4. The Glastonbury version of the tale was incorporated into the Irish *Glossary of Cormac*: p. 111 of the edition by J. O'Donovan and W. Stokes, Calcutta, 1868. Professor D. A. Binchy informs me that the linguistic evidence does not favour the supposition that the passage in Cormac may be an addition to the original text, or that it was written much later than 900. Thurneysen showed that the word *nGoidel* ('Glassdimbir nGoidel' = Glastonbury of the Goidel) is not found in the oldest manuscripts.—*Festschrift Ernst Windisch*, Leipzig, 1914, p. 24. There is room for further study of the interaction between Glastonbury and Ireland.

[2] AD p. 49.

[3] A. H. Smith, *op. cit.*, I, p. 34, s.v. bīcere.

[4] *Memorials*, p. 18. In the thirteenth century the *medarius* was one of the principal officers of the abbey.—AD p. 414.

to the Irish colony in the tenth century it was nothing of the kind. For them it was Becc-Ériu in their own tongue, meaning Little Ireland. A charter dated 971, portions of which may be genuine, refers to the chapel of "Bekeria, *alias* Parva Hibernia,"[1] and this bogus etymology has held the field ever since. In the *Oxford Dictionary of English Place-Names* Ekwall cites the charter of 971 as establishing the Old Irish derivation of the name. Max Förster includes Beckery in his list of Celtic place-names, and offers an all too ingenious conjecture as to its origin. On an islet of some twenty-one acres in Wexford harbour, now called Begerin or Beggery, stood a monastery founded by St Ibar in the fourth century. The Annals of Ulster record that this was plundered by Vikings in 813, and Förster suggests that the monks then took refuge in Somerset, bringing with them the name of their island home, which does in truth mean Little Ireland.[2] In 1958 Professor C. L. Wrenn, in the course of his O'Donnell Lectures at Oxford, alluded to this emigration from Wexford to Glastonbury, not as a guess by Max Förster but as a matter of known fact, which he placed in the seventh century.[3] It is instructive sometimes to watch history being manufactured.

As with place-names, so with personal names. A holy man named Beonna lay buried at Meare, three miles from the abbey. Beonna is a name which occurs frequently in that great repertory of Old English personal names, the *Liber Vitae* of Durham. It was borne by an abbot of Medeshamstede in the eighth century and a bishop of Hereford in the ninth; and in its possessive form, conjoined with elements like *ford*, *tree*, and the like, it enters into many English place-names.[4] The Irish, however, boldly identified the Beonna of Meare, latinized as Benignus, with their own St Benen, a disciple and successor of St Patrick. An inscription on his tomb, copied by William of Malmesbury, speaks of this identification.—

[1] CS 1277.

[2] M. Förster, *Der Flussname Themse und seine Sippe*, München, 1941, pp. 110, 111.

[3] C. L. Wrenn, 'Saxons and Celts in South-West Britain', *Trans. Hon. Soc. of Cymmrodorion*, 1959, pp. 43, 56.

[4] H. P. R. Finberg, *Lucerna*, London, 1964, p. 84; A. H. Smith, *The Place-Names of Gloucestershire*, Cambridge, 1964, II, pp. 104, 254.

Hunc fore Patricii dudum fortasse ministrum
Fantur Hybernigenae.[1]

There is a nice touch of reserve in the last line. "Fantur Hybernigenae"—so say the Irish. But with the passage of time all doubts were stilled. So bright an ornament of the early Irish church could not be suffered to lie at Meare. His remains were solemnly removed to a new shrine at Glastonbury, and thenceforth the Anglo-Saxon Beonna, *alias* Benen, *alias* Benignus, was firmly established as one of the Celtic saints who were alleged to have made Glastonbury illustrious long before the English occupation of Somerset.[2] Nor can it surprise us now to find the great French *savant* Ferdinand Lot affirming that Beonna is an "incontestably Irish name."[3]

These etymological vagaries are of some consequence, not only for their harmful effects on modern scholarship, but also for the insight they give us into the thought-processes—if that is the right word—of the Irishmen at Glastonbury. In quitting Ireland, these worthies did not leave behind the traditions of their native Church. By playing freely on the place-names and personal names of Somerset, they contrived to domesticate those traditions amid their new surroundings, and no word-play was too far-fetched for the purpose. Many parallels could be cited from the lives of the saints. As one of the greatest modern hagiologists has remarked, "more than one legend owes its existence to names incorrectly understood, or to resemblances of sound." Inscriptions misread, geographical names wrongly interpreted, have been fruitful sources of error.[4] If we share the misgivings that were freely expressed in the abbey itself, and if we believe that the apostle of Ireland

---

[1] AD p. 46.
[2] According to William of Malmesbury, AD 24, the bones of Beonna were removed to Glastonbury in 901. If this date could be accepted without hesitation it would go a long way towards proving that the Irish colony was active at Glastonbury from the time of Alfred the Great, who died in 899. But on a later page of the *De Antiquitate*, AD p. 113, the removal is ascribed to Thurstan, the first Norman abbot, and JG p. 162 gives the date as 1091.
[3] *Romania*, XXVII, 1898, p. 545.
[4] H. Delehaye, *The Legends of the Saints*, tr. V. M. Crawford, London, 1907, p. 47.

kept the vow which he himself says he made, to spend the rest of his life among the Irish, then we must conclude that under the monument in the old church lay the bones of somebody who may well have been no closer to St Patrick than the English Beonna was to the Irish Benen.

Patrick, *patricius*, is a title as well as a personal name. In the early English kingdoms it was applied to members of the royal family who held office as under-kings or ealdormen. In 681 King Æthelred of Mercia makes a grant of land to Malmesbury at the request of his *patricius* and kinsman Cenfrith.[1] In the same period Ine of Wessex grants an estate to a *patricius* named Hean.[2] If a personage holding this rank was buried at Glastonbury under a monument on which his title could still just be deciphered two hundred years later when the rest of the inscription had become defaced by time, the Irish were quite capable of identifying him with their national apostle.

It will be remembered that St Patrick's monument in the old church was matched in style if not in splendour by a monument on the other side of the high altar, dedicated to St Indract. About this personage conflicting stories were told. All agree that he was an eminent Irishman who met his death at the hands of the wicked English. According to one version, he and seven companions went on pilgrimage to Rome, but on their return journey were murdered by a robber at Shapwick, near Glastonbury. Another version lays the scene of the crime at Huish. Both accounts make Indract a seventh- or early eighth-century figure, and both ascribe his burial in the abbey church to King Ine.[3] This is to ante-date the historical Indract by a full century and a half.[4] For the truth about him we turn to the Annals of Ulster. There we read that in 849 "Indrechtach, abbot of Iona, came to Ireland with the *minda* of Colum-Cille," that is, with sacred objects which had belonged to, or been otherwise associated with, St Columba. Under 853 they say that "the successor of Colum-Cille, the best sage, was

---

[1] CS 58.
[2] CS 74.
[3] G. H. Doble, 'Saint Indract and Saint Dominic', reprinted from Somerset Record Soc. *Collectanea*, III, 1942, as No. 40 in the 'Cornish Saints' series.
[4] James F. Kenney, *Sources for the Early History of Ireland*, New York, 1929, p. 446.

martyred by Saxons on the fourth of the Ides of March."[1]

We are not told where Indract was killed, but it was presumably not in Iona nor in Ireland, and there is no difficulty in believing that he may have been murdered in Somerset on his way to or from Rome. The annals here are a year ahead of the true date, so Indract was killed on the 12th of March 852. His recorded practice of taking relics about with him on his travels may account for the presence at Glastonbury of certain objects associated with the early Celtic saints. The abbey claimed to possess relics of St Columba, *alias* Columb-cille.[2] In the chapel of St Mary Magdalen at Beckery they showed a scrip, a string of beads, a hand-bell, and some weaving implements which had belonged to the great St Bridget.[3] From the possession of these treasures it was but a short step to affirm that the sainted owners had visited Glastonbury in their lifetime, and even to assign dates for their coming: A.D. 488 for Bridget, and 504 for St Columba.[4]

Now the historical Indract was contemporary with a highly-placed Irish ecclesiastic named Patrick, who outlived him by eleven years. To be exact, his name was Máel-Pátraicc, that is: servant of Patrick. He was bishop and abbot-elect of Armagh, and thus a successor of the national apostle. The *Chronicon Scotorum* records his death under the correct date, 863: "Maelpadraig, son of Finchu, bishop and abbot-elect of Ard-Macha, went to his rest."[5] As long ago as the fourteenth century Higden in his *Polychronicon* suggested that the Patrick honoured at Glastonbury was not the apostle of Ireland, but an abbot of the same name who flourished about 850. In the seventeenth century Colgan, with a greater knowledge of Irish sources, repeated the suggestion.[6] It has the great merit of providing a historical Patrick to accompany the historical Indract. But while the circumstance that Indract met his death

[1] *Annals of Ulster*, ed. W. M. Hennessy, Dublin, 1887, pp. 357, 365.

[2] JG p. 451.

[3] AD p. 14.

[4] AD pp. 24, 25. There were some who did not shrink from asserting that St. Columba ended his days in the abbey.—*ibid.*, p. 25.

[5] *Chronicon Scotorum*, ed. W. M. Hennessy, Rolls ser. 46, p. 159.

[6] *Polychronicon Ranulphi Higden*, ed. J. R. Lumby, Rolls ser. 41, V, p. 304, and VI, p. 208; J. Colgan, *Acta Sanctorum Hiberniae*, Louvain, 1645, p. 366, n. 11. For a wrathful rejoinder to Higden, see JG p. 7.

at the hands of Englishmen may account for his burial and subsequent cult at Glastonbury, it is less easy to see why a contemporary abbot-bishop of Armagh should have found his way there, alive or dead. The bones that were held to be Patrick's may just as probably have belonged to a nameless companion of Indract. Or again, some Irishman may have brought with him objects believed to be relics of the national apostle. Once these were enshrined at Glastonbury, Irishmen of a later generation would have been all too apt to infer that Patrick had ended his days there. It is not a matter on which we can hope for certainty.[1]

Historical criticism may do its best—or worst, but the Glastonbury legends will always keep their hold over certain minds. The argument that what has been repeated for a thousand years and more *could* have been true, therefore it *is* true, is easily pressed into service, and to this day books are written about Glastonbury in that strain. We have seen the baleful effects on modern scholarship of the all too successful attempt to create a Little Ireland, so called, in tenth-century Somerset. Having opened a school for the sons of Anglo-Saxon thegns, the Irish teachers needed as much advertisement as they could get, and their fictions about Patrick, Benen, Bridget, and Columba are little more than extracts from the school prospectus.

These fables invested the abbey with a spurious antiquity reaching back some centuries into the pre-English past. They thus made room for further inventions, which other fabulists, and particularly the Welsh, were ready enough to supply. It was the peculiar lot of Glastonbury to be more thoroughly and successfully exposed to Celtic influences than any other English abbey, not excepting even Malmesbury, though Malmesbury had in very truth been founded by an Irishman. Towards the close of the eleventh century Welsh writers began

[1] The sixth-century biographer of St Bridget describes her monument as lying on the left, and that of St Conleth on the right, of the high altar in the church of Kildare. (". . . ecclesiae . . . in qua gloriosa amborum, hoc est episcopi Conleath et hujus virginis sanctae Brigidae, corpora a dextris et a sinistris altaris . . . requiescunt."—Migne, *Patrologia Latina*, LXXII, 788–9.) This suggests that the right was the place of honour reserved for the personage of higher rank. If so, the Patrick of Glastonbury may in truth have been a bishop.

ST PATRICK AT GLASTONBURY

to interest themselves in Glastonbury. Finding among the records of the abbey an early grant of land at a place called Ynyswitrin, probably in Cornwall, they gave out that this was the original British name of Glastonbury, *ynis*=island, and *gwidrin*=glass: a piece of linguistic puerility which still disfigures the Oxford Dictionary of English Place-Names.[1] It is common knowledge that the correct interpretation of placenames depends largely upon a study of the early forms. It is less commonly appreciated that such study demands a more rigorous criticism of sources than may reasonably be expected from philologists until experts in palaeography, diplomatic, and history have contributed their share.

Rhygyfarch, the earliest biographer of St David, writing *c.* 1080, ascribes the foundation of Glastonbury to the great saint of Wales.[2] In the next generation that enigmatic personage Caradoc of Llancarfan composed a life of Gildas in which he brings his hero to Glastonbury and works in a good deal of romance concerning Arthur and Guinevere.[3] After this it only remained for someone to discover that Joseph of Arimathea had landed in Britain in A.D. 63, built the first church at Glastonbury, and left descendants of whom King Arthur was one.[4] The monstrous edifice of fiction was then to all intents and purposes complete.

On the strength of its fabulous and sanctified antiquity the abbey attracted royal favour and abounding wealth. In 1086 it was by far the richest monastery in England.[5] A century later the local bishop tried to annex it to his see, but the abbey soon shook him off. After the great fire of 1184 a timely excavation brought to light the bodies of Arthur and Guinevere, and the abbey was rebuilt on a more splendid scale. When the Spaniards claimed precedence over all other Christian nations on the ground that they had been converted by St James the apostle, Glastonbury replied that its church had been consecra-

[1] H. P. R. Finberg, *Lucerna*, pp. 83–94.
[2] *Rhygyvarch's Life of Saint David*, ed. A. W. Wade-Evans, in *Y Cymmrodor*, XXIV, p. 10.
[3] Printed by Mommsen in *Mon. Germ. Hist.*, *Auctores Antiquissimi*, XIII, *Chronica Minora*, III, 1898.
[4] JG pp. 53, 57; J. Armitage Robinson, *Two Glastonbury Legends*, Cambridge, 1926.
[5] D. Knowles, *The Monastic Order in England*, Cambridge, 1949, p. 702.

ted by the Lord in person. In the sixteenth century, when Leland visited the abbey, he was allowed to borrow the Charter of St Patrick, and thus to refute Polydore Vergil, who had impiously questioned the existence of a monastery there in Arthur's day.[1] After the break with Rome it was useful to quote evidence that Christianity had flourished in England long before a papal missionary landed in Kent and founded the see of Canterbury. In 1572 the occupant of that see, Matthew Parker, used Joseph of Arimathea to good effect in restating this claim.[2] Even now, when no political or economic interest is served by perpetuating all this mythology, the authentic history of Glastonbury has yet to be written.

[1] J. Leland, *Collectanea*, ed. T. Hearne, 2nd ed., 1770–4, v, pp. 31, 42.
[2] M. Parker, *De Antiquitate Britannicae Ecclesiae*, ed. S. Drake, 1729, pp. 4, 5.

CHURCH AND STATE
IN TWELFTH-CENTURY DEVON

WHEN the dissolved abbey of Tavistock was granted to John, Lord Russell, ancestor of the earls and dukes of Bedford, its muniments and some of its library passed into the same hands. The muniments had been arranged in the first quarter of the previous century by an able administrator, John Mey, abbot of Tavistock from 1402 to 1422. Mey collected the original charters of the spiritualities and temporalities and stored them in boxes, assigning to each manor a box of its own. Then he set his clerk, John Ludegard, to copy them all into one great register, a volume of more than 400 pages.[1] Sir William Pole (1561–1635) made great use of this cartulary while collecting materials for a description of Devonshire. A copy of his notes which came into the hands of Ralph Brooke, York Herald, in 1608, and which is now in the library of Queen's College, Oxford, includes eight pages of memoranda from this source, headed by a note that the cartulary was then "in the Custody of ye Erle of Bedford."[2] In 1655, however, when the first edition of Dugdale's *Monasticon* was published, the cartulary was described as being in the hands of (*penes*) John Maynard, Esq.[3] On this account it is usually, and conveniently, known as the Maynard cartulary. It seems unlikely, however, that Maynard was its owner. In his day it was possibly still kept in the portion of the abbey which Maynard held on lease from the earl of Bedford.[4] At the beginning of the next century the learned antiquary William Wotton (1666–1726) consulted it when drawing up a list of the abbots for his friend Browne Willis, and according to Anstis, Matthew Hutton (1639–1711) saw it about five years

[1] B. M. Egerton MS. 3671, ff. 21, 22. Dugdale refers to the 220th folio of Mey's register.
[2] Queen's Coll. MS. clii, fo. 219 *b*.
[3] Dugdale, *op. cit.*, 1655, I, p. 995 *b*.
[4] Sir W. Pole, *Collections towards a Description of the County of Devon*, 1791, p. 340.

before his death.[1] Since then it has disappeared. It was not among the duke of Bedford's archives when these were catalogued in 1753–55, nor among the remnant of Maynard's collection which found its way into Lincoln's Inn library in 1818.[2] As Tavistock Abbey was the most important monastic house in the diocese of Exeter, and the only one which held of the Crown in chief by knight-service, the loss of its principal register is one which every student of south-western genealogy, manorial history, and place-names has had reason to deplore.

Besides this now missing volume, the duke of Bedford owned a smaller and older cartulary of Tavistock which may suitably be called the Russell cartulary. This consists of eighteen parchment leaves, measuring approximately $7\frac{1}{2}$ by 5 inches, in a covering of modern buckram. Most of the leaves are in good condition. There are two handwritings, both of the thirteenth century; and on the last page is a charter dated 1225. The Russell cartulary gives the texts of sixty documents, or rather fifty-nine and one duplicate. All but nine of these belong to the twelfth century. Five were printed by Dugdale from the Maynard cartulary and other sources; one more was printed in 1937;[3] the remainder were unknown until I came upon the cartulary in the muniment-room at Woburn and was permitted by the late duke of Bedford to publish a complete and annotated text.[4]

The charters make a welcome addition to our knowledge of Church and State in twelfth-century Devon, hitherto but sparsely documented. They fall into four groups, defined by the status of the grantors. There are royal writs; letters and confirmations from three primates; similar documents from the bishops of Exeter; and charters from a number of lay barons.

The royal series begins with a writ from Henry I on the sub-

---

[1] Bodleian MS. Willis 73, ff. 34 *b*, 42 *b*; BM Stowe MS. 1044, fo. 49.

[2] J. Hunter, *Catalogue of the Manuscripts in Lincoln's Inn Library*, 1838, p. xiv.

[3] Bishop Bartholomew's confirmation of an agreement concerning Leigh chapel, printed from BM Add. Ch. 29,000 by A. Morey, *Bartholomew of Exeter*, 1937, p. 157.

[4] 'Some Early Tavistock Charters', *English Historical Review* LXII, 1947, pp. 352–77 (hereafter cited as ETC).

ject of castle-guard.[1] Just as the abbot of Abingdon's knights mounted guard at Windsor, and the abbot of Bury's at Norwich, so the abbot of Tavistock's knights, we now learn, did duty at Exeter. But in future, the writ says, Tavistock need not send more than one military tenant to Exeter Castle. It does not say how many had been sent previously, and I know of no other document bearing on this aspect of the abbot's military obligations. As an incident of feudal tenure, castle-guard began to disappear at the end of the twelfth century; or rather, it was commuted for a money payment, the Crown finding it more convenient to employ permanent garrisons. The name of the abbey is coupled in this writ with that of the monk Osbert, successor of Abbot Wymund, who had been deposed for simony at Michaelmas 1102. The date of the writ is thus c. 1103, and from the fact that Osbert is styled monk, not abbot, it would seem that he was acting as prior or administrator during the vacancy. How long did this last? If the parallel case of Bury St Edmunds is any guide, it may have lasted until the settlement of the Investiture controversy and St Anselm's return to England in the summer of 1107.[2] The abbot of Bury had been deposed at the same time as Wymund, and for the next five years Bury was administered by Robert, a monk of Westminster, who finally, like Osbert of Tavistock, became abbot. We know that the see of Exeter remained vacant for four years, and the repercussions of the Investiture controversy may well have been audible even further west.

The next document is a writ from Henry I commanding that the manor of Denbury be taken out of the hands of Roger de Nonant and restored to Our Lady of Tavistock and her monks, its rightful owners.[3] One of the paradoxical features of this pious age was the difficulty of dislodging lay barons who had entered into possession of Church fiefs. The case of Denbury is one instance: we shall meet others presently.

A charter of c. 1103, attested by William Warelwast and Michael de Hanslope, is addressed by Queen Matilda from Exeter "to her servants of Lifton," that is, to the officials of Lifton Hundred. It announces that the queen has given Tavi-

---

[1] ETC I.
[2] Eadmer, *Historia Novorum*, ed. Rule, 1884, pp. 142, 188.
[3] ETC II.

stock Abbey all her customary dues from Ottery in Lamerton, dues which are specified as 22 pence and one amber of rye.[1] The amber, according to the Oxford English Dictionary, was a dry measure equal to four bushels. This charter adds one more name to the list of queen-consorts who, like Edith before the Conquest and Eleanor later in the twelfth century, drew a portion of their income from Lifton Hundred.

Next comes the original, and hitherto unknown, market-charter of the town of Tavistock. This takes the usual form of a writ to the sheriff of Devon, notifying him that the king has granted the abbey a market, to be held in Tavistock every week on Friday. The writ is dated from Stamford, and attested by William Warelwast, not yet bishop of Exeter, Alfred of Lincoln, Harding son of Eadnoth the Staller, and Walter Fitz Ansgar.[2] It is of some consequence to fix the date as nearly as possible, for without this market-grant Tavistock could not have become a borough. Fortunately the king's visits to Normandy, and William Warelwast's numerous diplomatic errands to the continent, provide both of them with alibis which simplify the problem. Alfred of Lincoln and Harding were both in attendance on the king in 1105; they witnessed a charter which he gave at Romsey in February of that year when just about to sail for Normandy.[3] There seems to be no other instance of an attestation by Harding in this reign. I believe, therefore, that Harding and Alfred of Lincoln were still with the king when he returned to England, and that the Tavistock market was granted in the late summer or early autumn of the same year 1105. Nothing that is known of Henry's movements or of the other two witnesses conflicts with this inference. Morever, throughout this year Henry was raising money for his Norman campaigns.[4] It was therefore a good time to approach him purse in hand. For a Norman king did nothing gratis, and a landowner eager for the right to levy market tolls must pay for the privilege. If these conclusions are sound, it follows that the Friday market at Tavistock is now more than eight hundred and sixty years old.

[1] ETC iii.
[2] ETC iv.
[3] W. Farrer, *Outline Itinerary of Henry I*, 1920, no. 115.
[4] Eadmer, *op. cit.*, p. 171.

The market-charter and the writ concerning castle-guard are both addressed to Geoffrey de Mandeville; the one concerning Denbury to Richard de Redvers and the same Geoffrey. In her paper on the hereditary sheriffs of Devon Mrs Rose-Troup assumed that William Fitz Baldwin, the date of whose death is unknown, was immediately succeeded by his brother or half-brother Richard, who became sheriff in or about 1107.[1] It looks, however, as if the post had been held during the first half-dozen years of the reign by an interloper,[2] either because Henry wished to break the hereditary succession, or because Richard Fitz Baldwin was not yet of an age to act as sheriff.

The only other royal writ from this reign is addressed to Bishop William [Warelwast], William Fitz John, and Geoffrey de Furnellis: it may therefore be dated c. 1130.[3] Its purpose is to enjoin the restitution of all demesne lands of the abbey which had been alienated without royal licence after the death of William the Conqueror, particularly Carey and Panson.[4] The earlier history of these places is of some interest. Carey does not appear in Domesday Book;[5] it must have been included in "Panestan," the modern Panson, which at some time after the Conquest had come by irregular means into the hands of Ralph de Pomeroy. A little later Ralph persuaded Ruald Adobed to accept it in exchange for three other manors.[6] Domesday Book is not in general an emotionally expressive document, but in recording this exchange it allows us to perceive that the jurors considered it an uncommonly smart piece of work on Ralph's part. Some time before 1103 Ruald became a monk in the priory of St Nicholas, Exeter, and his lands thereupon passed to the Crown or to his heirs, with the exception of Poughill, which he took with him to the priory,[7] and, as we now learn, Panson, which devolved upon Tavi-

---

[1] F. Rose-Troup, 'The Hereditary Sheriffs of Devon', DA LXIV, 1932, p. 412.
[2] cf. Farrer, op. cit., no. 88.
[3] cf. ibid., no. 604.
[4] ETC IX.
[5] The Domesday 'Kari' is Downacarey in Lifton Hundred.
[6] Exon Domesday, ff. 411b, 497, 343b.
[7] Oliver, op. cit., p. 119.

stock Abbey. For reasons which I am unable to follow, Reichel believed that Ruald's manor must be identified with West Panson, and that East Panson with Carey formed part of the abbot's manor of Werrington.[1] To me it seems plain enough that the Panestan of Domesday Book and of Henry I's writ included both East and West Panson, and was in fact conterminous with the present parish of St Giles on the Heath. The writ seems to have been efficacious only for a time, or perhaps not at all, for a quarter of a century later we find Henry II repeating his grandfather's injunction in very much the same terms.[2]

The primatial charters are mainly confirmations of episcopal grants which will be noticed in due course. Perhaps legatine charters would be a better term, for they were issued by the archbishops in their capacity of papal legates. They include a most interesting letter from Archbishop Theobald to Abbot Walter of Tavistock, written probably about 1158.[3] The letter states that the previous abbot [Robert Postel] had executed charters granting away some of the abbey lands without consulting his fellow-monks or at least without their consent; and Walter is reminded that the king had given him a mandate to revoke these grants. We happen to know from the Annals of Tavistock, a manuscript now in the Bodleian, that Abbot Walter had originally been a monk of Winchester.[4] It looks as if he had been put in by Theobald on purpose that he might tighten things up at Tavistock after the general anarchy of Stephen's reign. Such a mandate was no doubt more easily given than carried out; at all events, the purpose of the letter is to stimulate the abbot's zeal. He is told plainly that he will come to grief if he does not set to work more briskly to recover the lost lands. This sharp rebuke seems to have been effective, for shortly afterwards we come upon several deeds of restitution. Ironically enough, as illustrating what the abbot had to contend against, the very first of these is from the hand of his diocesan, Bishop Robert Warelwast, restoring Roger Cornu's fief to the abbot and convent, and acknowledging

[1] O. J. Reichel, *The Hundreds of Devon*, v, Black Torrington, 1932, p. 213.
[2] ETC xii.
[3] ETC xviii.
[4] MS. Digby 81, fo. 87a.

that he, the bishop, had been holding the said fief without any legal title to it.[1]

A tantalizing feature of the archbishop's letter is that it is defective just where it would have been of particular historical interest. There is, indeed, no lacuna in the manuscript, but there is an evident hiatus in the grammar and sense, and it is clear that the writer of the cartulary missed out a line or two. A phrase is left in isolation from its context just where the archbishop is describing the laxity of Abbot Walter's predecessor. The phrase is: *opera quedam esse remissa*. Theobald complains that certain works, which ought to have been exacted, had in fact been remitted. Dom Adrian Morey, an authority on the history of this period, agrees with me that this is not a phrase likely to have been used of monastic observances; it must therefore refer to manorial week-works and boon-works. Is it possible that we have here a gleam of light on Tavistock burghal origins? The essence of a borough, as is well known, was that each burgess held his messuage by payment of a quit-rent and owed little or no labour-service to his lord. Nobody knows exactly when Tavistock became a borough. The late J. J. Alexander believed that it became one in Henry II's reign; and I had come to the same conclusion by a somewhat different road. Archbishop Theobald's expression is not clear enough, in the absence of its context, to decide the question, but it fortifies an opinion tenable on grounds which are discussed elsewhere.[2]

Of documents emanating from the bishops of Exeter there are no fewer than fifteen. The series begins with a charter from William Warelwast confirming the abbey in possession of "the churches pertaining to the Honour of Sheviock"— that is, the churches of Antony, St John, and Rame. This charter throws an interesting sidelight on the process of subinfeudation, for it states that Abbot Geoffrey (1082–88) and the convent had kept these churches in their own hands when they settled the manors of Sheviock, Antony, and Rame upon a military tenant, Erbenald.[3] This was before 1086, for

---

[1] ETC XIX. In 1135 Roger Cornu held two knights' fees of the abbey, which Reichel identified, correctly as I believe, with Thornbury, East Pulworthy in Hatherleigh, and Nutley in Tavistock (DA XLVI, 1914, p. 223).

[2] Cf. pp. 109–11 below. [3] ETC VII.

both Abbot Geoffrey and Erbenald appear in Domesday Book.[1] During the episcopate of Robert Warelwast the abbey handed all three churches over to a certain Dean Andrew de Pidrewin, to be held "in farm" during his lifetime, the amount of the farm being fixed at 30s. yearly, payable in three instalments on St Rumon's day (30 August), Candlemas, and the Nativity of St John Baptist.[2]

The church of Milton Abbot is appropriated by Bishop Robert Warelwast, c. 1158, to the almonry and sacristary of the abbey, subject to payment of a suitable stipend to the vicar.[3] This seems to be one of the earliest known uses of the term 'perpetual vicar'.[4] The appropriation is confirmed by Archbishop Theobald[5] and later by Archbishop Baldwin.[6] The church of Lamerton, given to the convent by the lord of that manor, is appropriated to their use by Bishop Bartholomew, who defines the vicar's portion as half the total revenue,[7] and whose charter is confirmed by the archbishop, Richard of Dover.[8] A noteworthy use was made of this endowment some years later. It appears that the monks of Tavistock had a custom of feeding three poor men daily throughout Lent: a usage which appears in the customs of Fleury and other monastic houses. But in the time of Abbot Herbert, c. 1189, they decided, with the approval of Bishop John, and also of John, then vicar of Lamerton, to continue this charitable practice throughout the year, and their revenue from Lamerton church was earmarked for this purpose.[9]

The church of Abbotsham is appropriated by Bartholomew, in the time of Abbot Godfrey (c. 1168–73), to the sacristary with the special object of providing the abbey church with lights;[10] and that of Hatherleigh, by the same bishop somewhat later, to the infirmary for the support of sick brethren.[11] These

[1] Exon Domesday, fo. 180b et seq. Erbenald is there spelt Ermenald.
[2] ETC xv.
[3] ETC xvi.
[4] Dom Adrian Morey quotes Hartridge, *History of Vicarages in the Middle Ages*, p. 21, as giving no earlier instance than 1173.—*Bartholomew of Exeter*, 1937, p. 74.
[5] ETC xvii.   [6] ETC xliii.   [7] ETC xxv.   [8] ETC xxxi.   [9] ETC xlv.
[10] ETC xxvi.
[11] ETC xxxvii.

two appropriations were renewed in the following century by Bishop William Briwer, whose charter relating to Hatherleigh is dated from Dunkeswell, 17 September 1225, and includes among its witnesses the archbishop, Stephen Langton,[1] whose presence in Devon at the date mentioned is a fact not hitherto recorded.

There is a good example of the methods used by prelates at this period for bringing lay magnates to heel. Richard de Wicha, constable of the Scilly islands, has built a chapel in St Mary's parish church[2] on his own authority, and, what is worse, is causing divine service to be celebrated therein by a priest not episcopally licensed. Bishop Bartholomew sends a peremptory mandate: both Richard and his priest are to appear at Exeter on the morrow of Ascension-day and give an account of their proceedings.[3] A little later the same Richard is still more sharply admonished for having withheld his tithes, especially tithes of rabbits, from the prior and brethren of St Nicholas, Tresco, a dependency of Tavistock; and he is warned that if he does not pay them he will soon find himself under sentence of excommunication. In order to avert this peril, the culprit hastens to Tavistock, and there, in the presence of the abbot and convent, before St Rumon's altar, he takes his gospel oath that in future their monks in Scilly shall be defrauded of no single rabbit that is lawfully their due.[4] This, by the way, is the earliest known mention of rabbits in the British Isles.[5]

Perhaps the most interesting, and certainly the most curious, of these episcopal documents is one of Bishop Bartholomew's dated 1171: it deals with the church of St Paternus at North Petherwin. Apparently the celebrated Richard of Ilchester, archdeacon of Poitiers and later bishop of Winchester, procured a presentation to this church from Abbot Godfrey of Tavistock. This would be somewhere about 1169. Two or three years before that he had fallen in with a certain Ralph whom he had known as a furrier in the household of Robert,

---

[1] ETC LVII.
[2] or "in the parish of the same church."
[3] ETC XXVIII.
[4] ETC XXXII, XXXIII.
[5] *Agricultural History Review*, V, 1957, p. 86.

earl of Gloucester. This Ralph had been a cripple from birth, but now, in middle life, he had been cured by the intercession of St Nectan. At the time of his encounter with Richard of Ilchester he was on pilgrimage to Compostela. From him the archdeacon learnt that St Nectan's shrine at Hartland was still tended by hereditary priests, descendants of the chaplains Gytha, mother of King Harold, had installed there before the Conquest. Richard of Ilchester determined to reform this out-moded institution and to establish a house of canons regular at Hartland, a plan for which he readily secured episcopal sup-port.[1] In 1171 he resigned the church of North Petherwin into the hands of its patrons, the abbot and convent of Tavistock, with a proviso that for the next ten years an annual contribu-tion of six marks was to be paid in three instalments out of the vicarage revenue towards the Hartland building fund. There seems a touch of cynical humour in this plan of making one abbey contribute to the building of another, while the credit of the benefaction goes to a third party. It is carefully provided that the money shall be paid to the bishop of Exeter, who will see that it is properly applied; the object of this clause being to prevent Hartland from setting up any claim after the expiry of the stated period.[2]

The last group of documents to be considered are the deeds of gift, sale, or restitution by lay barons. Outstanding among these are a fine series from the Giffards, who in the course of Henry I's reign acquired the manors formerly held by Ruald Adobed, including Lamerton and Whitchurch, which adjoin Tavistock on the north-west and south-east. The Giffards ap-pear to have been good neighbours and generous benefactors. I suppose no landmark in south Devon is more striking in its way than the little church of St Michael which crowns the summit of the extinct volcano called Brentor. Its origin has always been something of a mystery. R. N. Worth, after re-porting the tradition that it was erected by a merchant, who, in peril at sea, vowed, if saved, to build a church on the first point of land he saw, says: "As the Tor belonged to the abbey of Tavistock, we may assume that the church was founded by

---

[1] G. H. Doble, *Life of St Nectan* (translated from a twelfth-century original), 1941, p. 21.
[2] ETC xxvii.

the monks."[1] But this assumption will no longer hold, for we now have it on the authority of the first Walter Giffard that his father built the church at his own expense and gave it to the abbey with a certain amount of land around the rock of Brentor. This takes the foundation back to the 1130's or thereabouts. It is noteworthy that as generation follows generation the abbey is careful to secure a charter from each new heir confirming his ancestors' grants. In the light of these charters existing genealogies of the Giffard family will need to be revised, for the line of succession from father to son as now revealed is: Robert, Walter I, William, Walter II, and Walter III.[2]

By a deed executed in the time of Abbot Walter(*c.* 1154–68), Robert de Regni, with Ranulf his uncle and Hay son of the said Ranulf, restore the land of Filleford—that is, Great Velliford in Hatherleigh[3]—acknowledging that they and their ancestors have long illegally withheld the service due from this land to St Rumon.[4] By a similar act, William de Marisco, *c.* 1180, restores Netherbridge, confessing that by rights it is demesne-land of the abbot's manor of Werrington.[5] The moral beauty of the restitution is a trifle dimmed by the fact that each repentant baron exacts a *quid pro quo*. The Regnis have to be paid four marks before they hand back Great Velliford. William de Marisco, however, is content with honorary admission to the brotherhood of Tavistock and a share in its spiritual blessings. He describes himself, and was usually described by others, as "William, brother of Earl Reginald," being either a son of Henry I by Sibil Corbet, or a son of the latter by her marriage with Herbert Fitz Herbert.[6]

Another pedigree upon which the cartulary throws new light is that of the Dawnays. I have already mentioned that at some time between 1082 and 1086 the abbot and convent had settled their Cornish manors—Sheviock, Rame, Antony, Tol-

---

[1] R. N. Worth, *A History of Devonshire*, 1886, p. 191.
[2] ETC XIV, XXXVIII, XLIX. Cf. *Devon & Cornwall Notes & Queries*, VI, p. 53, and DA XXXIV, 1902, p. 662 *et seq.*
[3] PND p. 145.
[4] ETC XXII.
[5] ETC XXXV.
[6] R. W. Eyton, *Antiquities of Shropshire*, VII, 1858, p. 159.

carne in North Hill, Penharget in St Ive, and Trewornan in St Minver—upon a certain Ermenald or Erbenald, who held them by knight-service. We now have a charter by which Henry Dawnay, or de Alneto, c. 1179, confirms a gift of some land in Sheviock which he says the monastery of Tavistock had from "Erbenald my ancestor."[1] A year or two later the same Henry surrenders the half-virgate of land in Tavistock which had been held by Ermenald, and in exchange takes back the land in Sheviock referred to in the former charter: that is, two acres at Trewrickle,[2] which no doubt were Cornish acres, a good deal larger than the English or statute acre.

Although the abbey had retained the churches belonging to the Honour of Sheviock in its own hands while enfeoffing Ermenald, and although its rights over the churches of Sheviock, Antony, and St John had been confirmed by three bishops of Exeter as well as by Archbishop Richard,[3] nevertheless Henry Dawnay claimed the advowsons and drove the convent to accept an unfavourable compromise, under which he became patron of Sheviock and St John while they kept Antony.[4]

At about the same time a dispute arose between Abbot Baldwin and one of his knights, William de Legh, who claimed the advowson of Leigh chapel. The convent asserted that this was a daughter chapel of Milton Abbot, the church of which was in their patronage. At last, by agreement between the parties, the question of fact was referred to a jury of three clerics and three laymen, who met in the presence of Bishop Bartholomew and on oath upheld the convent's claim.[5] After William de Legh's death, his daughter and co-heiress Alice, with her husband Robert Champeaux, executed a charter of confirmation,[6] as did also, a generation later, their son Roger Champeaux.[7] In the charter by Robert and Alice it is laid down that the chaplain of Milton Abbot must celebrate divine service at Leigh on Wednesdays, Fridays, Saturdays, and Sundays: a time-table which appears to leave him very little room for his duties at the mother-church.

---

[1] ETC xxxix.   [2] ETC xli.
[3] ETC vii, xv, xxxi.   [4] ETC xl.
[5] ETC. xxxvi.   [6] ETC xlii.
[7] ETC liv.

The Coffin family is represented by two deeds, both dating apparently from the 1170's. The purpose of the first is to record the settlement of a dispute concerning the boundary between Abbotsham and Alwington. The abbot and convent admit Richard Coffin and Peryn his heir to full honorary membership of their brotherhood. If it shall please God to inspire Richard with the wish to enter a monastery, he shall be received as a monk into their house. In the meantime, he shall be entitled to a monk's daily board as often as he comes to Tavistock. Further, the abbot pays him two marks in cash. In return for these concessions Richard allows the disputed boundary to be defined by the oaths of twelve good and lawful men of the neighbourhood.[1] In the other deed Elyas Coffin, with the consent of his wife Matilda and his heir William, grants to the monastery of Tavistock and to the church of St Peter, Monk Okehampton, one ferling of land called Northcombe. I have not identified this place: it is described as part of the manor of Monk Okehampton.[2] Elyas seems to take some credit for this piece of "beneficence," as he calls it, though he admits that the abbot and convent have paid him 20s., and given him a silver casket worth another 15s., not to mention one bezant paid to his wife and a silver buckle given by them to master William Coffin. The pious munificence of the twelfth century seldom became fully active until stimulated in some such fashion.

One of the latest deeds in the cartulary, and certainly the saddest, is executed by a certain Reginald de la Putte, who makes a grant in free alms to the abbey of his land of la Putte, which is no doubt Pitland, halfway between Tavistock and Brentor. In return for this grant, Reginald is to receive from the almoner of Tavistock daily for the rest of his life the corrody or board-allowance of a leper.[3] This agreement seems to have been made early in the thirteenth century. By the end of that century a regular hospital for lepers was established at the west end of Tavistock.

As might be expected of a monastery situated between the Tavy and the Tamar, the Tavistock cartulary includes more

[1] ETC xxix.
[2] ETC xxx.
[3] ETC liii.

than one reference to fishing-rights. Baldwin de Redvers, *c.* 1125, gives the abbey a tithe of all fish taken at Buckland.[1] Then, towards the end of our period, Abbot Herbert enters into an elaborate agreement with Roger de Valletort, lord of Trematon, concerning their respective rights in the Tamar salmon-fishery. Roger is entitled to take from the abbot's wood any timber that may be needed for the construction or repair of his salmon-trap. He may take fish there on any date between the fifteenth day after Candlemas and the Finding of Holy Cross; but not at any other time of the year. The abbot enjoys an unrestricted right of fishing in his own trap and in the water between his and Roger's; and he may take from Roger's wood any timber required for the construction or repair of his salmon-trap, excepting oak, ash, and coppice-wood.[2]

The documents illustrate several points of feudal custom. When a landholder enters into a transaction involving the rights of his overlord, those rights are carefully safeguarded. Thus Walter Giffard I, whose estates were held of the Honour of Plympton, formally notifies his confirmation of Robert Giffard's gifts to his lord Richard, earl of Devon.[3] During the minority of Walter's heir, the Honour of Plympton was in the hands of Reginald, earl of Cornwall, who confirmed the Giffards' gift of Lamerton church and notified the bishop and chapter accordingly.[4] When the boundaries of Alwington were formally perambulated, Richard Coffin's lord Geoffrey Fitz Baldwin was among those present, as was also Nicholas, the lord's heir. The custom of handing over some physical object in token of seisin is exemplified at the restoration of Great Velliford: a knife is placed in Abbot Walter's hand. Similarly the termination of the dispute over the churches of the Honour of Sheviock is typified by a public exchange of knives—in this case, folding knives—between Henry Dawnay and Abbot Baldwin.

Lastly, these documents throw more than one valuable side-light upon place-names. For instance, the English Place-Name Society found no example of the name Monkston in Brentor earlier than 1770. We can now point to it ("Munekes-

<hr>

[1] ETC VIII.   [2] ETC XLVIII.
[3] ETC XIV.   [4] ETC XXIV.

tune") in William Giffard's charter of *c.* 1171;[1] and what is more, we may infer that it was then recently invented, for in the charter given by William's father some fifteen years before, the place is merely a nameless portion of the Lamerton demesne. These charters also perpetuate some names which have gone out of use: for example, Little Brent, in Brentor; Coaching, in Whitchurch; and a parcel of glebe in Lamerton called Eatgodesland.[2] Perhaps the most interesting specimens of lost names occur in the definition of the boundary between Abbotsham and Alwington. In accordance with the custom of pre-Conquest land-books, these bounds are given in the vernacular, though the rest of the document is of course in Latin.[3] They include several places which are not to be found in the survey of Devon Place-Names. Thus they raise questions of identification which can be solved only by somebody with local knowledge.[4] Translated into modern English, they are as follows:

"From the double ditch on the west of Adjavin which lies between the land of Bideford and Abbotsham, up along the stream to the stream-head; and so to the Giant's Way. From the Giant's Way north over the hollow tumulus. From the hollow tumulus on the west of the way to the ditch which lies between Cockington and Abbotsham. From the ditch south to Trendlesbury. From Trendlesbury to Durnwell. From Durnwell to Woolacombe. From Woolacombe out to the sea."

[1] ETC XXXVIII.
[2] ETC XIV, XLV.
[3] ETC XXIX.
[4] For a discussion of the passage, see *Devon & Cornwall Notes & Queries*, XXII, 1942–6, p. 201.

THE BOROUGH OF TAVISTOCK

ITS ORIGIN AND EARLY HISTORY

AT THE time of the Domesday inquest there were only four towns in Devonshire. Exeter, the capital of the south-west, had been a place of importance ever since the Roman occupation. Barnstaple, Lydford, and Totnes, originally strongholds in the defensive system built up by Alfred the Great, had in course of time become trading centres, each with its own mint; and Okehampton, another fortified place, had made some advance towards borough status by 1086, having acquired a market and four burgesses. Throughout the rest of the county the population was made up of tillers of the soil and rural handicraftsmen, with a sprinkling of soldiers, barons, and ecclesiastics; but of townsmen we hear nothing.

A very different picture is presented by the Assize Roll of 1238, the earliest complete roll of this county which has been preserved. In 1238 Exeter and seventeen other boroughs sent delegations of their burgesses to meet the justices in eyre.[1] These delegations were distinct from those sent by the rural hundreds: they consisted of townspeople and they represented urban communities publicly recognized as such. Thus in the century and a half which had elapsed since Domesday thirteen towns had been successfully established. A development of such importance in the life of the county would repay systematic study, for in the making of towns example and emulation play a large part, especially when the towns arise in such rapid succession as they seem to have done in twelfth-century Devon. The more we learn about any one of these communities, the better we shall understand the rest.

[1] Honiton, Tiverton, Okehampton, Totnes, Plympton, Modbury, Tavistock, Lydford, Torrington, Barnstaple, Kenton, South Molton, Ashburton (twelve burgesses each); Bradninch, Bideford, Crediton, Colyford (six burgesses each). Kingsbridge is named as a borough, but was apparently not represented.—PRO Assize Rolls, J.I. 1, 174, m. 25.

As a contribution to the study of a phase of Devonshire history which remains virtually unexplored, I propose here to investigate the origin and early history of the borough of Tavistock. But first it may be useful to explain briefly what the term 'borough' meant in the twelfth century. A borough was a place where the tenements were held by burgage tenure.[1] That is to say, it was a place where the lord contented himself with a money rent, exacting from the inhabitants few or none of the manorial services he claimed from his rural tenants. The status of the burgess, therefore, was sharply distinguished from that of the serfs or *nativi* who formed so large a section of the rural population. They paid for their holdings chiefly by personal service of one kind or another; he paid his burgage rent, and was free of any liability for service in the fields. Burgage tenure was thus a species of freehold, roughly corresponding with the rural tenure in free socage.

A few boroughs were set up on sites previously uninhabited. Not so Tavistock, for here an important abbey was founded in the third quarter of the tenth century. By 1086 there were thirty-seven labourers and peasants in the abbot's lordship, as well as a dozen slaves employed on his demesne.[2] Tavistock was a large manor, covering an area of approximately eighteen square miles, and comprising a number of scattered hamlets; but some at least of this population must have been seated in Tavistock itself. All their main sources of livelihood were comprised within the boundaries of the future borough. It was the flat meadow ground beside the Tavy, with its rich grazing, which had probably attracted the earliest settlers. They would find building materials and fuel in the woods that fringed the surrounding hills and vales on the north and north-east, woods today remembered only by their names: Parkwood, Old Wooda, Waddon. And they would grow their corn on the southward-facing slopes between Glanville Road and the modern Launceston road. Beyond and above the township land of Tavistock lay the abbot's demesne, originally bounded on the west by the river Lumburn and on the east by

[1] J. Tait, *Medieval English Borough*, Manchester, 1936, p. 211; M. de W. Hemmeon, *Burgage Tenure in Mediæval England*, Cambridge (Mass.), 1914, p. 157; *British Borough Charters, 1216–1307*, ed. Ballard and Tait, p. liv.

[2] DB IV, p. 163.

the Wallabrook. In the centre of its upland portion stood his grange and sheep-farm, or *heordewic*. The demesne would require from each inhabitant of the township a portion of his time and labour. They would plough the lord's arable, cut his corn, and carry in the harvest; take turns in serving as reeve, woodward, and slaughterer; and perform a number of miscellaneous services, such as cleaning out the mill-leat, and riding about the manor or to distant townships on the lord's errands.

The first step in the transformation of this purely rural economy was taken when Henry I issued a writ in the following terms:

"HENRY, king of England, to Geoffrey de Mandeville and all the barons of Devon and Cornwall, French and English, greeting. Know that I have granted to St Mary of Tavistock and to the monks that they may have a market in Tavistock every week on Friday. And I grant to merchants that they may sell and buy whatever they please [there]; and no one is to do them wrong on that account. Witnesses: William Warelwast, and Alfred of Lincoln, and Harding son of Alnod, and Walter son of Ansgar. At Stamford."[1]

The limits of date for this charter are 1100, the year of Henry's accession, and 1107, when William Warelwast became bishop of Exeter. Detailed evidence, which I have discussed elsewhere, points to 1105 as the most likely date of issue.[2] In that year Henry was busy raising funds for a campaign in Normandy; and it would be interesting to know how much the monks of Tavistock contributed to his war-chest in return for the market-grant. Whatever the amount, it was profitably invested, for the Friday market at Tavistock has brought in a steady income ever since. Its tolls at this day amount to some £1500 a year.

Before the conquest Lydford had been the recognized commercial centre of the region between Dartmoor and the Tamar. Now, with a rival market already established at Okehampton, its interests were threatened from the other side. The Lydford burgesses, therefore, might well look with a jealous eye upon the newly won commercial autonomy of Tavistock. That the

[1] The original text is given on p. 125 below.
[2] See p. 92 above.

latter was not established without a struggle may be inferred from the fact that the abbot presently found it necessary to obtain this second writ:

"HENRY, king of England, to William, bishop of Exeter, and Richard Fitz Baldwin, and all the barons of Devonshire, greeting. It is my will and command that the abbot of Tavistock shall have his market in peace, as I have granted to his church and commanded by my writ; and no one is to do him wrong on that account.—Witness: Nigel de Albini. At Clarendon."[1]

This seems to have had the desired effect of damping down opposition. At Easter 1116 the king issued a third writ,[2] confirming the market-grant and adding a three-day fair, to begin yearly on the eve and to end on the morrow of the principal feast of St Rumon, the tutelary saint of the abbey: that is, from the 29th to the 31st of August. Like the market, this fair entitled the abbot to levy toll from buyers and sellers. By these grants Tavistock became, in the language of the Old English laws, which were still in force at this date, a *port*. The kings of Wessex had borrowed this word from the administrative terminology of the Carolingian realm; it meant a place of trade, not a sea-port. It is probable, though we have no record of the fact, that the abbot soon found it necessary to appoint an official styled a *port-gerefa*, or port-reeve, whose duty it would be to collect the tolls, to authenticate by his presence the more important sales, and to settle any disputes that might arise.

The acquisition of a market did not lead necessarily to the foundation of a borough; but a borough always presupposed an existing market. One of the leading authorities on English boroughs considers it possible that in some cases a market-grant may have led to the introduction of burgage tenure, or features of that tenure, without any formal act by the lord of the manor.[3] So far as Tavistock is concerned, that possibility may be ruled out. For when the curtain goes up early in the thirteenth century, revealing the fully constituted borough, it

[1] See p. 125 below.
[2] Dugdale, *Monasticon*, II, p. 496; for the date, see DA XLVII, 1915, p. 376.
[3] J. Tait, introduction to *British Borough Charters, 1216–1307*, p. li.

discloses a manorial transformation which cannot be conceived as having come about otherwise than by the lord's deliberate act. The Domesday manor of Tavistock has ceased to exist. In its place we find an urban district covering about half a square mile, called the borough of Tavistock, and a rural district comprising all the rest of the original manor except those portions which had been granted out as knights' fees. This rural district is known as the manor of Hurdwick, taking its name from the abbot's *heordewic*, or demesne sheep-farm. The abbey itself, though lying within the borough, is accounted a manorial *enclave* of Hurdwick.[1] The abbot's feudal and hundredal jurisdiction, as well as his manorial rights over the residue of the ancient manor, have been transferred to Hurdwick. On law-days its court acts as a hundred court for the entire hundred of Tavistock, comprising the abbot's estates in the four modern parishes of Tavistock, Tavistock Hamlets, Brentor, and Milton Abbot. And Hurdwick, not Tavistock, is henceforth the seat of the abbot's barony. At its court his tenants by military service attend to do homage for their lands in Devon, Cornwall, and Dorset, or to settle such debatable matters as the rotation of their garrison duty at Exeter.

The establishment of the borough, then, had involved a partition of the abbot's territory and jurisdiction; and however gradual a process had led up to it, the partition itself must have been accomplished by one decisive act. "When in the twelfth or the thirteenth century a lord wished to start a borough, he did so at a stroke."[2] Today when we contemplate the weather-worn antiquity of such towns as Tavistock, it is difficult to grasp the fact that they owe their being to acts of creation as deliberate as those which have originated Letchworth and Welwyn. Yet such is the account which Tavistock gave of its own origin. In 1275 a jury of Tavistock burgesses declared that "the site where the township and abbey of Tavistock now

---

[1] The earliest extant document referring to the manor of Hurdwick is an undated deed of *c.* 1235 (W. D. Bdle 8, no. 1). In a lease granted 8 Jan., 1729–30, the abbey courtyard is described as being situated "in the parish of Tavistock, within the Manor of Hurdwick" (C Bdle 1, no. 20); and the Bedford Office surveys mention "the Scite of the Abbey within the Manor of Hurdwick."—H. Smith's Survey, 1726, fo. 3.

[2] Hemmeon, *op. cit.*, p. 166 *n.*; A. Ballard, *The English Borough in the Twelfth Century*, Cambridge, 1914, p. 65.

stand belonged at one time to Ethelred, king of England before the conquest. . . . A certain abbot of the same place founded (*fecit levari*) the aforesaid town: it is now worth eight pounds a year."[1]

"A certain abbot": if only they had remembered his name! Their forgetfulness may justify us in concluding that the borough had been founded before their grandfathers' time; let us say, before 1185. On this point corroboration is provided from an unexpected source. The cartulary of Buckland Priory in Somerset includes a slightly faulty transcript of a deed which may be translated as follows:

"In the name of our Lord Jesus Christ: be it known to the sons of holy mother Church, both now and in time to come, that I, *Robert de Crebor*, and William my father, have given and granted to the brethren of the holy Hospital of Jerusalem our land of Hole with all its appurtenances; and one acre of meadow on the bank of the Lumburn, by the hedge on the south side, as *Godfrey, son of Hugh*, held it; and fourpence from our burgage in Tavistock, to be rendered to the said brethren yearly on the feast of St Rumon by whomsoever shall hold that burgage. Also that for [the souls of] all our friends, living and deceased, we have given and granted [and] confirmed by this present charter the aforesaid land to the above-named brethren in pure and perpetual alms, reserving twelve pence yearly to be paid to us and to our heirs on the feast of St Rumon for all services, including the king's service, which shall be discharged, when it becomes due, out of those twelve pence; with common easements of our land in all places for persons inhabiting the aforesaid [land of Hole]. In presence of these witnesses: *R., dean of Tavistock*; Robert, the priest of Tavy; Richard Clerk of Cudlip; Hugh Clerk of Whitchurch; *Robert de Vespont*; Geoffrey; *Roger Ruby*; *Baldwin Giffard*; *Paine de Rowden*; *Roger de Harrogrove*; *Walter, his brother*; Robert Ruff, brother Michael of the Hospital; and many others."[2]

This document is undated; but the nine persons whose names I have italicized are mentioned in another Buckland charter, which is dated 1185.[3] In connection with this grant to the

---

[1] *Rotuli Hundredorum*, I, p. 81.   [2] P. 126 below.
[3] *Cartulary of Buckland Priory*, ed. Weaver, p. 146, no. 258.

Hospitallers, it is perhaps significant that a certain Radulfus de Hospitali, or de Hospicio, was one of the royal administrators who managed the temporalities of Tavistock Abbey from the death of Abbot Baldwin in 1184 until Easter 1186, when a new abbot was appointed.[1]

It seems then that by 1185 there were tenements in Tavistock that could be described as being held 'in burgage'. A noticeable feature of the document just quoted is that the grant is made, not by William de Crebor with the consent of his son and heir, but by the son, who speaks of his father as co-proprietor but takes it upon himself to act in their joint names. If the father was that William "de Creuebere" whose name occurs in a list of military tenants holding under the abbot in 1135,[2] he would be an aged man, possibly in his dotage, at the time of this grant. The point is worth making because it suggests that the burgage tenement had already been in the family's possession for some years.

The limits of date for the foundation of the borough are thus reduced to 1105, the probable year of the market-grant, and, at the lower end, 1185. No document has been discovered which provides any further clue, and therefore this is all that can be said with certainty upon the question of date. Six abbots in succession ruled Tavistock during the period for which evidence is lacking. Of these, Abbot Walter is, on general grounds, perhaps the likeliest candidate for the title of founder. His term of office (c. 1155–68) coincided with a rapid and considerable expansion of the Dartmoor tin-trade, which must have intensified the demand for houses in Tavistock. The industry was regulated by a code known as the 'assize of mines',[3] the details of which have not been preserved; but it may well have anticipated the charter of 1201 in requiring that tin should be put on sale only in certain boroughs and market towns appointed for the purpose, and that serfs engaged in digging for tin should be exempt from legal pursuit by their lords.[4] If so, the lord of a manor situated, like Tavistock, at the very edge of Dartmoor would have the strongest possible inducement to set

---

[1] Pipe Roll Society, XXXIV, p. 204, and XXXVI, p. 204.
[2] *Red Book of the Exchequer*, p. 250.
[3] Pipe Roll Society, XXXVIII, p. 169.
[4] G. R. Lewis, *The Stannaries*, Cambridge (Mass.), pp. 235, 238.

up a borough town. For his serfs, if they were enterprising enough to stake out tin-claims on the moor, would be protected by the Crown, which had a fiscal interest in the mines and cared little if the lord's arable were left untilled. A fragmentary copy of a letter from Archbishop Theobald to Abbot Walter has been preserved, from which it appears that certain labour services due from the tenants had been remitted by Walter's predecessor.[1] Faced with a choice between attempting to retrieve the services in the face of strong local and governmental opposition, and waiving them by the introduction of burgage tenure, a prudent abbot would not hesitate.

It has already been observed that the creation of the borough divided Tavistock from Hurdwick. There is no reason to suppose that this delimitation, once made, was ever altered, for the boundary, as perambulated and recorded in 1738,[2] shows every sign of having been drawn with the set purpose of including within the borough just so much arable, woodland, and meadow as pertained to the agricultural population of the older township, but no more, since the new burgess population would live mostly by trade or handicraft. Beginning at a rivulet which flowed into the Tavy half a mile south-west of the abbey, the boundary went northward up a lane dividing the arable fields of the township from an ancient farm called Pixon. At about two-thirds of a mile from the starting-point it turned eastward, and ran between the 450- and 500-feet contour-lines across Waddon and Billingsbear Wood; then, after taking in some two-thirds of Old Wood, it reached Exeter Lane. Here it turned sharply northward so as to include a portion of what was later known as Common Close, presumably a stretch of grassland in which the township had enjoyed rights of pasture. It then cut across Parkwood to the Tavy, the right bank of which formed the southern boundary.

The total extent of the borough is said to have been 325 acres. Less than half this area is built up even now; indeed, as recently as 1945 corn was being grown beside the Launceston road, on part of the ground where, in all probability, the men of the primitive township cultivated their arable strips. At first sight it may appear strange that the boundary, at its

[1] See p. 95 above.
[2] DA LXXIV, 1942, p. 199.

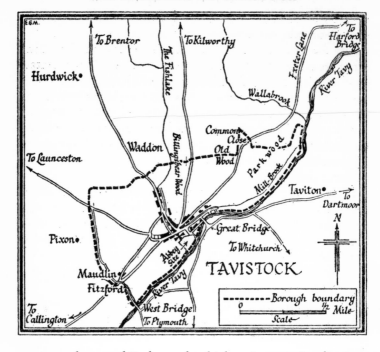

eastern end, crossed Parkwood, which, as its name implies, was enclosed woodland belonging to the abbot. The seeming anomaly, however, was dictated by the construction of a new mill-stream. Hitherto there had been only one mill in Tavistock. It was situated on or close to the site of the present Guildhall, and was driven by water from a little stream known as the Fishlake. It is described in Domesday Book as serving the domestic needs of the monastery.[1] Standing as it did within the abbey precinct, and belonging therefore to the manor of Hurdwick, it could not meet the requirements of the growing borough. Accordingly a new mill was built outside the precinct, on the site of the present Town Hall, and supplied with power from an artificial channel called the Mill-brook, water being drawn off from the Tavy by means of a weir in Parkwood, about a mile away to the east. As the borough boundary was taken across Parkwood to the head-weir, the whole course of the Mill-brook lay within the borough, and no dispute could

[1] DB IV, p. 163.

arise between Tavistock and Hurdwick over the responsibility for scouring it. The channel from the Fishlake was diverted into it just outside the abbey gateway, and henceforth the Millbrook drove both mills, old and new.[1]

The borough was provided not only with a town mill: it had also its own court. This met in the open air, at the junction of Market Street with what is now called Pym Street. Here stood the shambles, or stalls upon which meat and fish were exposed for sale on market-days. In the local dialect they were called shammels; and from the circumstance of its meeting in the midst of them the borough court of Tavistock was known as the Shammel-Moot.[2] Though liable to be summoned every three weeks, in practice the court would not assemble more than twelve or thirteen times a year, if so often. Invariably, however, there would be two 'great courts' or law-days at or about Michaelmas and Holy Cross Day (May 3) when justice would be done on petty criminals. For female disturbers of the peace the borough had its tip-cart or tumbrel, at Tavistock as at Totnes called a skelving-stool (elsewhere a cucking-stool);[3] and for male offenders a pillory standing at the foot of Kilworthy Hill.

At the Michaelmas law-day the jury of burgesses—or portmen, as they called themselves[4]—selected two or more candidates for the office of portreeve. As his name implies, the portreeve discharged within the borough duties not unlike those of the reeve in rural manors; both of them in formal documents are styled *prepositus*.[5] The portreeve was the lord's agent for

---

[1] DCNQ XXII, 1946, p. 369.

[2] See p. 127 below. The name does not occur in later documents. A deed of 1315 granting "certain stalls in the middle of the street of the borough of Tavistock" is endorsed: "Shamelys in Tauystok" (W. D. Bdle 84, no. 9); and cf. the "Fisshe-Shamells" at Totnes (DA XII, 1880, p. 232). At Coggeshall, Essex, the court was held at the Shambles in the market-place.—S. and B. Webb, *The Manor and the Borough*, 1908, p. 65 n.

[3] DCNQ XXII, 1946, p. 368.

[4] An inference from field-names. There were two closes in Tavistock called Portmene-closes, and a piece of land near Old Wood called Portmanlond.—Tavistock Abbey White Book, ff. 1, 22b, 38b.

[5] A certain amount of ink has been wasted in discussion of the Latin title "senior," attributed to the portreeve of Tavistock by R. N. Worth in his *Calendar of the Tavistock Parish Records*, p. 65. The undated deed of *c.* 1275 in which Worth imagined he had found this title refers to quite a different

collecting reliefs, amercements, burgage rents, and other seignorial dues.[1] No extant document reveals where lay the dividing-line between his functions and those of the town bailiff, an officer who makes his first appearance in 1281; nor indeed is it absolutely certain that the bailiff who in that year accompanied the borough jurors to the eyre, or the Richard Blacksmyth, "tunc ballivus ville," who witnessed a deed in 1322,[2] was a different official from the portreeve. Numerous fourteenth-century charters show the latter witnessing conveyances of burgage tenements. As the highest elective officer of the borough court he enjoyed a precedence of honour, and sometimes no doubt of leadership, over his fellow-townsmen. To this limited extent, during his year of office, he ranked as the chief citizen of Tavistock. A garden in the borough was reserved for his use, but this seems to have been his only perquisite;[3] and the fact that the office was rarely held more than once by the same person suggests that it was not an object of ambition. The portreeve who rendered account in 1497, Richard Lybbe, is styled *prepositus* as usual on the roll, but in a conveyance executed two or three days earlier he is described as "mayor of Tavistock."[4] This unauthorized use of the mayoral title, which had its parallel in other Devon boroughs, and which occurs intermittently at Tavistock between 1449 and 1556, amounted to nothing more than a fitful and rather half-hearted attempt to dignify an officer whose origin and essence lay in the service due from a tenant to his lord.[5] Not for him, whatever he might call himself, the power and preeminence enjoyed by the chief magistrate of an incorporated borough.

---

officer: Henry de Kestelwyk, "tunc Sen' Tauystoke"—doubtless an abbreviation of *senescallus*, meaning steward.

[1] *Calendar of the Tavistock Parish Records*, pp. 8, 20, Cf. DA XVI, 1884, p. 174 (portreeve of Sutton Prior), and XXXVIII, 1906, p. 303 (portreeve of Hatherleigh). At Ashburton the portreeve and burgesses used a common seal (*ibid.*, LVI, 1924, p. 57), but this seems to have been exceptional.

[2] W. D Bdle 2, no. 19.

[3] *ibid.*, B Bdle 117, no. 18; Tavistock Abbey White Book, fo. 37*b*.

[4] *Calendar of the Tavistock Parish Records*, p. 81.

[5] Cf. DA LXIX, 1937, p. 277. A list of the Tavistock portreeves from 1272 to 1501 is given in DA LXXIX, 1947, pp. 148–151, and of those from 1682 to 1884 in DA XLVI, 1914, pp. 173–75.

In themselves neither Shammel-Moot nor town mill portended any notable relaxation of seignorial control. The abbot was still lord of Tavistock. It was his steward who presided in the Shammel-Moot and appointed the portreeve, for although the port-men had now the right to put forward their own candidates for that office, the decision between these rested with the lord's representative, and if none of the candidates proved acceptable, the outgoing portreeve might be left in office for another year. Corn ground for burgesses at the town mill was subject to deduction of a percentage by way of toll; and this toll-corn was either sent to the lord's granary, or sold, the proceeds being then paid into the lord's exchequer. Alternatively, the abbot might grant a lease of the mill at a fixed annual rent, in which case the lessee claimed the toll-corn, and sometimes, to make certain of his profits, exacted more than custom allowed, notwithstanding the clamour of the townspeople. When, in 1275, the Tavistock jury declared that the borough was worth eight pounds a year, they meant that this was the average total of the abbot's receipts from burgage rents, fines imposed upon delinquents, and tolls of market, fair, and mill.

The jury's valuation is confirmed by a surviving rent-roll of the borough for the year 1291,[1] when the portreeve accounted for a sum of £7 8s. 4½d., derived mostly from burgage rents. More than half the burgages pay rents of eightpence. The next commonest amounts are sixpence and fourpence. It seems probable that eightpence had at first been the standard rent, as it was at Exeter, and that the smaller payments represent partitions of the original holdings. Ten persons, three of them women, were charged twopence each "for liberty to buy and sell" in the borough without paying toll. They were presumably non-residents, for market-tolls were not exacted from tenants in burgage. This is proved by an 'extent' or survey, drawn up in 1414, of the sacristan's property, where a typical entry reads: "Gregory Sargeaunt holds one tenement in Tavistock, with a garden, and with liberty as a burgess of the town so that he shall be free of toll through the whole borough."[2] From the same document it appears that when a burgess in-

---

[1] W. D Bdle 84, no. 2.
[2] White Book, fo. 32.

herited a tenement, the lord claimed a succession-duty, or 'relief', of 2s. 6d. If a burgess died intestate, leaving no heirs of his body, his tenement passed into the lord's hand by escheat.[1]

The earliest extant borough court roll belongs to Elizabeth's reign; but among the unpublished documents in the possession of the duke of Bedford are two deeds which throw much light upon the borough and its institutions in the early thirteenth century.[2] By the first of them one Robert Clerk, in return for five marks of silver paid to him by Ralph, son of Muriel, surrenders to the aforesaid Ralph all his right over a messuage in Tavistock with its appurtenances: which messuage the grantor's father had built and held in free burgage, rendering therefor eightpence yearly at Michaelmas to the sacristan of Tavistock for all charge and service. This conveyance is described as taking place "in full Shammel-Moot" during the abbacy of William de Kernet: that is, between 1220 and 1224; and the name of the builder of the house, the grantor's father, is given as "Robert, chaplain of Tavy." It is tempting to identify him with that "Robert, priest of Tavy," who witnessed Robert de Crebor's grant to the Hospitallers in 1185.

The second document may be a little older than the first. It deals with a plot of ground in Tavistock, described as lying between the house which belonged to Osmar the smith and that of Semar the cobbler. In consideration of a *gersuma* or premium of one mark of silver paid to him by Roger Cruci and Matilda his wife, Laurence Colbert grants them this plot with all the liberties and free customs pertaining thereto within and without the borough of Tavistock, to be held of the grantor and his heirs at a yearly rent of tenpence, payable at Michaelmas. The transaction is authenticated by the charter and seal of the grantor, who further states that he has given seisin to Roger and Matilda and has received their homage "in the Shammel-Moot, before the whole township of Tavistock, with my friends present and consenting." Furthermore, Sir Reginald de Ferrers, the landlord from whom the grantor holds the piece of land in question, has confirmed the transaction by his charter.

[1] DA LXXIX, 1947, p. 153.
[2] See pp. 126, 127 below.

The reference to homage is curious, for homage was an incident of feudal tenure, and as such had no place in boroughs. It is true that grants by burgesses in other towns occasionally purport to be made "for the homage and service" of the grantee; but the author of the standard work on burgage tenure considers this to be mere verbiage, a high-sounding imitation of feudal terminology.[1] The imitation seems however to have been carried rather far at Tavistock, for the language of Colbert's grant leaves very little room for doubt that Roger and Matilda went through some sort of performance in the borough court which was regarded by those concerned as a true render of homage, though the conveyance would have been just as valid if they had spared themselves the trouble.

In some boroughs, as at Bury St Edmunds under Abbot Samson's charter of 1190, the sale of inherited tenements was not allowed, though tenements acquired by purchase could be sold without restriction. At Tavistock we have seen Robert Clerk selling a messuage left him by his father; and there is at least one other thirteenth-century deed which expressly conveys lands of inheritance within the borough.[2] It seems clear that the "liberties and free customs" of Tavistock included a virtually unlimited freedom of sale.

This 'mobility' of the burgage tenement, in an age when the conveyance of all other real estate was hedged about with strict rules, formed a great attraction in the eyes of persons with money to invest. From the three documents already quoted we can see how this attraction operated in the vicinity of Tavistock. Sir Reginald de Ferrers, lord of the adjacent manor of Bere Ferrers,[3] takes a plot of ground and lets it, still vacant, to an under-tenant, who in turn sublets it to a third party. Robert, the chaplain of Tavy St Mary or Tavy St Peter (it is impossible to say which), was clearly a well-to-do ecclesiastic who combined a distaste for celibacy with a shrewd appreciation of house property. Robert de Crebor was a military tenant of the abbey, holding Crebor near Tavistock with certain lands in Hatherleigh by the service of half a knight's fee.[4]

[1] Hemmeon, op. cit., pp. 50, 51.
[2] W. D Bdle 2, no. 12.
[3] DCNQ xxi, 1940, p. 60.
[4] W. D Bdle 9, no. 1; The Book of Fees, p. 780.

Being charitably disposed towards the Hospitallers, he creates a rent-charge in their favour upon his tenement in the borough, which is occupied by a subtenant. All this points to a brisk traffic in burgage property. The purchase-price of Robert Clerk's house, five marks, is exactly one hundred times as much as the burgage rent of eightpence which the abbey gets from it "for all charge and service." It is interesting to compare this with the four and a half marks paid at the same period for a shop in Bath, where the burgage rent was sixpence.[1]

Borrowing for a moment the vocabulary of a later age, we may say that the squires and parsons of the neighbourhood have been quick to avail themselves of the opportunities for investment provided by the new borough. The abbot, on his part, has offered them building sites on easy terms. Waiving all predial services, he stipulates only for a modest burgage rent, an occasional 'relief', suit of court, and suit of mill. But what of the unfree or half-free inhabitants of the existing township? Have they too been emancipated from manorial burdens? For answer we turn to a memorandum endorsed on the first membrane of an 'extent' of Hurdwick, dated 1416. "Note well that on the death of every abbot of the monastery of Tavistock, and of every professional monk there, eighteen tenants of the town of Tavistock, whose names are severally inscribed below, shall watch the body of the same for one night from sunset until sunrise of the day following, and shall receive from the abbot, prior, or almoner for the time being two shillings and sixpence for bread and drink during the said time, and shall bear the whole charge of that time for themselves and all others coming thither for that purpose and watching according to custom. Likewise the same tenants shall have on the morrow or on the burial-day of the said abbot or monk one meche-loaf, three pottles of beer, one main dish of meat or fish, and one subsidiary dish of meat or fish, according as the day may require . . .

"Item, the almoner, or any other person by order of the abbot if there be one, or of the prior for the time being, shall charge the aforesaid tenants upon their oath then to be taken,

---

[1] Hemmeon, *op. cit.*, pp. 67, 81. At Lydford the burgage rent was 4d. (*Dartmoor Preservation Assoc.*, I, p. 152). At Bradninch it was 6d.; at Barnstaple 8d. (average); and at Okehampton 1s.—Hemmeon, pp. 67 sqq.

to watch the body of the deceased faithfully during that time. If any of the aforesaid tenants shall absent himself from these vigils, he shall pay to the lord abbot and to the convent one pound of wax, to be levied at discretion by their bailiff. For the performance of these watches the said tenants shall be fore-warned by the bailiff of the town of Tavistock at the behest of the abbot, the prior, or the precentor, or on other sufficient mandate from his superior . . ."

Then follows a custom which had nothing to do with burials:

"Item, each of the said tenants shall go to the manor of Plymstock to summon the reeve there and bid him warn the other tenants of that manor to send and carry corn to the said monastery of Tavistock, and to do other carriage-service according to the custom of the aforesaid manor [of Plym-stock]. A tenant thus making summons shall have, on his arrival, one whole three-quarter loaf for his pains.

"It is shown in ancient muniments that they are under obligation by reason of their tenure to do and observe all the above-named duties."[1]

Having written thus far, the compiler forgot to carry out his intention of giving the tenants' names, nor did he state where their tenements were situated. It need hardly be said that their duties would as a rule be performed in rotation. Relays of watchers might take turns in the abbey church, and there could be no need to send more than one messenger at a time to Plymstock. Yet the number eighteen is surely not without significance. We seem here to catch a glimpse of Tavistock at the moment of its transition from a rural township to a borough town. Outside the abbey gate are eighteen cottages inhabited by labourers and hinds of servile status who owe their lord a miscellany of services. By creating a borough, the lord turns them into burgesses, making them free of all service henceforth, except that they must still provide an occasional postal service between Tavistock and Plymstock when the lord's granary needs replenishing, and must still grace with their presence the solemnities of burial in the abbey church.

It remains uncertain whether the abbot embodied his con-

[1] W. D Bdle 84, no. 29, m. 1 b. The omitted portions relate only to the abbot and convent.

cessions in a charter or proclaimed them orally. If there was a charter, it has long since disappeared, and all trace of it is now irrecoverably lost, unless indeed the great register of Tavistock Abbey, commonly called the Maynard cartulary, which vanished at the end of the seventeenth century, should ever come to light again and be found to include a transcript of the missing document. There was no need for the abbot to seek royal confirmation of his act, for the foundation of the borough, while it established a new relationship between the abbot and the men of Tavistock, made little difference to outside parties. Only in judicial matters, when the justices in eyre came down to Exeter or the sheriff went round Devon on his tourn, was there any contact between the borough and the king's representatives. We have seen that by 1238 Tavistock was represented at the eyre by a delegation of its own burgesses. This privilege can hardly have been acquired without a royal grant, but there is no record of such grant in the Charter Rolls. It may have been purchased from John Lackland during the period of approximately four years, beginning in December 1189, in which the absent king allowed him to rule Devon, Cornwall, and five other counties, as a quasi-independent principality.

In 1258 there occurred, for the first and only time on record, a clash between the borough and its lord. At that time the abbey was undergoing a financial crisis. In November 1257 royal letters-patent were directed to all its tenants, informing them that the monastery was in debt, and requesting them to help the new abbot, Henry de Northampton, with a voluntary subsidy.[1] The response to this appeal was presumably insufficient, for the abbot shortly afterwards laid an arbitrary tax, or 'tallage', of ten marks (£6 13s. 4d.) upon the borough. During the vacancy preceding his election the prior and convent had purchased the right to act as custodians of the abbey. This entitled them to keep for their own use the revenues that would otherwise have accrued to the king during voidance, including "tallages of their men," a form of impost to which, as a rule, only serfs were liable on the estates of private lords. The king, however, still claimed and exercised the right to tallage boroughs on his own lands, and Abbot Henry seems to have

[1] CPR 1247–58, p. 602.

maintained that the grant of custody had put his convent in the same position as the king so far as this right was concerned. When the burgesses of Tavistock refused to pay, he called in the sheriff to distrain upon them. An appeal to the king followed. On the 18th of June 1258 the sheriff was forbidden by a royal mandate either to distrain for the tallage himself, or to let the abbot do so. It was explained that the king had not intended the grant of custody to reduce any tenant of the abbey to servitude.[1]

In 1294, confronted with the prospect of a war with France, Edward I obtained from parliament a tax on personal property at the rate of a tenth in rural districts and a sixth in "cities, boroughs, and market towns." No definition of these terms was given; it was left to the assessors, acting in concert with the sheriff of the county, to select such trading centres as could best support the burden of the higher tax. It is not known what Devonshire towns were chosen, but there is reason to believe that they were few in number,[2] perhaps not more than the five, including Tavistock, which received the sheriff's writ in the following year. The higher rate of tax was henceforth to be a distinguishing mark of boroughs which the Crown recognized as such. In 1295, with a view to fresh taxation, the sheriffs were instructed to send up two knights from each county, two citizens from each city, and two burgesses from each borough, to attend a parliament at Westminster. The sheriff of Devon returned representatives of the shire, of the city of Exeter, and of five towns: Totnes, Barnstaple, Plympton, Tavistock, and Torrington; the members for Tavistock being Ralph de Sachevill and Walter le Wise.

From what has been said about the circumstances of their summons, it will be obvious that to Sachevill and Wise, and still more to their constituents, parliamentary representation was a most unwelcome source of expense. Far from being proud of the franchise, more than one borough attempted to shake it off. There is no indication that Tavistock made any such attempt; and indeed its burgesses must have been well aware that no petition for release coming from their town

[1] CPR 1247–58, p. 560; CCR 1256–59, p. 313.
[2] J. F. Willard, 'Taxation Boroughs and Parliamentary Boroughs', *Historical Essays in honour of James Tait*, Manchester, 1933, p. 422.

would stand any chance of succeeding. For in 1305 its ancient importance as a centre of the tin-trade was confirmed by a royal charter establishing or re-establishing Ashburton, Tavistock, and Chagford as the three stannary towns where all tin raised within the county of Devon was to be weighed, stamped, and put on sale.[1]

With occasional interruptions, the borough was represented in parliament by two members until 1868, when the two members were reduced to one. Its parliamentary history has been narrated elsewhere by an able pen;[2] but one curious detail may be mentioned here. In 1703 an ex-portreeve of Tavistock informed the Committee of Privileges that the franchise belonged to freeholders of inheritance living within the borough and presented as such by the jury of the borough court; and he added that such freeholders were still called "the abbot's burgesses."[3]

The abbots had seen to it that their town was provided with all necessary services. Mention has already been made of its cornmill, market stalls, pillory, and skelving-stool. The Fishlake, augmented by a tributary called the Buddle, flowed down Market Street in an open channel whence the inhabitants could help themselves to water. The residential and commercial quarter radiated outwards from the abbey gate. About fifty yards east of the main gateway stood a small chapel dedicated to St Matthew, which the monks believed to be more ancient than their abbey.[4] This may well have served the needs of the lay population until the close of the twelfth century, but then or soon afterwards the new parish church of St Eustace was built on its present site.[5] John, "chaplain of Tavistock," attests

[1] Lewis, *op. cit.*, p. 239.

[2] J. J. Alexander, in DA XLII, 1910, pp. 258 sqq.; XLIII, 1911, pp. 371 sqq.; LXIX, 1937, pp. 260 sqq.

[3] *Journals of the House of Commons*, 1702–04, p. 121.

[4] DCNQ XXII, 1942, pp. 56, 57.

[5] A bull of Celestine III, dated 1193, alludes only to the abbey church and to the parish "chapels" (Dugdale, II, p. 498). Had a parish church existed at that date, it would almost certainly have been mentioned by name in the bull, with the others belonging to the abbey. The earliest authentic reference to St Eustace's occurs in 1265 (*Register of Walter Bronescombe*, ed. F. C. Hingeston-Randolph, p. 266); but the dedication is an unusual one, and Eustace occurs as a Christian name at Tavistock in 1238.

a charter *c.* 1177; his successors in the following century are styled vicar.[1] Eastward from the parish church ran Brook Street, most of which belonged to the sacristan, an official whose duties kept him much at home, and whom it was therefore convenient to endow with burgage rents. West Street led towards a ford over the Tavy, later known as Fitz-ford, which was superseded halfway through the fifteenth century by a stone bridge.[2] Another bridge, on the site of the present Abbey Bridge, served the private needs of the monastery, and a third, the "great bridge" as it is first called *c.* 1260, a narrow five-arched structure with cutwaters on either side, was built about two hundred and forty yards upstream.[3] At the western extremity of the borough stood "the hospital of St Mary Magdalene of Tavistock," first named in 1244,[4] and intended chiefly for sufferers from the then prevalent disease of leprosy.

The rent-roll of 1291, already quoted, calls up a picture of the town at the close of the thirteenth century: a picture which, however, does not include the sacristan's property. The burgages which owed rent to the abbot consisted at that date of 106 messuages, 53 of which had gardens adjoining; 12 "tenements"; 2 "tenements with gardens"; and 35 detached "gardens, with liberty." In some cases a holding is divided into moieties, each paying half the original rent; but the "liberty" (of transfer, exemption from toll, and so forth) is then attached to one moiety, and the other is described as being "without liberty." Fifteen residents pay twopence each for having foot-bridges across the Fishlake or the Mill-brook; and one pays

[1] A. Morey, *Bartholomew of Exeter*, Cambridge, 1937, p. 157. At Totnes the change of title from chaplain to vicar occurs *c.* 1216.—DA LVII, 1925, p. 274.
[2] A charter dated 1460 refers to West Bridge as "le newbrig."—W. D Bdle 2, no. 129.
[3] *Calendar of the Tavistock Parish Records*, p. 65. The Great Bridge was pulled down in 1764. Only one document known to me refers to the forerunner of the present Abbey Bridge. It is a letter, dated 26 August 1743, informing the steward of the Tavistock estate that the writer has been looking for some large moor-stones to repair a breach in the Mill-brook. "Hunsdon has taken several out by the riverside opposite to the Lower Abbey Gate" [i.e. the water gate] "that were formerly part of the ancient bridge there."—John Wynne to Robert Butcher, W. Table 4 B, Drawer 1.
[4] PRO Assize Rolls, J.I. 1, 175, m. 11*b*. It stood on the site of the tenements known lately as Old Workhouse Cottages.

twopence "for an encroachment by the great bridge." The "lepers of La Forde" pay 1s. 2d. for their hospital—described as "a messuage and garden, with liberty"—near what was later known as Fitzford. There is an edge-mill for which Osmund the Smith pays fourpence, and a tan-mill for which the sacristan pays sixpence. One burgess, Ralph de Sachevill, the M.P. of 1295, is unique in owing a pound of wax for his messuage instead of a money rent. Six tenants are stated to owe rent "and other service." Was this the service of taking messages to Plymstock and assisting at funerals, for which, as we have seen, eighteen burgesses were liable? If so, the other twelve must have been tenants of the sacristan.

It is interesting to compare the rent-roll of 1291 with the account rendered by the portreeve in 1497. In that year the gross rental, £7 19s. 5½d., was reduced to £6 4s. because fifteen tenements were in hand, one was derelict, an unspecified number, with an aggregate rental of 5s. 9d., were lying vacant, and one or two, like that of the abbey laundress, and the vicar's house in St Matthew Street, were rent-free. Thirteen courts were held during the year, their proceeds amounting to £1 7s. 2d.; and a 'relief' of 12s. 6d. was collected. When fourpence had been paid to the clerk who engrossed the account, there remained a net total of £8 3s. 4d. Thus the abbot's income from the borough remained as nearly as possible stationary for two hundred years. It should be mentioned, however, that for some unexplained reason the portreeve of 1497 does not account for market tolls or the profits of St Rumon's fair: items which in 1535 were reckoned as being together worth, upon an average, another £1 per annum.[1]

Between the city which ranked as a shire incorporate, receiving royal writs direct from the Crown and having its own sheriff—a status which Exeter itself did not attain until 1536 —and the village into which a local lord had introduced burgage tenure in its most elementary form, the gradations of burgality were manifold. At or near the lower limit stood rural market-centres like Denbury and Hatherleigh, two villages which belonged to the abbots of Tavistock and received from them the name of boroughs, with certain liberties, but never achieved public recognition. Modest as their franchises were,

[1] *Valor Ecclesiasticus*, II, p. 381.

those of Tavistock itself were at first hardly more extensive. For this reason, and because its foundation-charter has not been preserved, Tavistock is ignored by the three writers (Ballard, Tait, and Hemmeon) who have thrown most light upon the early English borough. Some other writers tacitly assume that only the king's towns were of any consequence. In reality, quite a number of seignorial boroughs grew up into flourishing towns, while some of royal creation failed utterly, like that abortive borough of Newton which Edward I set up in the Isle of Purbeck. A town might owe its being to a charter, but its well-being rested upon trade and population. When the quotas of taxable capacity were fixed in 1334, Tavistock was placed fifth among the Devon boroughs, after Exeter, Plymouth, Barnstaple, and Dartmouth, Totnes being sixth and Torrington seventh. By 1445, when the quotas were revised, it had superseded Dartmouth in the fourth place; and it still held that position in the assessment of 1523.[1] As a stannary town, a thriving centre of the cloth trade, and a parliamentary borough, Tavistock easily escaped the obscurity and insignificance which characterized many Devonshire boroughs of seignorial creation.

APPENDIX OF DOCUMENTS

A

HENRICUS Rex Anglie. Goifredo de Mandeuilla. & Omnibus Baronibus Francis & Anglis de Deuenesira. & de Cornubia. Salutem. Sciatis me concessisse Sancte Marie de Tauistocha. & monachis. ut habeant mercatum in Tauistocha in vnaquaque ebdomoda. die veneris. & concedo mercatoribus ut uendant. & emant. quicquid uoluerint. & nullus eis super hoc iniuriam faciat. T. Will' o Warewast. & Alured' de Linc'. & Harding' filio Alnodi. & Walt'o filio Ansg'i. Apud Stanford'.

(Russell Cartulary, fo. 1b. For a description of this cartulary, see EHR LXII, 1947, pp. 352 sqq.)

B

H. rex Angl' Will'mo Ep'o exonie & Ric' fil' Bald' & Om'ibus Baronibus deuenesire sal'. Volo & p'cipio q'd Abbas de tauistoca

---

[1] PRO Lay Subsidy Rolls, E179, Bdle 95, nos. 10, 99; Bdle 97, no. 186.

habeat inpace Mercatu' suu' de tauistoca. sic' dedi Eccl'ie & p'cepi p' breue meu' & nullus ei sup' hoc iniuria' faciat. T. Nig' de Albini'. Ap. Clarendona'.

(Original charter, formerly D. Bundle 84, no. 3; now in Devon County Record Office.)

C

IN nomine domini nostri i'hu x'ri sciant tam presentes quam futuri sancte matris ecclesie filii quod Ego Robertus de Crawabara & Will's pater meus dedimus fratribus sancti hospitalis Jerusalem & concessimus terram nostram de Hole cum omnibus pertinenciis suis & unam acram prati super ripam lambre iuxta fossatum in australi parte sicut Godafridus filius Hugonis tenuit & quatuor denarios de burgagio nostro in Tauistoke Reddendo ipsis fratribus annuatim ad festum sancti Rumoni quicumque illud Burgagium tenuerint Et quia predictam terram prenominatis fratribus in puram & perpetuam elemosinam exceptis duodecim denariis annuatim ad festum sancti Rumoni nobis & heredibus nostris reddendis pro omnibus seruiciis Nam seruicium Regis ex illis duodecim denariis cum contigerit fiet & communia aysiamenta terre nostre in omnibus locis predictam [terram] inhabitantibus hominibus pro omnibus amicis nostris vivis ac defunctis dedimus & concessimus [&] hac presenti carta confirmauimus. Hiis testibus R decano Tauist' Roberto Sacerdote Tauy Ricardo Clerico de Cudelep Hugone Clerico de Witychircha Roberto de Vespont Galfrido Rogero Ruby Baldewino Giffard Pain' de Ruadun Rogero de Harragraua Waltero fratre eius Roberto Ruffo fratre Michaele de Hospitali & multis aliis.

(Cartulary of Buckland Priory, now in the possession of the Somerset Archaeological and Natural History Society, at Taunton Castle. The curator, Mr H. St George Gray, kindly supplied a photograph of the page. The bracketed words are missing in the cartulary text.)[1]

D

SCIANT presentes & futuri quod ego Robertus Clericus filius Roberti Capellani de Taui dedi & concessi & Presenti carta Confirmaui Radulfo filio Muriel Quoddam Mesuagium Cum pertinentiis In Tauistok. Illo videlicet Mesuagio Cum pertinentiis Quod pater meus construxit & Tenuit In Burgagio libero. Reddendo Inde Annuatim Sacristarie Tauistoch' octo Denarios ad festum Sancti

[1] Baffled by the haphazard use of capitals and the absence of punctuation, the Rev. F. W. Weaver gave a decidedly erroneous translation of this document in his edition of the cartulary, Somerset Record Society, xxv, p. 153, no. 274.

Michaelis pro omni seruicio & omni exactione. Tenendum &
Habendum sibi & Heredibus suis Libere saluo & Quiete Ita Quod
ego & Heredes mei In prefato Mesuagio nec Inpertinentiis Jus
Amplius Clamare Non Possimus. Ego autem & Heredes mei
Tenemur Warantizare predicto Radulfo & Heredibus suis prefatam
Donationem & concessionem meam Contra omnes Homines &
omnes feminas. & Pro Hac mea Donatione & concessione dedit
mihi sepedictus Radulfus Quinque Marcas Argenti In Recogni-
tionem. Facta uero fuit Hec donatio & concessio mea In Pleno
Shamelimoto Tauistok' Will'o de Kernet Tunc Temporis Abbate
Tauistok' predicto Radulfo & Heredibus suis Rata & stabilis et
Inperpetuum Duratura & sigilli mei Inpressione Confirmata. Hiis
Testibus [? Bal]dwino de Taui. Alano Maresscallo. Will'o filio
Matillidis. Augustino filio Roberti filii Nyel. Radulfo Porleu &
multis aliis. [*Seal missing.*]

(W. B Bdle 117, no. 1.)

E

SCIANT Presentes & futuri Quod Ego Laurencius Colbertus Con-
silio & assensu & Consensu amicorum meorum Dedi & Concessi
Rogero Cruci & Matillidi vxori sue & heredibus ipsorum pro
seruicio & Hummagio suo vnam Placiam in villa Tavistoch' que
Jacet Inter Domum que fuit Osmari fabri & Semari sutoris Tenen-
dam de me & Heredibus meis iure hereditario ipsis & Heredibus
suis cum omnibus Libertatibus & Liberis Consuetudinibus ad Eam
Placiam pertinentibus infra Burgum Tavistoch' & Extra. Reddendo
Inde singulis annis decem denarios ad festum sancti Micahelis. Pro
omnibus seruiciis mihi & heredibus meis ipsi & heredes sui. Pro
hac autem Concessione dedit mihi memoratus Rogerus Cruci &
Matillis uxor eius Unam marcam argenti in Gersuma. Tenemur
igitur Nos & Heredes nostri Warantizare Placiam prenominatam
pretaxatis Rogero & Matillidi & Heredibus suis & omnes Libertates
ad eam placiam pertinentes sicut prescriptum est Contra omnes
homines & feminas. Hanc autem Donacionem & Concessionem
Nostram Concessit & Confirmauit quantum ad eum pertinet
Dominus Reginaldus de Ferres Eisdem Rogero Cruci & Matillidi
vxori sue & heredibus ipsorum per Cartam suam sicut dominus meus
de quo Eam Teneo. Et ut Hec mea donacio & Concessio futuris
Temporibus stabilis & firma sine doli machinacione habeatur
sigillo nostro & presenti scripto Eam Confirmauimus & Coram
omni villeta [*sic*] Tavistoch' in Scamellimoto presentibus amicis
nostris & Consencientibus cum placia prenominata & cum presenti
carta nostra sepedictos Rogerum Cruci & Matillidem uxorem suam

seisiauimus & hummagium ipsorum Recepimus. Hiis Testibus. Radulfo de Ferreres. Nicholao de Hauton. Roberto de Witechurche. Radulfo Gave. Godwino Neel. Waltero filio Godwini. Augustino filio Roberti Neel Will' Le Dinbur. Waltero & Rogero filiis Augustini Nutte & multis aliis. [*Seal missing.*]

(W. D Bdle 2, no. 1.)

THE OPEN FIELD IN DEVON

IT HAS been generally agreed that Devonshire lies outside the area formerly cultivated under the open-field
system. The map which serves as frontispiece to Gray's
monograph on the subject shows the western boundary of the
open-field area beginning in the west of Dorset and passing up
northward across Somerset so as to exclude Devon, Cornwall,
and west Somerset.[1] Dr and Mrs Orwin, while revising and
correcting Gray's data at several points, are emphatic where
the south-western counties are concerned. "In *Lancashire,
Devon*, and *Cornwall*, there is nothing to indicate that the
system [of open fields] was ever followed."[2] Professor Darby
illustrates his remarks on the history of the English village
with a reproduction of Gray's map. According to Stenton, the
open-field system "is not found in Devon," and according to
Douglas Jerrold "it was never introduced into Devon, Cornwall, or the borderland of Wales."[3]

One well-known fact, which at first sight appears irreconci-
lable with these pronouncements, has not been entirely overlooked. I refer to the existence at Braunton, in north-west
Devon, of an open field of some 350 acres, divided into arable
strips. In 1889 there were stated to be 491 strips, or 'lands' as
they are called locally, divided among fifty-six proprietors.
"The lesser plots appear as a rule to approximate in area to half
an acre, more or less, and the others to be multiples of this
quantity, or very nearly so; very few, however, exceed the
limit of two acres. Some persons own very many of the strips
scattered all over the field; that is to say, several strips in almost
every division of it. Others have a few only, one here and

[1] H. L. Gray, *English Field Systems*, Cambridge (Mass.), 1915, frontispiece
and p. 63.
[2] Orwin, *The Open Fields*, Oxford, 1938, p. 61. This statement is corrected
in the second edition (1954).
[3] *An Historical Geography of England before A.D. 1800*, ed. Darby, p. 194;
F. M. Stenton, *Anglo-Saxon England*, Oxford, 1945, p. 277; D. Jerrold,
Introduction to the History of England, 1949, p. 259. Clapham, *Concise Economic
History of Britain*, Cambridge, 1949, pp. 86, 88, is notably cautious.

there. But in all cases the strips of one owner are everywhere separated from each other by interposed strips of other owners . . . The line of demarcation between any two strips is commonly indicated by a narrow unploughed balk . . ."[1] There is no sign of those alternate ridges and furrows which in scores of midland parishes testify to former methods of cultivation. The perfectly flat surface of the Great Field is broken only by the grass balks, which at Braunton are called *landsherds*. These turf boundaries, most of them little more than a foot wide, are more economical of space than any hedgebank, and do not harbour so many rabbits, but on the other hand they propagate couch-grass and are infested by countless rats. Today the proprietors number only twenty, two of them holding each a single land. The lord of the manor sold all his strips between 1875 and 1889; at the earlier date he owned seventy-three, in seventeen divisions of the Field. In 1843, the date of the tithe award, the division called Higher Thorn, with an area of 20.367 a., contained thirty lands, and Middle Thorn, which is 15.92 a., contained nineteen. These have now been reduced to twenty-four and fourteen respectively. Where the larger owners have succeeded in consolidating their lands the intermediate *landsherds* have disappeared; but those which remain are numerous enough to show quite clearly the original size and shape of the strips.[2]

Concerning this field Gray propounds a theory which seems designed to explain it away. According to him, "Its position on the map and its low-lying character suggest that it is land at some time reclaimed from the marshes; the two other manors in Braunton not adjacent to the marshes have no open field . . . The extensive scattering of the strips may have been due to the gradual reclamation of the area, each furlong having been subdivided by lord and freeholders as it was improved . . . If these conjectures be correct, Braunton Great Field was of

[1] J. B. Phear, 'Notes on Braunton Great Field', DA xxi, 1889, p. 202. This valuable paper is accompanied by a plan of the Field. For a more recent account, illustrated by two photographs, see J. A. Venn, *Foundations of Agricultural Economics*, Cambridge, 1923, p. 14.

[2] For information concerning the present state of the Field I am indebted to a well-known local resident, Mr A. H. Slee, under whose guidance Dr W. G. Hoskins and I went over the ground in April 1949.

relatively recent origin."[1] The Orwins accept this conclusion, and add some conjectures of their own. "The Great Field is probably a reclamation, comparatively recent, from the river estuary, rather than a survival of ancient cultivation. The tenants occupy their holdings in it in conjunction with enclosed fields on the higher land adjacent, and probably the Great Field was once common grazing, which was allotted in blocks to those who had grazing rights in it when the silting of the estuary had reached a level at which the grazing of this rich soil could give place to cultivation."[2]

In the course of this study it will appear that open fields were at one time by no means rare in Devonshire. But before examining the data from other parts of the country, it will be advisable to clear up once for all the doubts which have been expressed concerning Braunton Great Field. The evidence has been accessible in print for the last fifty years, and is incontrovertible. An entry in the Calendar of Close Rolls shows that on the 20th of March 1324 the escheator of Devon made an assignment of dower to Eleanor, widow of Ralph de Gorges, lord of the manor of Braunton Gorges. The deceased had held 75 acres of arable in demesne, and of these the widow received 26½ acres, made up as follows.

1 a. in the *cultura* Underfayrlinch, in two parcels;
1 a.   „   „   at Schorteland;
1 a.   „   „   at Le Aliene;
2 a.   „   „   of Myddelforlong, in two parcels;
3 a. in four parcels on La Merlane [*sic*; cf. next item];
3 a.   „   „   in the *cultura* under La Morlane;
1 a. in the *cultura* Bysoutheye;
1 a.   „   „   Bywestegreneweye;
1 a.   „   „   Byestegreneweye;
1 a.   „   „   Bywestestriclane;
2 a. the most southern in the *cultura* at La Putte;
2 a. in the *cultura* Byestecharthurn [*sic*; cf. next item];
2 a.   „   „   Bywestelathurn;
1 a.   „   „   at La Crofta;

[1] Gray, *op. cit.*, pp. 262, 263.
[2] Orwin, *op. cit.*, p. 46, modified but not retracted in the second edition, p. 51.

1 a.	,,	,,	on Smerham;
½ a.	,,	,,	at La Longeland;
1 a.	,,	,,	Byestesmaleweye;
1 a.	,,	,,	at La Cok;
1 a.	,,	,,	called Stonacre;

26½ a.

Here is documentary proof that dispersed arable strips were to be found at Braunton six hundred years ago.[1] What is more, a number of these strips lay within the area of the present Great Field. The field is divided into a number of shots or furlongs, each bearing a distinctive name; and several of the names are recognizable in the document just quoted. "La Putte" is clearly Pitlands; "La Longeland" is the present Longlands; "La Crofta" is now divided into Higher and Lower Croftner. The "greeneweye" can be identified from the tithe map as Greenaway Lane, being the southern portion of what is now called Second Field Lane. The *culturae* east and west of the thorn-tree ("By-este-la-thurn" and "By-weste-la-thurn") lie today in Higher, Middle, and Lower Thorn.

At this point a glance at the six-inch Ordnance Survey map will be found instructive (Fig. 1). Although surrounded by outlying hamlets, Braunton itself presents the appearance of a typical 'nucleated' village. On its western side, immediately to the north of the Great Field, are fifty or more small enclosed fields, which, by their minute acreage and oblong shapes, irresistibly suggest that they are fossilized remnants of strip cultivation. A number of other fields presenting the same appearance are to be found adjoining the Great Field on the west and south. It is in these enclosures that we must locate some of the strips named in the allotment of 1324. The acre "under Fairlinch" lay at the foot of the slope which bears that name, due west of the village. Further south, the six acres by and under Moor Lane ("La Morlane") now lie outside the Great Field. So also do two oblong fields adjoining Pitlands

[1] CCR 1323–27, p. 333; PRO Inquisition post mortem, C 134, File 81, no. 23. The widow also received half an acre of meadow and "the middle close of pasture in the park."

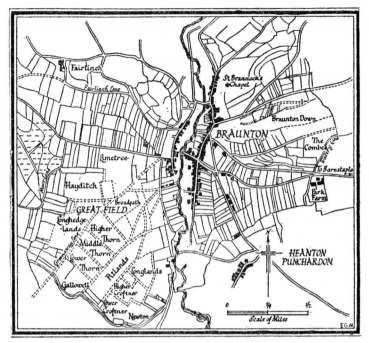

Fig. 1. BRAUNTON. Based upon the Ordnance Survey map, 1903 edition, with the sanction of the Controller of H.M. Stationery Office.

on the south, which are almost certainly identifiable with "the two southernmost acres in the *cultura* at La Putte."

Passing to the east of the village, we enter the manor of Braunton Abbots. Here, between the village and Park Farm, we observe another group of strip-shaped enclosures. The six-inch map reveals their original character; but discoveries to which the map affords no clue are to be made by climbing Watery Lane. On the left, around the steeply sloping flank of the Combes, are unfenced strips, of late years cultivated as allotments; and on reaching the top of the hill one comes upon a new series of arable strips and grass balks, a repetition of the Great Field on a smaller scale. Up here on Braunton Down, three hundred and fifty feet above sea level, open-field cultivation is being carried on today as it has been without a break from time immemorial. It looks as if the manor of Braunton Abbots had been superimposed upon the former east field, and

133

that of Braunton Gorges upon the west field, of the ancient Braunton field system.[1]

Nothing, therefore, could be further from the truth than Gray's asserion that only one of the Braunton manors contains any open field. As for the "relatively recent origin" of the Great Field, we have seen that it is over six hundred years old; and so far from being the result of gradual "reclamation" from the estuary, it is but the shrunken remnant of an open-field system which at one time reached up to, and still partly occupies, the highest ground in the parish. The real problem that awaits solution is why the process of enclosure has been so much less completely carried out at Braunton than elsewhere.[2] It is to be hoped that someone will undertake a detailed study of the Great Field, tracing its history from the remote past and providing a full description of its recent and present management. The Field may well be a thousand years old, and certainly merits as painstaking an investigation as has been devoted to the surviving open fields at Laxton and elsewhere.

The Braunton pastures lay in the area of marsh-land, over a mile wide, between the Great Field and the estuary. Within living memory, however, the Field itself was thrown open for common grazing for a month or two after Michaelmas. Grazing rights exercised in common over the fallow field, and over the cornfield after harvest, are a well-known characteristic of common-field agriculture; and there is evidence that it was not confined to Braunton. In 1249 Walter del We, of Ford in

[1] If so, we should expect to find some tenants holding lands of equal extent in both manors. As a matter of fact, some did. For example, in 1502 John Fortescue of Wear Giffard held 50 a. in Braunton Abbots, valued at 20s., by fealty and a rent of 3s. 2d., and 50 a. in Braunton Gorges, also valued at 20s., by fealty and a rent of 2s. 4d.—*Calendar of Inquisitions post mortem*, 2nd Ser., II, p. 390.

[2] The custom of the manor here has been too strong even for the Crown, as appeared some years ago, when the Air Ministry proposed to turn the Great Field into an aerodrome. The plan had to be dropped "because the land is shared by some fifty or sixty owners whose farms are on the hills to the north, and the transactions would have been too complicated, apart from throwing out of gear some fifty established farms, the value of which (at an average rental of £1 an acre) depended very largely on the possession of a portion of the field."—*The Land of Britain: Report of the Land Utilisation Survey*, ed. Stamp, Part 92, Devonshire, p. 515.

Milton Abbot, complained to the justices in eyre that the abbot of Tavistock had deprived him of his common pasture in Leigh and of the pasture he was accustomed to have in the abbot's arable after the corn had been removed; and a similar complaint was made by one John Furlang against the lord of Rushford on the other side of Dartmoor. Both plaintiffs recovered seisin, with damages.[1] In the same year the abbot of Dunkeswell gave one of his tenants leave to plough up all but a specified portion of Hackpen Hill near Uffculme, but reserved the right to depasture his own cattle there after harvest; at the same time he waived his right of common in the tenant's other lands.[2] In 1332 there is a reference to the pasture of 20½ arable acres at Chilton, a hamlet in the parish of Thorverton.[3]

The examples quoted relate to disputes or agreements between individuals, not between an individual and a community. We have no means of knowing whether the successful plaintiffs were suing as representatives of a community without declaring themselves as such, or solely on their own account. In either case, a series of agreements between individuals might well produce results indistinguishable from the communal system exemplified at Braunton.

At Woodbury the demesne arable consisted in the thirteenth century of 100 a. valued at 1d. each and 80 a. taken in from the waste. These last were valued at 2d. an acre in 1288, but by 1321 they had gone back to waste. There remained the original hundred acres, which evidently lay in open field, for in 1362 they were described as "one ploughland, worth nothing when unsown, because the land lies in common" (*que nichil valet quando jacet frisca, quia terra jacet in communi*).[4] In the same year a hundred acres of demesne arable at Stoke Fleming were valued at 2d. each when sown, and nothing when unsown, for the same reason.[5] A ploughland at Chittlehampton is valued in 1353 at 6s. 8d. "and no more, because the whole of it lies in common."[6] A similar description of the arable at Loddis-

---

[1] PRO Assize Rolls, J.I. 1, 176, mm. 7, 11*b*.
[2] *Devon Feet of Fines*, I, p. 232, no. 462.
[3] PRO Inq. post mortem, C 135, File 31 (14).
[4] *ibid.*, C 133, File 54 (4); C 134, File 66 (21); C 135, File 168 (3).
[5] PRO Inq. post mortem, C 135, File 169 (4).
[6] *ibid.*, C 135, File 122 (7).

well (80 a.), Ideford (40 a.), and Battishorn in Honiton (80 a.) suggests a three-field system, for in each case we are told that two thirds of the acreage can be sown, while the other third lies fallow and in common (*jacet ad warectum et in communi*).[1]

These figures are extracted from descriptions of property appended to inquisitions post mortem: a class of document which Gray used extensively for other counties, but not at all for Devon. Quite a number of Devon inquests, however, provide information with a possible bearing on field systems. After enumerating the full extent of the demesne arable, they go on to state the number of acres which "are tilled" at the moment or "can be tilled" in any given year. Some examples are given in the table opposite.[2] The proportion could be read as indicating a two-field system in the first three manors, and a three-field in the next four, but the others cannot be reduced to any common formula. In some cases the first figure may include areas of grassland which were ploughed up from time to time but not regularly cultivated. Some of the manors, again, may be suffering from the after-effects of the Black Death and later epidemics, a shortage of manpower causing a higher proportion of the land than usual to remain untilled.

The cartulary of Canonsleigh, now one of the Harleian MSS. in the British Museum, contains a number of manorial extents drawn up in 1323. From this source we learn that the demesne arable at Netherton in Farway consisted of

> 45 a. in Estfeld;
> 43 a. in Myddelfeld cum Chelshamcrofte;
> 45 a. in Westfeld.
> _____
> 133 a., valued at 3d. an acre.[3]

Northleigh, an independent estate before the Norman Conquest, had been absorbed into the great Mortain fief, and

[1] PRO, C 135, File 155 (12). This was in 1360. The sown portion was valued at 1d. an acre at Loddiswell and Ideford, 2d. at Battishorn; and the fallow at *nil*.

[2] From *ibid.*, C 135, File 260 (3), File 150 (11), File 166 (6), and File 169 (4.)

[3] Harl. MS. 3660, fo. 178.

Year	Demesne	Total arable acreage	Acres actually tilled
1377	Sampford Courtenay	80	40
,,	Chawleigh	60	28
,,	Kenn	145	60
,,	Musbury	60	40
,,	Hulham	30	20
,,	Stedcombe	100	66
,,	Colyton	105	60
,,	Aylesbeare	107	30
,,	Chulmleigh	100	38
,,	Towsington	120	30
,,	Exminster	120	106
,,	Okehampton	100	30
,,	Plympton	100	74
,,	Tiverton	86	31
1360	North Molton	200	30
1362	Kingsteignton	100	33
1362	Stoke Fleming	300	100

subsequently partitioned. The abbess of Canonsleigh held one half of the manor, and her arable consisted of

> 11½ a. in Campo Australi juxta Wytemor;
> 15 a. in Middelfeld;
> 14 a. in Northfeld.
>
> ———
>
> 40½ a., valued at 2d. an acre.[1]

Both at Netherton and Northleigh we seem to be in presence of a three-field system. By contrast with these manors, the demesne arable at Canonsleigh itself appears to have lain in scattered parcels, many of them already enclosed. It is described as follows:

[1] *ibid.*, fo. 176.

18½ a. in forlang' juxta grangiam Curie versus Occidentem

19 a. 1 r. in Nythereforlang;   [in Overeforlang;

18½ a. in Pylelonde;

19 a. 1 r. in Eldemarnelonde;

12½ a. in Haybeare;

 9 a. in Nyenakerlond;

12 a. in Pugeham juxta terram Pouke de Geffreyeshulle;

22½ a. in Knollelond;

28½ a. in Seleham;

 2½ a. 1 r. in Langemede;

12 a. in Les byrches;

 8½ a. in La Legh;

 4½ a. in una cultura super la Knolle;

 3½ a. in alia cultura super la Knolle juxta volatile Wode-

 3½ a. in Wollelegh;   [coccorum;

50½ a. in tota terra Byestebrok.

—————

245 a. 1 r., valued at an average of 4d. an acre.

At Rockbeare the abbess had 202 a. of arable in sixteen parcels, all apparently enclosed.[1]

One or two references dating from the thirteenth century may be quoted from the unpublished cartularies of Otterton and Newenham. In the first, there is record of an exchange of certain acres "in parva furlanga de Churlebroke" in the manor of Yarcombe; and it is provided that the vicar of Yarcombe shall have thirty acres of arable "lying together" (*que simul jacent*), and not intermixed as some of the other holdings evidently were.[2] In the second, there are references to land "in Axminster field" on the west of that township, and to scattered acres, some of them in Cleyfurlong, others in "the furlong above Rudmede."[3]

Among the surviving muniments of Tavistock Abbey is a charter whereby Richard de Ocbear, lord of the small manor, or sub-manor, of Ogbear in the parish of Tavistock, conveyed

---

[1] Harl. MS. 3660, ff. 167, 143.

[2] G. Oliver, *Monasticon Dioecesis Exoniensis*, 1846, p. 251, no. vii, and p. 258, no. 52.

[3] BM Add. MS. 28649 (Prince's copy of Sir W. Pole's extracts from the Newenham cartulary and other documents), ff. 424, 428, 433.

to Walter his son, in return for a payment of 100s. and a yearly rent of 6d., a close, a curtilage, and two ferlings of land in Ogbear, made up as follows:

4 a. between the river Lumburn and Ogbear;
10 a. in the furlong between la Torre and Ogbear;
11 a. in Yerkysburghe furlong;
2½ a. in Broken-Cross furlong;
2½ a. west of Broken-Cross furlong;

_____

30 a., and also 1 a. of meadow.

The charter is undated, but the names of the witnesses date it _c._ 1302.[1] It is noticeable that two thirds of this arable lay in blocks within two furlongs, but whether the strips were contiguous or scattered is not clear. The account rendered at Michaelmas 1393 by the reeve of Denbury, another manor belonging to the abbot of Tavistock, shows that whereas barley was then cultivated on about seven acres of seemingly enclosed ground described as "the lord's land at Hewelegh," wheat was being sown on sixteen acres of "the lord's land in divers furlongs in the Combes" (_in diversis culturis in le Combes_). This is exactly the phrase that would have been used in reference to the still existing unfenced strips in the Combes at Braunton. Another fifteen acres of the demesne arable "in divers furlongs" were given up to oats.[2] At Tavistock itself the broad expanse of gently undulating downland that stretches from the west end of the borough to the left bank of the Lumburn was cultivated in the thirteenth century by tenants of the abbey whose plough-lands lay intermixed in selions. The same open-field pattern was repeated on the steeper ground across the Lumburn, between Newton and Woodovis.

It will be remembered that the turf balks which divide the strips at Braunton are known as _landsherds_. This word is clearly derived from the Old English _landscearu_, which from the eleventh century onwards becomes _landscore_.[3] Generically it

[1] W. D Bdle 41, no. 2.
[2] W. G Bdle 5, no. 3.
[3] _Crawford Charters_, pp. 48, 49, where it is pointed out that _landscore_ is not phonetically developed from _landscearu_, but is the result of the replacement of _-scearu_ by another word, _score_, probably of Scandinavian origin.

means any sort of boundary, and in this sense it is applied as a name to certain farms—Landskerry in Milton Abbot, for example, and Langsford in Petertavy—which are situated near the boundaries of their respective parishes.[1] In the specific sense of a turf boundary between open-field strips its use is not confined to Devon, for the balks that divide the "lawnds" or arable strip-lands in the isle of Portland are still called "lawndsheds," and in 1525 a tenant at Compton, near Winchester, was reproved for ploughing up a boundary or "land-sherde" between two holdings.[2] What does appear to be peculiar to Devon is the usage whereby tenants of arable in open field are said to hold *on* or *by landscore*. This expression is equivalent to the "acre under acre" of tenth-century charters, and to the holding "in stitchmeal" of seventeenth-century Cornwall.[3] It was in current use a generation or two ago at St Marychurch, where an estate map drawn up *c.* 1775 indicates that most of the strips had been enclosed, but some remained divided only by grass balks.[4] Certain lands within the borough of Plymouth are said to have been held by landscore.[5] A survey of Lord Dynham's estates, drawn up in 1566, notes that at Woodhuish "the landes for the most parte lyeth by londes score in twoe commen feldes." The same document informs us that one holding at Newton Poppleford included "three parcels of land lying by the bounds called landscores, with land of other persons, containing 2½ acres"; and that one at Ilsington consisted of "divers parcels of land called *lez Shotes*, lying in common about the bounds called *lez londscores* with the lands of William Dyggen."[6]

Woodhuish is in the parish of Brixham, which can be shown from other sources to have been an open-field area. In 1334 Sir Henry de Pomeray granted a lease of a house there "and

---

[1] PND pp. 215, 232.

[2] C. D. Drew, 'Open Arable Fields at Portland and Elsewhere', *Antiquity*, XXII, 1948, p. 79; J. S. Drew, *Compton near Winchester*, p. 69. Gray, p. 174, quotes a reference to "the ancient landshares" at Haverfordwest.

[3] Gray, *op. cit.*, pp. 52, 263.

[4] DA XVIII, 1886, pp. 434, 440.

[5] R. N. Worth, *History of Devonshire*, 1886, p. 204; cf. DCNQ XXII, 1942, pp. 93, 94.

[6] DA XLIII, 1911, pp. 276, 280, 282. The printed text reads "in *the* common," but Gray, p. 261, is probably right in preferring the reading given here.

land in Bremele Furlong."[1] Gray overlooked this document, but he found in a survey of 1523 that every tenant of a ferling in the manor of Brixham was entitled to common pasture for sixty sheep, two cows, and one horse "in communibus campis," which he interpreted as meaning open arable fields.[2] That this interpretation is correct has been demonstrated by Mr A. H. Shorter, who went over the ground and was rewarded with a view of strips exactly one furlong in length. He found three surviving strip patterns, east, south, and west of Brixham, in each case associated on the tithe-map with the field-name Landscove, apparently a local variant of landscore. "In two bundles, most of the strips are still separated one from another by grass-covered balks one to two feet higher than the ground on either side." Mr Shorter has collected references to landscores in about a dozen parishes, and many others are to be found in Devon tithe awards.[3]

Some of the documents which have been cited here as evidences of strip cultivation reveal an early tendency towards enclosure. The curtailment of pasture rights of which we have seen tenants complaining in mid-thirteenth century is probably to be explained by attempts at enclosure on the part of landlords. There is clear evidence that the prior of Otterton and the abbot of Newenham were engaged at that time in consolidating their arable by purchase and exchange.[4] In the following century we find a higher value set on enclosed ploughland than on strips in the common field. At Ermington, for instance, the demesne arable in 1324 consisted of 36 a. *in communi*, valued at 2d. an acre, and 82 a. in severalty, valued at 6d.[5] Two years later twenty acres, presumably enclosed, belonging to the lord of Bovey Tracy, were valued at 6d. each, twice as much as the 189 a. of demesne ploughland lying *in diversis culturis*.[6] The tenants of the dean and chapter at Nor-

[1] HMC 15th Report, Appendix VII, p. 137.
[2] Gray, *op. cit.*, p. 259.
[3] DCNQ XXIII, 1949, pp. 372–380; DA LXXXII, 1950, pp. 271–80.
[4] For Otterton, see Oliver, *op. cit.*, p. 257, no. 19, and p. 258, nos. 52, 62–65. In 1293 Edmund, earl of Cornwall, confirmed exchanges made by the abbot of Newenham "in Axminster field" and elsewhere.—BM Add. MS. 28649, fo. 424; other exchanges are recorded on fo. 433.
[5] PRO Inq. post mortem, C 134, File 81 (3).
[6] *ibid.*, File 99. Twenty-seven years later the demesne arable at Bovey

ton, in Newton St Cyres, testified in 1303 that the lessee of the manor had been active in enclosing arable and meadow.[1] In making provision for the vicar of Brixham, Bishop Stapeldon took account of the possibility that arable land might be converted into gardens and orchards, and *vice versa*.[2] A survey of the Tavistock manor of Hurdwick drawn up in 1387 refers to eight "parcels" of land in the open-field area of Bowrish and Downhouse, occupied by as many tenants; but over "parcel" a later hand has written "close" in each case. By 1549 the arable lands of Devon were reported to be among the most completely enclosed in England.[3]

The narrow, oblong enclosures on the edge of Braunton Great Field, already illustrated (Fig. 1), are highly characteristic. They show that a very slight measure of consolidation sufficed to encourage the erection of hedgebanks. In this respect the Devonshire practice resembled that of Norfolk, where Nathaniel Kent, writing in 1794, observed that comparatively few common fields remained, "for notwithstanding common rights for great cattle exist in all of them and even sheep walk privileges in many, yet the natural industry of the people is such, that wherever a person can get four or five acres together, he plants a white thorn hedge round it, and sets an oak at every rod distance, which is consented to by a kind of general courtesy from one neighbour to another."[4] Often a good deal less than four acres would suffice. The plans of some Norfolk estates display single strips enclosed as long rectangular "pightles."[5] Such closes visibly perpetuate and, as it were, fossilize the ancient strip pattern. In Devon groups of them, each representing a few strips thrown together, are noticeable at Boode, Halsinger, and Winsham, three Braunton

---

Tracy was reported to consist of 24 a., worth 10s.; 37 a. in the east of the manor, also 10s.; 70 a. in the north, 40 a. in the west, and 25 a. in the field called Heathfield, all valued at 2d. an acre (*ibid.*, Miscellaneous Inquisitions, C 145, File 169, no. 4).

[1] *Reg. Stapeldon*, p. 297.

[2] *ibid.*, p. 86.

[3] *Discourse of the Common Weal*, quoted by W. E. Tate in DCNQ xxII, 1942, p. 6.

[4] Quoted by Gray, *op. cit.*, p. 308.

[5] *ibid.*, pp. 310, 311.

hamlets; at Croyde and North Buckland, in the parish of Georgeham; and at Goodleigh, three miles inland from Barnstaple. The eighteenth-century estate maps of Cliston and Clist Gerrard, in the parish of Broad Clyst, exhibit the same pattern. Round each of these hamlets is a patchwork of intermixed arable strips enclosed by hedges.[1] A map of Widworthy, prepared in 1780, reveals similar enclosures.[2] The six-inch Ordnance map shows clusters of them at Kingston in the South Hams, where in 1326 the lord of the manor had 862 a. of arable *in diversis culturis*.[3]

In the light of this evidence it seemed worth while to exam-

Fig. 2. KENTON. Re-drawn from the tithe map of 1840 with the sanction of the Tithe Redemption Commission.

[1] *The Land of Britain*, p. 501.
[2] *Ex inf*. Lt-Colonel J. Ramsden.
[3] PRO Inq. post mortem, C 134, File 99. He also had 536 a. at Tawstock, similarly described.

ine some of the maps prepared in connection with tithe awards at various dates between 1838 and 1847. For this purpose two dozen parishes were chosen at random. All but six displayed the characteristic vestiges of strip cultivation. In some cases the 'church-town' from which the parish takes its name presented the appearance of a nucleated village like Braunton, with enclosed strip-fields adjoining on one or more sides. In others, outlying hamlets were surrounded by strip-systems of their own. The pattern was unmistakable at Kenton (Fig. 2), Sidbury (hamlets of Sidford and Burscombe), Woodbury Salterton, Halberton, Cornwood (hamlet of Lutton), Wembury (hamlet of Down Thomas, Fig. 3), Sheepwash, and Combe Martin. It was present, though less obviously, at Shebbear, Crediton, Witheridge, Winkleigh, Chawleigh, Denbury, Kentisbeare, Exminster, Sampford Peverell, and Uffculme. To this list Mr Shorter adds Ashburton and Topsham. There is every reason to believe that a thorough scrutiny of tithe maps, Ordnance Survey maps, and aerial photographs would bring to light similar vestiges in scores of Devon parishes.[1]

On the other hand, the thirteenth-century selions and furlongs at Tavistock have left no trace upon the ground; and Mr Shorter points out that the strip-fields west of Halberton are not to be seen on the present-day map, having been amalgamated since 1838 into fewer and larger units. A large-scale map, drawn in 1820, of Molland, an extremely hilly parish on the southern edge of Exmoor, shows groups of fields divided into strips. They are dotted about the parish,

[1] The parishes which yielded no evidence were Lifton, Coryton, Yealmpton, Modbury, Dartington, and Stokenham. For Ashburton, see DCNQ XXIII, 1949, p. 379. Mr Shorter informs me that an advertisement appeared in *Trewman's Exeter Flying Post*, 16 June 1780, as follows. "To be Sold. The Fee-simple of an undivided 4th Part of SEVEN FIELDS, about 19 acres; and a 4th Part of a 3rd undivided PART of a FIELD, about three Quarters of an Acre; and a 4th PART of HALF an ACRE, undivided, in a Common Field, about 5 acres, all in Topsham, and in the several Occupations of "[six persons]. Mr Shorter says: "Topsham must once have been a true nucleated settlement with open fields. The field-patterns today, and still more the tithe map, suggest it. The field in front of my house is exactly a furlong, slightly curved, and enclosed by hedgebanks." It may be added that the division and sub-division of property in land, so clearly illustrated by the advertisement, was bound to produce a pattern of strips.

Fig. 3. HAMLET OF DOWN THOMAS. Re-drawn from the Wembury tithe map of 1840 with the sanction of the Tithe Redemption Commission.

forming islands of strip cultivation in a district already for the most part enclosed.[1] By 1842, when the tithe map was prepared, they were no longer visible. The Braunton tithe map indicates that in 1843 there were fourteen arable strips, belonging to about a dozen proprietors, on the sloping bank of Knowl Water, south of Park Wood and the old Barnstaple

[1] *Ex inf.* Dr W. G. Hoskins.

road. Neither the shape nor the appearance of the two fields in which this ground is now enclosed gives any hint of its former pattern. Here too every trace of strip cultivation has been obliterated. It follows that while the existence of ancient strips is frequently betrayed by the present form of their enclosures, or by that shown on old maps, the absence of the characteristie strip configuration is no proof that strips did not exist there in the past. And since the evidence of Braunton shows that unfenced strips were cultivated on steep hillsides as well as on comparatively level ground, we have to face the possibility that every parish in Devon may once have had some open field.

Ever since Maitland used the map of north-east Devon to point a dramatic contrast between the "land of hamlets" and the "land of villages" further east, the south-western counties have been classed as a region of dispersed settlement.[1] That the small hamlet and the isolated farmstead were to be found there at a very early date is not to be denied. But the nucleated village is not peculiar to the midlands. Dr A. L. Rowse has already shown that Cornwall had its open fields,[2] and enough has been said here to demonstrate that they were a far more prominent feature in the agrarian landscape of Devon than has been admitted hitherto. Strip cultivation, intermixture of holdings, the dispersal of the lord's arable in common fields, grazing rights exercised in common over the ploughland of the manor: all these features of the open-field system have their parallels in Devon, though some of them had begun to disappear before the thirteenth century was over. The only characteristic of the midland system for which no decisive evidence has been forthcoming is the symmetrical grouping of strips in two or three large fields. The three-field symmetry at Netherton and Northleigh may have been accidental; it is not found on the other Canonsleigh estates. In many parishes the furlongs may have been scattered about in accordance with the contours of the ground and the nature of the soil and sub-soil. On the whole it seems likely that in Devon, as in East Anglia, the furlongs, whether contiguous or scattered, formed the constitutive element of the agrarian framework.[3]

[1] *Domesday Book and Beyond*, pp. 16, 17.
[2] *Tudor Cornwall*, pp. 32–36.
[3] Cf. Gray, pp. 313, 314.

One other resemblance to the East Anglian system is brought out in the survey of the Dynham estates from which I have already quoted. Woodhuish in Brixham, as we saw, was a manor where the arable lay "for the most part"—but not all—by landscore in two common fields. The holdings were rated in ferlings, to each of which belonged some twenty-seven acres of "arable land lying at large in the fields and *lez Breches*."[1] Altogether there were 652 acres, but we are not told how many lay in the fields and how many outside in "*lez Breches*." Now 'breach', 'break', or 'breck' is the word regularly used in Norfolk and elsewhere to signify a portion of common pasture broken up for cultivation. When the break had been cropped for a year or two, it reverted to grass, and the process might then be repeated on another section of the common. This shifting or temporary cultivation of the waste, or outfield, as it was called to distinguish it from the continuously tilled 'infield' furlongs, used to be regarded as distinctive of Celtic agriculture. It was certainly practised in Scotland and Cornwall down to the eighteenth century. But recent writers have found traces of it in Northumberland, Cumberland, Sherwood Forest, Warwickshire, and the East Riding of Yorkshire, as well as in the brecklands of Norfolk; Gray quotes an early example from Kent without recognizing it as such; and one cannot help suspecting that the "peculiar sort of arable island surrounded by the common pasture" on Shawford Down in Hampshire, so described in Mr Drew's admirable history of Compton, should be added to the list. As Clapham says: "There can be little doubt that, if we knew medieval England completely, we should meet plenty of it."[2]

---

[1] DA XLIII, 1911, p. 282.

[2] Gray, pp. 223, 232; M. W. Beresford, 'Lot Acres', *Economic History Review*, XIII, 1943, pp. 74–79; J. Saltmarsh and H. C. Darby, 'The Infield-Outfield System on a Norfolk Manor', *Economic History*, III, 1935, pp. 30–44; Clapham, *Concise Economic History of Britain*, pp. 48, 87, 89. Gray, p. 280, cites a conveyance dated 20 Henry III (1235–36) of some 48 arable acres at Barfreston, Kent, of which 34 a. lay in open field and 14 a. in six parcels lay "in the midst of the pasture" on North Down and Little Down. This looks like outfield cultivation. So do the lynchets on Shawford Down which J. S. Drew, *op. cit.*, p. 159, describes as "conforming in shape to the long narrow Saxon type" and yet lying right outside the three-field system of the village.

The cultivation of the waste or outfield in Devon is a well attested practice. A thirteenth-century grant of Blackmoorham in Tavistock gives the tenant right of common for his cattle over the whole waste of Whiteborough Down "when it lies untilled; but it shall be lawful for the abbot and convent to cultivate the said waste whenever they shall think fit." In 1310 two and a half ferlings at Newton in the same parish were granted with common pasture for all the grantee's cattle that could winter upon Luscombe Down "when the said waste lies untilled and not let off."[1] The custom of Hemyock and Clayhidon was that "the Tenaunts may breake upp or eare any parte of the lordes' waste to sowe any grayne in, payenge for every acre iiijd. as longe as they shall sowe hit."[2] At Great Torrington 163 acres of the common were known as 'tillage lands', in which the lord of the manor and certain tenants yearly exercised the right of growing spring corn, and excluded their fellow-commoners until the corn was harvested. At Okehampton some 250 acres of common were set apart in the same way, but here winter corn might be sown.[3] Marshall, at the close of the eighteenth century, noted extensive marks of cultivation on the Blackdown Hills in east Devon. So also in the west of the county: "The better part of these open commons have evidently heretofore been in a state of aration, lying in obvious ridges and furrows, with generally the remains of hedgebanks corresponding to the ridges." A little later Vancouver observed similar traces on the "ancient moorlands" of north Devon.[4]

The infield in Devon might be the enclosed arable of an individual farm: what the south-western farmer called his inground. It was not necessarily a common field, though it might take that form in Devon as it did in eighteenth-century Scotland. The outfield, being part of the lord's waste or common pasture, would, while under cultivation, take on the

[1] W. D Bdle 3, no. 1, and Bdle 21, no. 3.

[2] DA XLIII, 1911, p. 290.

[3] J. J. Alexander and W. R. Hooper, *History of Great Torrington*, 1948, p. 80; C. Vancouver, *General View of the Agriculture of the County of Devon*, 1813, pp. 275, 289.

[4] W. Marshall, *Rural Economy of the West of England*, 1796, I, p. 32, II, pp. 46, 48, 132 sqq.; Vancouver, *op. cit.*, p. 274.

character of open field, a complex of intermingled strips, in which the lord might take a share if he thought fit; and it would of course be subject to a general right of pasture after the corn was cut. Eventually perhaps it would lend itself particularly well to piecemeal enclosure. According to Vancouver, it was not permissible for any individual commoner to enclose and appropriate an area of common pasture, even when that area was an appurtenance of his particular farm, unless his fellow-commoners gave their consent. On the other hand, "in cases where vestiges of the old mounds remain, or the site of them can be distinctly traced, the individual's right to enclose seems permanent and indisputable."[1] When a man had been permitted, "by a kind of general courtesy" among neighbours, to surround a parcel of three or four strips with a hedgebank, and others had in course of time followed his example, the outfield would become just such a network of fossilized strips as we have seen at Down Thomas and elsewhere (Fig. 3). The field pattern of Sheepwash may be instanced as a case in point. This village, once a market town and seignorial borough, is situated in the valley of the Torridge. Its name implies that it was by origin a pastoral settlement. The tithe map reveals two groups of enclosed strips north and south of the village, which anyone familiar with the midland lay-out would take to be the north field and south field of a two-field township; and the notion is encouraged by an entry in the calendar of Elizabethan Chancery proceedings to the effect that Sheepwash had "two great open common fields adjoining to the borough." But the tithe award gives the names of these fields as North Common and South Common, and on closer inspection the Chancery pleadings make it clear that they were really common pastures

---

[1] Vancouver, *op. cit.*, p. 290. In 1742, when a tenant of the duke of Bedford began to enclose the portion of Ramsdown, in Milton Abbot, which belonged to his farm, the local agent wrote: "The plot he is enclosing is called Slemans Corner, and there is old banks round it as if it had formerly been enclosed. There is likewise old banks on other places of the Down which looks like Enclosures as well as that, and have formerly been ploughed, as appears by its lying Ridge and Furrow, and are called by other names. I desired him to desist from enclosing any further till I could hear what his Grace's pleasure is."—Bedford Office, Bloomsbury, Devon Letters 1738–63: J. Knight to R. Butcher, 19 January 1742.

which the inhabitants were converting into ploughland at the close of the sixteenth century.[1]

Some historians regard the infield-outfield system as a phase in the evolution of agricultural technique. Thus, Clapham describes it as "the next stage beyond that of constantly shifting arable fields," and Gray outlines a hypothetical process by which it might graduate into a three-field system.[2] But the truth is that its early history is quite unknown. We are on surer ground if we take the open-field system to be a genus, of which the two-field system and its probable derivative the three-field form one species, and the infield-outfield another. The two probably evolved side by side, moulded by the contrasting qualities of the highland and lowland landscapes. Grazing rights over the fallow field, and over the other field or fields when not under crops, were a cardinal feature of the midland system. In Devon, on the other hand, there was grassland to spare. Every occupant of land in the county, with few exceptions, enjoyed the right of depasturing commonable beasts on Dartmoor gratis outside the forest area, and within the forest on payment of small customary fees. Apart from that great central waste, the majority of parishes had their own tracts of heath and moorland. In such a region there was no absolute necessity to leave a half or a third of the ploughland under grass every year. So far, then, from being an eccentric

---

[1] Bartholomew Thorne, who in 1600 divided with the Holland family the lordship of the borough of Sheepwash, declared that he was accustomed to receive from each free tenant of the borough a "common rent" of sixpence yearly which entitled the tenant to depasture his cattle on North and South Commons; but that of late John Westlake and divers other tenants had broken up and ploughed North Common without his licence and in breach of ancient custom. The other tenants afterwards compounded with him, but Westlake refused to do so. Thorne therefore impleaded him of trespass in the Court of Queen's Bench. Westlake then counter-attacked in Chancery. His case was that "certain parcels of land, known, bounded, and mered in certain, but lying in common without any enclosure" in the two fields, belonged to him as part and parcel of his burgage, and that he paid one entire rent for the same to the lord of the borough (PRO Chancery Proceedings, C 2 Eliz., W 12, 35). The first part of this statement might well be true, and perhaps there had been occasional tillage in the past. The pleadings are silent on that point, but it seems clear that in 1600 a definite conversion took place of pasture into arable.

[2] *Concise Economic History of Britain*, p. 48; *English Field Systems*, p. 225.

deviation from the midland norm, or a survival of primitive conditions which the more 'progressive' midlands had left behind, the infield-outfield system existed in its own right here and throughout the highland zone, as indeed it did wherever there was a superabundance of rough pasture.[1]

Whether any of the open fields in Devon were managed on the three-field principle, and how far the strip pattern still so plainly visible up and down the county is to be associated with the cultivation of the outfield: these are questions which cannot yet receive more than tentative answers. A systematic investigation of the subject is now urgently required. In this enquiry fieldwork, assisted by air-photographs and six-inch maps, will play a large part, but the topographical evidence will need to be controlled and amplified by documentary research. Court rolls, manorial surveys, and deeds of sale will throw much light on the morphology of Devon villages and hamlets; and the search will add a new chapter to the agrarian history of England.

[1] Rotation of crops is not discussed here because, as Clapham has observed, it is quite independent of field systems (op. cit., p. 54).

MORWELL

THE southern portion of the parish of Tavistock Hamlets consists of a hog's-back or ridge of high ground separating the valleys of the Tamar and the Tavy. Until 1836 the crest of the ridge was open downland, providing common pasture for the adjoining farms. Along it ran the ancient trackway from Bere Ferrers. On either side of the down, and at a somewhat lower level, there was a fringe of cultivated land, beyond which the hill-sides, thickly clad with timber, fell steeply, and in places almost perpendicularly, to the banks of the two streams four hundred feet below.

At the time of the Domesday inquest the whole of this area was included in the manor of Tauestocha, seat of Tavistock Abbey and its principal demesne. But this great manor was no longer an undivided whole. William the Conqueror had imposed upon the abbot the duty of contributing fifteen men-at-arms in time of war, and the abbot, like other churchmen in the same plight, had found that the most convenient way of organizing this service was to create a permanent endowment for it: in other words, to carve out portions of his lands and settle them as 'knights' fees' upon the requisite number of military tenants. Domesday Book shows half a dozen of the abbot's knights holding each a portion of Tavistock and parcels of land on his other manors. If any of them failed to attend the muster, it was the abbot who was called to account. This might happen at any time, so long as he provided only for his exact quota. To insure himself, therefore, against possible defaults, he endowed one or two additional knights. Many of his brother abbots did the same. But it was a policy very apt to embroil them with their monks, for the monks, being less directly involved, were not so easily convinced of the need for supernumerary knights. At Tavistock, especially, they might with good reason shrink from any addition to a burden already heavier than that borne by many a richer house. Consequently when Abbot Wymund (c. 1091–1102) proposed to create a new military holding in favour of his brother William, they suspected him, not unjustly perhaps, of jobbery. But in spite of their opposition Wymund had his way.[1] The new fief consisted of an isolated holding on the edge of Dartmoor, named Cudelippe, the modern Cudlipptown, and "Roweburgh," which I believe to have been what is now called Morwell.

Roweburgh, or Roborough, means 'rough hill', and is a common enough place-name. Previous writers have identified Wymund's Roborough with Taviton, a sub-manor of Tavistock situated on the left bank of the Tavy.[2] The only reason for doing so is that Taviton lies in the Domesday hundred of Walkhampton, otherwise known as the hundred of Roborough. There was a manor of Roborough belonging to the abbey in the hundred of Fremington, but it makes no appearance in the fee-lists, and none of its tenants held by knight-service.[3] Morever there is no sign of any tenurial connection between Cudlipptown and either of these manors. Taviton appears regularly in the fee-lists as held, together with Whitham, an adjoining part of Tavistock, by the abbot himself for half a knight's fee; and there is evidence that it had been so held from the time of Abbot Baldwin (c. 1174–84), who recovered it from the descendants of Ermenald, the Domesday holder.[4] Between Cudlipptown and Morwell, on the other hand, there was a connection which we shall find persisting for centuries. Morever, a hitherto unpublished document to which I shall presently refer discloses that there was a landmark in Morwell, the exact position of which cannot now be identified, but which lay between Morwell Barton and Morwellham, and which was known in the thirteenth century as Parva Rueberge: in English, Little Roborough. Thus topography and feudal records both favour the identification of Wymund's Roborough with Morwell.

The effect of the abbot's grant was to create a new manor, carved out of the portion of Tavistock described at the begin-

---

[1] Reasons have been given in my *Lucerna* (pp. 176, 177) for believing that the transaction was really a *quid pro quo*.

[2] Reichel, *The Hundred of Tavistock*, DA XLVI, 1914, p. 231; Alexander, *The Beginnings of Tavistock*, DA LXXIV, 1942, p. 190, where Taviton is misprinted "Tavistock."

[3] DCNQ XXIII, 1948, p. 241.

[4] *Feudal Aids*, I, pp. 355, 404, 449; ETC XLI.

ning of this essay. Its boundaries are not defined in any document that I have seen, but they can be made out from particulars given in two fifteenth-century surveys.[1] Beginning at a landmark by the river Tamar known formerly as Sharptor, but now as Chimney Rock, the boundary followed a track called Hilly-path which led directly from the rock to Golya-worthy, the modern Gulworthy. Skirting the western edge of that farm, it went round some acres of pasture called Golya-down (now represented by two fields named Higher and Lower Gullaton), then turned southward and for the best part of a mile followed the line of the modern road. In doing so, it took in a group of fields called Stoberlands, on the opposite side of the road from Hurlditch Horn. Stoberland, in the 1414 survey, appears as Studburghe; very probably, like Studborough in Northants., it derives its first element from the Old English word *strūt*, meaning strife, contention, and indicates a boundary-point which at some time or other gave rise to controversy.[2] From this point the Morwell boundary turned south-eastward and made for the highest point of the whole ridge, where at one time there stood a beacon. This was just inside the present Morwelldown Plantation. Then, taking in the cultivated area of Rumonsleigh, it turned westward and ran straight across the down to the well-spring, or *moorland well*, to which Morwell owes its later name. From that spring, hard by Morwell Barton, a rivulet flows down the combe formerly called Lobscombe or Luscombe, and joins the Tamar at Morwellham. This is the southern boundary-line of the manor, and the Tamar is of course the western.[3]

[1] Extent of Hurdwick, 1416 (W. D Bdle 84, no. 29); Extent of Morwell, 1414 (transcript in the Tavistock Abbey White Book).

[2] Gover, Mawer, and Stenton. *The Place-Names of Northamptonshire*, p. 29.

[3] Rumonsleigh is the farm now known as Hartshole, the original name being preserved in Rumonsleigh Cottages close by. For Luscombe, or Lobscombe, see p. 163 below. It seems probable that the whole ridge was originally called Luscombe Down. In process of time this name was confined to the tract between Blanchdown and Gulworthy. South of this lay some acres known as Masseleesland, from Robert Massely, who rented them for a shilling a year in 1347. Then came Morwell Down, which extended eastward as far as the Firebeacon. The smaller expanse between the beacon and Shillamill wood was called Hurdwick Down because it lay within the manor of that name. To the south of Morwell Down, between

Of the territory thus bounded very little was suitable for tillage. Apart from the demesne of Morwell Barton and the flat ground beside the Tamar at Morwellham, the only considerable farmlands were Rumonsleigh and Gulworthy. In this neighbourhood a '-worthy' signifies a piece of down-land enclosed for purposes of cultivation; and it is possible that in Wymund's time Gulworthy was still part of the open down. In the eyes of the abbot and his brother the value of the manor would lie not in its corn-crops, but in its pasturage, its timber, and perhaps most of all in its riparian rights. For the Tamar salmon fishery has always been profitable, and from a very early date Morwellham has served as the port of Tavi-stock, the river being navigable as far as this by vessels of ten feet draught.[1]

Wymund was removed from office in 1102. Fourteen years later Henry I issued a writ prohibiting any increase in the number of the abbot's military tenants over and above those endowed during the Conqueror's reign, and annulling Wymund's grant of Roborough and Cudlipp.[2] It has been too readily assumed that the twin properties were thereupon restored to the abbey demesne. England has had no greater king than the first Henry, but even his mandates were not invariably carried out. We have some reason for doubting whether they were so in this case. For in 1166 Abbot Walter reported to the Exchequer that on the last day of Henry I's reign sixteen knights' fees had been held of the then abbot: that is, one more than there should have been if Henry's writ had been strictly enforced. He added that further encroach-ments had taken place during the civil war of Stephen's reign, a seventeenth fee having been extorted by Richard de Cole-ville and a further half fee by Geoffrey and William de Lega.[3]

Maddacleave and Blackmoorham, lay Whiteborough Down, on the southern edge of which stood a building formerly known as Gawton Moor-house. A moorhouse is a shelter for travellers. This one was later converted into a dovecote, the picturesque remains of which have been described and illustrated by Mr G. W. Copeland, DA LXXV, 1943, p. 270.

[1] Bradshaw's *Canals and Navigable Rivers of England and Wales*, 1928, p. 359.

[2] Dugdale, *Monasticon*, II, p. 496.

[3] *The Red Book of the Exchequer*, p. 250.

In 1193 a papal bull enumerating the possessions of the abbey mentions Ruaburga, which may have been Morwell but was more probably Roborough in the hundred of Fremington. To have two manors called by the same name was inconvenient; it is therefore not surprising to find Morwell emerging into documentary light of day under its modern name, as it does in 1194. In that year the government of Richard I seized the lands of all those accused of siding in rebellion with John Lackland; and among the lands thus confiscated were "Morwalla" and "Cudelyppa." The Pipe Roll drawn up at Michaelmas 1194 shows the royal escheator, William de Ste Mère Eglise, accounting for the year's revenue, 14s. 7d. from Morwell and 9s. 11d. from Cudlipp. In the following year the Pipe Roll reveals the owner's name. It was Ralph Archdeacon ("Radulfus Archidiaconus"), who now proffers ten marks to recover his inheritance "of which he was disseised for being with Count John,"[1]

The Archdeacons were a family who later rose to great eminence. Their origin is obscure. If Morwell and Cudlipp are to be identified with the sixteenth fee 'of old feoffment', the two manors may have passed to the Archdeacons by direct descent from Wymund's brother William. If, on the other hand, they were among the additional fees extorted during Stephen's reign, the descent must have been from one or other of the extortioners named by Abbot Walter. Both hypotheses may be commended to experts in feudal genealogy, especially as Geoffrey de Lega and William his son are named as holding fees of both old and new feoffment, and the next document to which we come shows a lady of the de Lega family holding Morwell in dower as an Archdeacon's widow.

The document in question is not an original, but a fourteenth-century copy preserved among the duke of Bedford's muniments.[2] The original was witnessed by seven persons, three of whom appear as jurors for the hundred of Tavistock on the Assize Roll of 1238; it may therefore be dated c. 1235–40. It is a grant by Matillis de Lega, who describes herself as lady of Morwell in the time of her widowhood, to William, son of Adam de Welraddon, of the whole land of Morwellham

---

[1] Pipe Roll Society, XLIII, p. 22; XLIV, pp. 48, 134.
[2] W. D Bdle 39, no. 5.

for a yearly rent of five shillings, payable half at All Saints and half on St Rumon's day. At this date the port of Morwellham was evidently in full working order, and its harbour-dues were valued as a source of income, for although William is allowed the right of landing his own goods without paying toll, the lady of the manor reserves to herself the wharf (*domus portus*) and a roadway fourteen feet wide between manor-house and quay. The boundary of the land demised to William starts from the rivulet which flows into the Tamar on the north side of the port. Then, moving inland, it goes to a spot in line with a heap of white stones opposite the parson of Calstock's garden; thence out to the said heap of stones, and on to another heap; thence to the corner of the hedge made by Walter Merchant, and along the hedge to the corner of the *codretum* (whatever that may be) at Little Roborough. This last name is the clue, previously missing, which has enabled us to identify Morwell with the Roborough named by Henry I. From Little Roborough the boundary runs to a boundary-mark under a forked oak; after which it moves eastward, the remaining points mentioned being: the foot of the Morleteweie; the old road from the port; the *codrum* at the higher end of the houses; the eastern corner of a ditch; the white stone called Gremure; and the rivulet that formed the starting-point. The grantor reserves to herself suit to her manor-court of Morwell, royal service (that is, payment of scutage and other feudal dues) as for two ferlings of land, and the oven or furnace (*clibanus*) which Roger Austin made on the east side of the roadway. (Was this a lime-kiln or a smelting-house for tin?) She grants the tenant a right of way up to the downs between her demesne and Lobbahole, common pasturage throughout the manor, timber from her wood for repairs, and the right to take broom, furze, and bracken for strengthening the Red Ford (*vadum rubrum*) at "la Horaston."[1]

[1] The "white stone called Gremure" is obviously a (*ge*)*mære stan*, or boundary stone; cf. the "great stone called Graymare" which in 1613 marked the parish boundary of Cardinham (G. H. Doble, *History of the Church and Parish of S Meubred, Cardynham*, p. 13). Lobbahole is no doubt a watering-place for cattle, situated somewhere in Lobscombe or Luscombe. With "la Horaston" compare the Horestones in Witheridge and Bishop's Tawton, both from *har stan*, another term for a boundary stone. As for the red ford, there are plenty of streams in Devon with reddish-looking water, but the

This Matillis, or Matilda, was doubtless the Matilda de Moruill whose name appears on the Assize Roll of 1238 as co-defendant with Odo and Michael le Arcedeakne (? her sons) against one Robert Sparke, who alleged that they had illegally dispossessed him of a certain waste in "Cudelip," his free holding. Matilda declared that Sparke was her bondman and a runaway (*nativum et fugitivum suum*), but brought no evidence in support of this assertion, and the court decided that Sparke should recover his tenement with 40s. damages.[1]

In 1262 Thomas Archdeacon granted Morwell to Hereward de Marisco in exchange for two Cornish manors, Redwery *alias* Roseworthy in Gwinear, and Ryvers in Phillack. Immediately after this transaction Hereward made over Morwell to the abbot and convent of Tavistock in pure and perpetual alms.[2] In the Taxation of Nicholas IV (1291–93) the annual value of the manor was put down as £2 10s., so that it had more than doubled in value during the previous hundred years.[3]

Morwell is not mentioned in any of the fee-lists compiled from time to time for the information of the Exchequer. The irregularity of its origin may account for this omission. Its outlying dependency, Cudlipp, in the hundred of Roborough, appears in the lists of 1303, 1346, and 1428 as being held by the abbot in pure and perpetual alms for one-third of a knight's fee.[4] The relationship between Morwell and Cudlipp is more clearly brought out in documents compiled by the abbey for its own use. Thus, a survey of Morwell drawn up in 1414 opens with the entry: "Cudlyppe. William Coryton holds all his lands and tenements there of the manor of Morewill by the service of three-eighths of a knight's fee for the same, suit of Morewill court yearly from court to court, scutage, and relief." In a list of fees at the end of the White Book, which was compiled in the abbey about 1488, Morwell and Cudlipp are shown as held together for one fee.[5]

---

mention of broom, furze, and bracken suggests at least a possibility of confusion between *rēad* and *hreod* (reed).

[1] PRO Assize Rolls, J.I. 1, 174, mm. 7, 24.
[2] W. D Bdle 39, nos. 1–3.
[3] *Taxatio Ecclesiastica*, p. 153.
[4] *Feudal Aids*, I, pp. 354, 402, 448.
[5] White Book, ff. 30*b*, 38*b*. This manuscript contains copies of a number

The abbot, having got back this delectable manor into his own hand, took care not to let it go again. It provided him with a country seat to which he could resort whenever he felt inclined for rural tranquillity, or for a run with the hounds in his neighbouring chase of Blanchdown. In 1391 the chapel of the manor-house was licensed for divine service.[1] A surviving account-roll drawn up by the abbot's steward for the year ending Michaelmas 1429 shows various items of expenditure amounting to 12s. 9½d. for repairs at Morwell Barton, including repairs to the cellar. It also allows us to see how the cellar was replenished, for there is a payment on account of the carriage by water from Plymstock and Plymouth to Morwellham of three casks, one pipe, and one "hoggeshead" of wine. The Barton house appears to have been rebuilt in the time of Abbot Dynyngton (1451–90). It is a quadrangular structure, with a pinnacled gatehouse very much like the surviving Court Gate of the abbey; and it still remains with little outward alteration.

An 'extent' or survey drawn up on the 1st of October 1414, upon the oaths of Bartholomew Wyndsore, John Harrye, William Drake, and other tenants, throws much light on the administration of the manor at this time. The sum of the yearly rental is given as 63s. 7d. and one rose. Besides this there was a fluctuating revenue from court perquisites, the Tamar fishery, and sales of timber. The woods of Morwell, from north to south, appear in the survey under the names: Impham wood, Thilkeholmes and Bywewood, and Sheepridge wood.[2] Cudlipptown was not the sole outlier: there was another at Tuell in the parish of Milton Abbot. As Tuell is in the neighbourhood of Leigh Barton, the original home of the de Lega family, one may hazard a guess that Matilda de Lega had brought it with her in dower when she married one

---

of manorial surveys from 1411 onwards. It was probably compiled for the use of a travelling official such as the abbot's steward. The incoherences complained of in J. J. Alexander's account of it (DA LXIX, 1937, pp. 253 sqq.) arise from the additions made from time to time with a view to bringing the contents up to date.

[1] *Register of Thomas de Brantyngham*, ed. F. C. Hingeston-Randolph, p. 732.

[2] The name Sheepridge is nowadays improperly given to the wood on the south side of Luscombe, adjoining Maddacleave wood.

of the Archdeacons. It was rated at three ferlings, and was held of the manor of Morwell by knight-service. In this respect it did not stand alone, for there were no socage tenants; all the freeholders held by military service. That is to say, each of them was under obligation to discharge a fraction of the lord's liability whenever the Crown should levy scutage or other feudal 'aid'. Most of them paid rent as well. There is one freeholder, John Colmestor, whose tenure is peculiar in that he owes suit of court to Morwell but pays his rent to the neighbouring manor of Hurdwick. He seems to have done so in respect of Golya-down, or Gullaton, which in 1415 figures on the rent-roll of the convent almoner, though in 1375 it had been demised to Colmestor as part of Morwell. Colmestor also does one day's reaping on the demesne, or pays 2d. in lieu thereof at the lord's choice, for the right of taking heath on Morwell Down. Several other tenants pay 1s. 6d. or 1s. 8d. yearly for pasture on the down.[1]

Twenty years before this survey was drawn up the house of commons had drawn attention to a loophole in the Statute of Mortmain. They pointed out that if a freeborn heiress married a serf on a monastic manor, her children would be serfs and the lord would thus acquire a title to her property, without any special licence from the Crown. The commons asked that a remedy might be ordained, but the Crown declined to alter the existing legislation.[2] In the survey of Morwell there is a case in point. A house and some enclosed land at Gulworthy are held by William Drake as tenant-at-will: "which house and land escheated to the lord by the death of Walter Page because the same Walter was a born serf (*nativus*) of the lord's, and had the land aforesaid with the house to him and his heirs in fee simple in right of Matilda Hunte his wife; of which said Matilda Hunte by the same Walter was begotten Alice Page, who is the lord's born serf. Therefore the said land came to the lord."

The abbot of Tavistock had from time immemorial enjoyed

---

[1] John Colmestor's family took its name from a tongue-shaped wooded promontory, half a mile due north of Newton, which is named Kylmanstor 1309, Colmanistorr 1340, Colmystorr 1375, and, in the eighteenth-century rentals, Kemmester.—W. D Bdle 8, no. 4; Bdle 41, nos 19, 20.

[2] *Rotuli Parliamentorum*, III, p. 319.

the right of fishing in the Tamar. Towards the end of the twelfth century this right had been defined by an agreement between Abbot Herbert and Roger de Valletort, who as lord of Trematon controlled the opposite bank.[1] But in February 1352 orders were given by the Black Prince's council to distrain the abbot and cause him to show by what title he had made a weir in the Tamar "within the prince's manor of Calstock" and was taking great abundance of salmon there; for it was said that the whole water of Tamar belonged to the prince as lord of Trematon and duke of Cornwall. The abbot, in reply, produced a copy of Roger de Valletort's charter; and the council, having studied this, gave orders that the abbot should be left undisturbed.[2] The weir in question, variously known as Gulworthy Hatch or the Over-hatch, was situated on or very close to the site of New Bridge. In the following year William Stacy of Tavistock offered the duchy £8 a year for a seven-year lease of Calstock weir, which until then had been let for £6. This weir stood some three-quarters of a mile below Gulworthy Hatch. Stacy's offer was accepted; but on hearing of it the abbot promptly offered £10, whereupon the prince's advisers cancelled Stacy's lease, awarded him £3 as compensation for his expenditure on the weir during the nine months of his tenancy, and on the 1st of October 1354 granted a perpetual lease of the weir and of the whole river between Gulworthy Hatch and Okeltor to the abbot and his successors for all time.[3] The 1414 survey shows that the abbot sub-let a number of 'lewes' or fish-traps, reserving to himself a moiety of the fish taken, and also the following rents:

Wympull Water	8s.	Forde Lew	18d.
Wympull Lew	2s.	Gyade Lew	2s.
Guddegyrie	2s.	Stone Lew	12d.
Kyte Lew	2s.	Troddepoll	3s.
By Lew	12d.	At Stone	6d.
Barbygan	6d.	Okelator	20s.
Scobbe	6d.	Nunnepoole	23s. 6d.

Occasionally the abbot found himself in conflict with dwellers

[1] ETC XLVIII; see above, p. 102.
[2] *Register of Edward the Black Prince*, II, pp. 27, 31.
[3] *Register of Edward the Black Prince*, II, pp. 54, 58, 71.

on the opposite bank. The parson of Calstock, for example, brought a suit against the abbot in the consistorial court of Exeter, claiming tithe of the fish caught at the Over-hatch. The case dragged on for sixteen months; at last judgement was given in favour of the abbot. Worsted on this ground, the parson launched a second attack from a new base. He complained to the council of the duchy that whereas his predecessors time out of mind had enjoyed the right to have four "settels"—probably some kind of wicker trap—affixed to the soil of their glebeland beside the Tamar for taking salmon and other fish, the abbot was now denying him this right. On enquiry it was found that the exercise of the right had been interrupted not by the abbot but by a previous lessee.[1] In the time of Abbot Peryn (1523–39) there were proceedings and counter-proceedings both in Star Chamber and in the Court of Requests, occasioned by the riotous behaviour of certain Cornishmen who had tried to destroy Gulworthy Hatch.[2] Finally, in 1535, Henry VIII ordered a general destruction of weirs, and in November of that year it was reported that all those in Devonshire were down.[3] Shortly afterwards the building of the present New Bridge was begun by Sir Piers Edgcumbe.

From 1501 onwards Morwell Barton, with Morwellham but without the fishery, was let out on lease at the yearly rent of £5 12s., and six quarters of wheat. Some further income, estimated in 1535 at a total of £5 7s. 3d., was derived from the sale of timber and the proceeds of the manor-courts.[4] In 1539, less than four months after the dissolution of Tavistock Abbey, Morwell was included in the grant of its possessions to John, Lord Russell, ancestor of the earls and dukes of Bedford. It has continued in his descendants ever since. Morwell Barton became a farm-house, the ducal family, when rusticating near Tavistock, preferring to stay at Crowndale, the reputed birthplace of Sir Francis Drake.[5]

[1] *Register of Edward the Black Prince*, II, pp. 74, 90.
[2] PRO Star Chamber Proceedings, St. Ch. 2, Bdle xxx, no. 115, and Bdle xxII, no. 56; Court of Requests, Req. 2, Bdle IX, nos. 52, 6.
[3] *L. & P. Hen. VIII*, IX, p. 279, § 833.
[4] *Valor Ecclesiasticus*, II, p. 381.
[5] *Letters of a Grandmother*, ed. G. Scott Thomson, 1943, pp. 89, 90.

Among the manuscripts preserved until lately in the Bedford Office is a volume compiled in 1758 by John Wynne, and entitled: "Plans and Particulars of all the Timber and Coppice Woods belonging to His Grace the Duke of Bedford in the County of Devon." This gives a description of the Morwell woodlands under the following names, which may be compared with those previously quoted from the survey of 1414: Impham Ball wood, Weir wood, Hay wood, Impham Plain wood, Umple Rocks wood, Waterhall wood, Woodyates wood, and Belkamore wood. Waterhall is probably Waterhole, the spot referred to by Matillis de Lega as Lobbahole; and the Umple (or Whimple) Rocks are the famous eyrie now known as Morwell Rocks.[1] In 1774 the old way from the down to Morwellham, Luscombe (or, as Wynne calls it, Lobscombe) Lane, was superseded by the present road, which runs a little east and south of its predecessor and has a fork leading to Newquay.[2] About fifty years later the ancient highway from Bere Ferrers was made into a turnpike road, intersecting the road from Morwellham at a spot still marked on the Ordnance map with the name of a former inn, The Rock. The enclosure of the down began to be mooted soon afterwards. In a letter dated 5 September 1827 the steward of the Bedford estates, Andrew Wilson, wrote: "The only proper spot for the erection of a Toll bar under the recent Turnpike Act is situated in the Centre of the Down, but it will be impossible to prevent the evasion of tolls as long as the Down is unenclosed."[3] Eventually the toll-house was built facing The Rock. It stands to this day, a charming slate-hung cottage, its front presenting the appearance of an octagon, with a porch to shelter the keeper while he collected toll.

[1] The name Whimple is now applied to a farm on the Cornish bank. Properly speaking it belongs to the pool immediately below Morwell Rocks. It is a compound of two British words corresponding to the Welsh *gwyn pwll*, or 'white pool' (cf. PND p. 579).
[2] The old road appears in documents from 1375 onwards as "the highway from Morwellham to Brentor." It led directly to and over Middle Lumburn Bridge, then turned north-eastward towards Hurdwick, where it joined the main road from Tavistock to Brentor. It can still be followed as far as the point where it crossed the Lamerton road, but the part between that road and Hurdwick—Pocket Lane, as it was formerly called—has disappeared.
[3] Bedford Office (Tavistock) Letter-book, 1824–62.

The Act for the enclosure of Morwell Down was passed in 1828; but the enclosure award, affecting an area of six hundred statute acres, was not made until 1836. Allotments in fee simple were made to those property owners who had rights of common on the down, the general public receiving no compensation for loss of access to an open space so highly suitable for exercise and recreation. Mrs Bray, however, writing in 1833, refers to a new road lately cut through the Morwell woods. "This was, but a few years since, cut under the immediate direction and at the expense of the duke of Bedford; and this act of munificence has afforded to the public at large so much delight, and thrown open to them such a glorious ride through scenes of almost matchless grandeur and beauty in their kind, that it deserves the most honourable mention." Mrs Bray goes on to speak of Morwell Rock, as it was now generally called, remarking: "Though truly it is a magnificent object, it has no right alone to engross the name, since all the rocks around it are likewise those of Morwell, and several are quite as beautiful as this; but it having been considered the greatest lion of its neighbourhood for so many years, the good folks who are accustomed to go thither in the summer months to boil their tea-kettles will not be prevailed with to think it can have a rival, far less an equal."[1]

Two batches of Morwell court-rolls are preserved among the duke of Bedford's muniments. The first of these runs from 1449 to 1614. During that period two courts were held every year, nominally at Michaelmas and Easter. Morwell was one of a group of small manors near Tavistock for which the abbot's steward held a combined court; but the proceedings were of little interest.[2] By the nineteenth century only one court was held, in October. Rolls are extant from 1801 to 1818, the last date at which a court is known to have been held. The number of jurors varied between six and ten. A reeve and a tithing-man were sworn, but the chief business clearly was to pay rents and to eat the dinner which the lord provided for his tenants. The following bill is dated 8 October 1814:

[1] A. E. Bray, *Traditions of Devonshire*, 1838, III, p. 279.
[2] The other manors were Ogbear, Parswell, Ottery, Foghanger, West Liddaton, Week, Hole, and Petertavy.

His Grace the Duke of Bedford. Dr. to George Bloye
For the Expenses of Morwell Court.

Round of Beef	0. 16.	9
Goose	5.	0
2 Qts. Brandy	18.	0
2 Qts. Rum	11.	0
9 gallons Beer	18.	0
Dressing Dinner, Bread, Vegetables, Servants, Etc.	15.	0
	4. 3.	9

The soil of Morwell must have been worked for minerals at an early date, how early it is impossible to say. The oldest document I have come across is an indenture dated the 20th of November 1566 by which Francis, earl of Bedford, granted John Fitz of Fitzford and certain other persons licence to work the tin-mines in Morwellham, on condition of rendering to the earl the eighth dole: that is, one-eighth of the unsmelted ore. On the same date the earl gave a similar concession to John Toker and others for a tin-work in Hay Wood. A tin-work called Morwellham-parks is mentioned in 1577, and in the following year the earl himself took a share in another working situated in the field called Eastern Town *alias* Well Park, adjoining Morwell Barton.[1] Joseph Drake, one of the Drakes of Buckland Monachorum, who died in 1708, left by will to his wife "all his tin bonds [? bounds] and shares in tin-mines upon Morle Down [*sic*] and Luscomb Down."[2] A number of old tin-mines are shown on the map drawn up to illustrate "A Survey of the West Part or Division of the Parish of Tavistock, taken between the years 1765 and 1769 by Gilbert Aislabie." Two of them are near Hurlditch Horn, one just beside the farm, the other in Down Park *alias* Tin Pit Park, a field across the road where now stands a deserted engine house. Further indications of mining activity are to be found in Wynne's survey of the woods. His map shows two stamping mills near Weir Head and an old smelting-house adjoining Impham Quay. But as the duke of Bedford's tin-

[1] Bedford Office: Ancient Deeds relating to the Tin Works.
[2] E. F. Elliott-Drake, *Family and Heirs of Sir Francis Drake*, 1911, II, p. 171.

dues for the thirty-one years ending 1786 amounted only to
£69 10s. 10½d. from the whole of his Devonshire estates,
production cannot have been on a big scale.[1]

It should be mentioned here that the last tin 'coinage' held
in the county of Devon took place at Morwellham in 1838,
when 756 blocks of tin, weighing together approximately 126
tons, were 'coined' or stamped with the arms of the duchy of
Cornwall to signify that a duty of 1s. 6¾d. per hundredweight
had been paid to the duchy. In the same year coinage duties
were abolished.[2]

Of much greater importance was the copper-mining which
began in earnest during the last decade of the eighteenth
century. There had been some earlier attempts, of slight
consequence, but the first mine that really flourished was
Wheal Friendship, in the parish of Marytavy, opened in 1796
or '97. The prosperity engendered by this enterprise affected
the whole neighbourhood. Among other things it created a
demand for additional means of transport, which was met in
1803 by an Act of Parliament authorizing the construction of
a canal from Tavistock to Morwellham. When the canal had
been taken as far as Crebor, some two miles outside Tavistock,
it became necessary to cut a tunnel through the heart of Morwell Down. In those days only hand drills and black powder
were available for blasting the hard rock; but under the direction of John Taylor, the very able manager of Wheal Friendship, this notable feat of engineering was successfully accomplished. Vancouver, who wrote during the progress of the
work, says: "The tunnel is cut 8 ft. deep and 6 ft. wide, having
a depth of 3 ft. 3 in. of water to answer the purpose of naviga-
tion. The whole distance through the hill is estimated at 1400
fathoms, and costs £14 per fathom, exclusive of the air-shafts,
the first of which is sunk at the distance of 200 fathoms from
the north end of the tunnel, is 28 fathoms deep, and 4 ft. in
diameter. No. 2 is sunk at a distance of 500 fathoms from the
first point and is 55 fathoms deep. No. 3 is at the distance of

[1] Accounts of the Duke of Bedford's Canal- and Mine-Dues: MS. volume
formerly in the Bedford Office, Tavistock; Richard Turner's Notebooks,
ibid. (Aislabie's map and Wynne's survey were also preserved in the Office.)
[2] H. T. De la Beche, *Report on the Geology of Cornwall, Devon, and West
Somerset*, 1839, pp. 586–90.

1100 fathoms from the place of beginning, and is 48 fathoms deep."[1] The canal emerges from this tunnel at the head of Luscombe and is carried round the north side of the combe for about half a mile, terminating at the edge of the hill 240 feet above Morwellham quay. The barges were there fastened upon trolleys, which ran down the grooved rails of an inclined plane, controlled by a windlass and chain, to the quay below. The canal was opened on the 24th of June 1817, having cost £68,000 to construct.[2] Rachel Evans, writing in 1846, describes it as "a scene of busy industry, with its unloading barges, and shouting sailors, and hammering workmen, and train of waggons ascending or descending the inclined plane. A quantity of ore is here shipped off to distant smelting-houses. It is curious to enter the well swept yard, and observe the different wooden shafts down which distinct ores from various mines are poured. Then it is to be collected, and placed on board the vessels bound for distant quarters. These ships in return bring coals, and lime-stone, and many other commodities."[3]

The richest mines, Wheal Tamar, Wheal Crebor, and Wheal Crowndale, lay on one and the same lode north of the canal, and outside the boundaries of Morwell, while the richest of them all, the famous Devon Great Consols, lay still further away, in Blanchdown. Within the territory of the manor there were however several which proved not wholly unremunerative. Wheal Impham, opened in 1799 and still working in 1815, was given up by 1822.[4] West Crebor and Colcharton had some success. Between 1857 and 1869 East Wheal Russell sold 9089 tons of copper for £49,863. Russell United, which in 1870 was 60 fathoms deep and employed 30 people, sold 11,400 tons; the company was not wound up until 1893.[5] The peak of mining activity, however, in the Tavistock neighbourhood as in the west of England generally was reached in

[1] C. Vancouver, *General View of the Agriculture of the County of Devon*, 1813, p. 382.

[2] W. White, *History, Gazetteer, and Directory of Devonshire*, 1850, p. 624.

[3] *Home Scenes, or Tavistock and its Vicinity*, p. 98.

[4] "Duke of Bedford's Canal- and Mine-Dues;" Lysons, *Devonshire*, p. cclxxxiv.

[5] J. H. Collins, *Observations on the West of England Mining Region*, 1912, p. 573.

the 1850's. After that the story is one of progressive decline. Mrs Rundle Charles in 1896 wrote: "Last autumn I went once more to Morwellham after years of absence. The quays were deserted. The men were all away working in the fields, or in mines some miles off. Not a ship was on the river . . . The canal, once a new and successful enterprise, was unused, partly because the mines whose ore used to be carried in its barges were closed, partly because the railway had superseded it."[1]

After about seventy years of dereliction the canal has lately been put to a new use; it now provides the neighbourhood with electricity.[2] But grass grows on the quay at Morwellham, and no vessel weighs anchor from the little port. The woods and fields of Morwell remain enfolded in a rural peace which can hardly be matched and assuredly not surpassed for beauty by any stretch of country in the south-west.

[1] *Our Seven Homes*, p. 68.
[2] The work was carried out in 1933-34, when over 20,000 tons of mud and silt were removed from the canal. See the account by F. E. Pitt in *Journal of the Institution of Electrical Engineers*, XCII, 1945, pp. 111 sqq.

THE TRAGI-COMEDY OF
ABBOT BONUS

WHEN a man endowed with no more than average wisdom and strength of character is forced into a struggle against hopeless odds, the outcome will naturally be either tragedy or tragi-comedy. In the case of Abbot Bonus the tragic and comic elements were closely intertwined. Bonus himself was just a human misfit, of no particular importance. His story, however, exhibits a famous bishop in no very creditable light, and to the student of ecclesiastical history it may suggest one or two reflections on such debatable themes as the system of papal 'provisions' and the desire of monasteries for immunity from episcopal control.

At the beginning of 1325 the monks of Tavistock were called upon to fill the vacancy caused by the death of Robert Champeaux, who had ruled the abbey very creditably for over thirty-nine years. There were two candidates, both monks of the house. Robert Busse was chosen by a majority of the electors; but his rival, John de Courtenay, son of Hugh, baron Courtenay of Okehampton, could muster influential friends outside; and his supporters were emboldened by that fact to repudiate the choice of the majority. On hearing of the dispute, the government ordered Bishop Stapeldon to hold an enquiry; but the monks refused their bishop's arbitration and appealed to the Holy See. A grant which the late abbot had secured in 1315 empowered them to keep the management of the abbot's property in their own hands during voidance, instead of handing it over to the royal official who would normally have administered the estates for the king's profit.[1]

At this time Edward II's uneasy reign was drawing to its close, while John XXII ruled the Church from wind-swept Avignon. The Pope appointed Raymond, cardinal de Fargis, to adjudicate upon the case. Two monks of Tavistock, John Fromund and Richard Mountori, associated themselves with

CPR 1324–27, pp. 62, 89, 106, 109, 113, 179; CCR 1323–27, p. 283.

John de Courtenay in appealing against the election of Robert Busse. On the 15th of November the complainants, through their proctors, handed in a lengthy statement of their objections to the abbot-elect.[1]

To explain away the majority vote, they alleged that it was brought about by corrupt bargaining. Seven of the electors had gained their first admittance to the monastery through Busse's influence with the late abbot, but only after they had bribed him and taken their gospel oath to uphold his interest on all occasions. Even before the late abbot's death he had conspired with them to procure his own election, and had promised to distribute the various household offices among his supporters. A list of these promised appointments is given. Richard de Wylle was to be prior; Roger de Pountyngdon sacristan; William de la Wille almoner; Alexander de Leghe cellarer; Richard de Esse precentor; John de Bremdon chamberlain and granger; John de Schalounes *salsarius*; and Reginald Drake prior of Scilly.

Not content with thus rigging the election, Busse went to Exeter in September 1324, and sought the professional advice of Master Richard de Langatre, of the diocese of Lincoln, a noted fortune-teller, or—as the appellants more colourfully put it—a consultor of unclean and malignant spirits. Whereupon Master Richard set his magic arts in motion, and elicited from the demons an encouraging reply. This was matter of common report in the city of Exeter.

When the election was over, Busse took possession of the treasury, and also of a silver casket which had been deposited there by the king's officers. In February 1325 he left the monastery by night, taking with him £1200 in cash. Later in the same month he returned with an armed escort and removed gold and silver plate to the value of £800.

Having said their say about the election itself, its antecedents and immediate sequel, the complainants now proceeded to open their case in earnest. According to them, Busse was disqualified by birth, and by the excommunication he had incurred for breaches of ecclesiastical law. They also accused him of embezzlement, assault, battery, manslaughter, and sexual misconduct.

[1] W. Table 4A, Drawer 2, Tavistock Addenda.

As to birth: he was the son of a priest, Master Robert de Yoldelond, and of that priest's concubine Joan Busse. In proof of which, they pointed out that he was christened Robert, and surnamed Busse.

For a period of twelve years, beginning in 1312, Busse, in partnership with John Prince of Tavistock and other laymen, purchased salt, hides, wool, and livestock, usually at fairs, and re-sold them at a profit. With his lay associates he also lent money out at interest, evading the Church's laws against usury. On the 13th of August 1313 he stole £100 from his reputed father, taking with him as accomplices two uncles of his, who were afterwards convicted of the theft and hanged. Once he paid £40 to his brother-in-law without the abbot's knowledge. In the space of two months, at Exeter, he gave away trinkets (*jocalia*) to the value of £60, the property of the house, to actors, actresses, whores, and other loose and disreputable persons.

In 1322, sitting as judge in the hundred-court of Tavistock, he sentenced to the gallows one David de Cornilii, convicted of stealing oxen from the prior of Bodmin. He caused Nicholas le Lokeyer's ears to be cut off; grievously beat two clerks; and assaulted his servant Luke Croker, breaking several of his ribs. In August 1324 he armed certain men of Tavistock with cudgels and led them in a murderous attack on the men of Buckland Abbey.

It will be seen that the complainants were now warming to their work. They proceeded to accuse Busse of having incurred excommunication by disguising himself, on several occasions between 1310 and 1322, in lay costume. He had done this for the purpose of carrying on amorous intrigues. Five women are named, including Catharine, wife of John Busse (a sister-in-law, perhaps?), and Eleanor, wife of Michael Dorrant, his own godmother. By Christina Lucas he is said to have had two sons. In the light of these charges an accusation of homosexual proclivities would not have looked very plausible. The appellants therefore contented themselves with recalling that he had been rebuked by the late abbot for urging that leniency should be shown to a convicted pervert: proof enough that his opinions on the subject were unsound.

In short, if his opponents were to be believed, no more infamous monk had ever disgraced the order of St Benedict.

On the 19th of November Busse's proctor entered a denial of all the above allegations, and offered to prove them false, calumnious, invented out of malice, immaterial, and insufficient (!) to upset the election.

Depositions had been taken from several witnesses; and after two adjournments the cardinal ordered these to be read publicly. Most tantalizingly for us, the transcript of this evidence, and of the remainder of the pleadings, is missing. From other sources we learn that the verdict was given in favour of Robert Busse.[1] The whole of the evidence on both sides having been lost or perhaps destroyed, posterity can only take note of this fact, that Courtenay and his two supporters failed to make out their case before the competent tribunal at the time.

It must be repeated that Busse had been chosen by the majority of the electors; and according to Bishop Grandisson, an independent witness, the majority of the Tavistock monks at this period were "good and satisfactory men."[2] It must also be remembered that in the fourteenth century litigants did not pull their punches. They, or their lawyers for them, regularly painted the other side in the most lurid colours, fully expecting the court to discount their allegations by at least one half, and reckless of any scandal that might recoil upon themselves or the institution to which they belonged.

The Holy See, while giving its verdict in favour of the abbot-elect, understood that he and his opponents could hardly be expected to live happily together after so baleful a dispute. Accordingly Busse was persuaded to resign Tavistock and to accept a papal nomination to the Cluniac priory of Montacute.[3] Encouraged by this news, the Courtenay faction made a fresh effort. On the 20th of August 1327 letters were sent in the king's name to the Pope and to the vice-chancellor of the Holy Roman Church, insisting on Courtenay's merits and family connections, and stating that the abbey had suffered no small detriment from the long vacancy.[4]

This had now lasted over two and a half years: a costly busi-

---

[1] *Calendar of Papal Letters*, II, p. 265.
[2] *Register of John de Grandisson*, ed. F. C. Hingeston-Randolph, p. 98.
[3] *Calendar of Papal Letters*, II, p. 257.
[4] *Reg. Grandisson*, p. 33.

ness, for by the terms of the grant under which the prior and convent acted as custodians they were obliged to pay the Crown sixty marks during the first four months of voidance and a hundred marks a year thereafter.[1] Moreover, both factions had done their best to prevent the assets of the house from falling into their opponents' hands. Busse, as we have seen, had removed the contents of the treasury, and on the other side John Fromund, with a band of seventeen laymen, prominent burgesses of Tavistock, had broken into the abbey, assaulted the officials, and carried away a quantity of books and plate, the property of the late abbot.[2]

At last, on the 30th of October 1327, the papal decision was announced. John de Courtenay's election was declared null and void. Taking the appointment into his own hands, the Pope gave Tavistock a new pastor in the person of Bonus, abbot of the small monastery of St Orientius at Larreule in the diocese of Tarbes and county of Bigorre.[3] Evidently it was hoped that Tavistock would recover its tranquillity more speedily under a newcomer, a complete stranger to both factions. As a native of Aquitaine, Bonus was by birth a subject of the English king. He seems to have had powerful supporters. The cardinals de Pelagrua, de Garvo, and de Mota espoused his interests,[4] and may have thought they were doing him a service in procuring his transfer to a more important house. While these considerations help to explain his appointment, his own motives for accepting it remain unfathomable, though we may hazard a guess that the Tavistock representatives, being Devonshire men, had not understated the attractions of their home.

The appointment of Busse to Montacute was resisted by the abbot of Cluny, who maintained that the right of nomination belonged exclusively to him. Then there was more litigation, and before it had run its course the much-harassed Busse was

[1] *Calendar of Fine Rolls*, 1307–19, p. 246.

[2] CPR 1327–30, p. 211; cf. *Reg. Grandisson*, p. 408.

[3] *Cal. Papal Letters*, II, p. 265; cf. *Gallia Christiana*, I, p. 1257, and J. M. Besse, *Abbayes et Prieurés de l'Ancienne France*, III, pp. 37, 77. Hingeston-Randolph, following Oliver and Browne Willis, calls the abbot *Robert* Bonus. This mistake rests on a confusion between him and the disappointed candidate, Robert Busse.

[4] *Reg. Grandisson*, p. 97.

dead.[1] Meanwhile the see of Exeter, vacant by the sudden death of Bishop Berkeley, had been filled by the Pope's appointment of his favoured pupil and chaplain John de Grandisson. The new bishop was in his thirty-sixth year. Believing his diocese to be in urgent need of reform, he addressed himself to the task without delay and with a vigour that more than once outran discretion.

Before starting on his journey to England, Bonus was obliged to borrow money in order to meet the charges of the pontifical exchequer. A proposal to endow the papacy with a permanent income-tax of one shilling in the pound on the ecclesiastical revenues of Christendom had been made at the council of Vienne, but nothing had come of it, and the papal government relied largely upon heavy casual taxes, such as the tax on new appointments made or confirmed by the Pope. Under this head Bonus was charged 1000 florins, or £133 6s. 8d. of English money.[2] As if this were not enough, he found, on landing in England, that the royal government took strong exception, not to him personally, but to his appointment by the Pope, for Tavistock was a royal foundation and it was therefore arguable that the king's rights as patron had been infringed. Consequently he was not allowed to proceed until he had given an undertaking to pay, at call, 500 marks into the royal exchequer.[3]

On the 10th of May 1328 he raised a fresh loan of £100 on the security of his lands and chattels in the county of Devon.[4] A month later Bishop Grandisson issued a mandate for his induction. The demoralized and impoverished abbey at last received its abbot, himself heavily in debt. During the vacancy no new monks had been admitted. Among the survivors of the older generation were Courtenay and his disgruntled faction, jealous of the newcomer, perhaps eager to catch him out. The customs of the country were decidedly peculiar. And to complete his misery, Bonus, a native of sun-baked Gascony, found himself living at the edge of Dartmoor, under grey skies and

[1] *Cal. Papal Letters*, II, p. 277.
[2] W. E. Lunt, *Financial Relations of the Papacy with England to 1327*, Cambridge (Mass.), 1939, p. 681.
[3] *Calendar of Fine Rolls*, 1327–37, p. 89.
[4] CCR 1327–30, p. 385.

what must have seemed to him incessant rain. For an unfortunate monk in this plight there was, however, one alleviation. As Bishop Grandisson had said when writing to his friends at the papal court, the diocese of Exeter might be situated at the outside edge of Christendom, but it did import a plentiful supply of claret from Bordeaux.[1] To keep the damp out, therefore, and to help him forget his creditors, Bonus called for wine. Small wonder if, as the painful months wore on, his potations grew, at times, excessive.

Relations with the bishop went wrong from the start. Grandisson announced his intention of visiting the abbey, and required that no new monks should be admitted in the meantime, for such admissions, he said, might disturb the peace of the monastery. He was persuaded to revoke this order, in an interview which took place at Chudleigh; and on the 4th of August he sent the abbot and convent a mandate to admit William de Inwoldesleghe as a monk of their house; but four days later he renewed the former prohibition in peremptory terms.[2] On the 22nd Bonus was present at the bishop's enthronement, and when taking leave of him after the ceremony remarked that unless some novices were speedily habited and tonsured, the bishop, when he came to Tavistock, would find an empty choir. To this Grandisson replied: "Very well; do as you please." A fortnight later he wrote demanding to be informed whether certain novices had recently been tonsured in defiance of his late inhibition. The abbot replied that the admission and tonsuring of monks was a matter which pertained, of custom and of right, to the abbot and convent alone. He reminded the bishop of their conversations at Chudleigh and Exeter; pleaded the urgency of the case; and begged him not to take offence at what had been done.[3]

So far, the abbot was on safe ground. Had he contented himself with a firm but respectful statement in these terms, his position would have been morally as well as legally unimpeachable. Unfortunately for himself, Bonus was not the kind of man who knows when to stop. He went on: "You are aware, Father, that we can be worth as much to you perhaps as some

[1] *Reg. Grandisson*, p. 98.
[2] *ibid.*, pp. 368, 369.
[3] *ibid.*, pp. 393, 395.

175

of those who incite your person against us with their desperate lies; and you will be better able to carry out your plans with the assistance of our money and our service than with those of the men whose constant aim it is to stir up your displeasure against us, blameless as we are." Then he proceeds to inform his outraged diocesan that, according to what his monks have told him, the abbey used to be wholly exempt from episcopal jurisdiction. Nevertheless he is ready to obey the bishop in all things lawful, and so far as may be without prejudice to the abbey or to the Roman Church. And he concludes by wishing Grandisson long life and perfect health.

When the bishop read this letter, he saw at once that he had made a false step. He allowed a month to pass before writing again. Then he informed the abbot that certain magnates were urging him to make a visitation of the abbey, but that he preferred the path of good counsel, and would therefore pay the house a friendly visit, not a formal visitation, on the 7th of October. If, after that, the desired end were not attained by means of charity and sweetness, the whole responsibility would rest upon the abbot.[1]

It was plain that, given time, Bonus could be relied upon to compass his own downfall; and Grandisson, perceiving this, was content to wait. Years afterwards, while turning the pages of his official register, he came upon a transcript of the abbot's letter. Drawing an indignant pen thrice from top to bottom of the offensive screed, he wrote in the margin: "Fool!" and added, with a play of words on Bonus: "That abbot's name was Good, but he was a scoundrel, a near-heretic!"[2]

From the 7th to the 9th of October the bishop was at Tavistock. It is not known what passed on this occasion, except that Grandisson again pressed the convent to receive William de Inwoldsleghe, and took it upon himself to recommend Richard de Esse for the office of *salsarius*.[3] In the meantime Bonus had obtained a rescript from Canterbury forbidding Grandisson to molest him or his monastery. Grandisson, writ-

---

[1] *Reg.*, p. 405.

[2] *Iste abbas qui dicebatur bonus erat pessimus quasi hereticus.* A facsimile of the page is given by Hingeston-Randolph as frontispiece in Part II of his edition of the Register.

[3] *Reg.*, pp. 1524, 412, 197.

ing to thank a correspondent who passed on this news, denied that he had ever cited or molested the abbot, "that son of inconstancy and double-dealing," although he and his house needed correction more than any in the diocese.[1] At the same time he wrote to the prior, apparently behind the abbot's back, promising to shield him and the monks against all oppression by their superior.[2]

Bonus had been accompanied to England by two esquires, his fellow-countrymen. To one of these, John de Brusci, he owed some money, but presently he dismissed the man without settling the debt. The other, named Everard, a former servant of the cardinal de Garvo, also fell foul of his master, unfortunately at a moment when the abbot had taken more drink than usual. A disgraceful scuffle ensued, in which Everard was nearly killed.[3] Grandisson at once saw how these incidents could be used to discredit Bonus at headquarters. He wrote off to the Pope, lamenting that his Holiness had been "got round" (*circumventam*) in the matter of the Tavistock appointment. According to him, Bonus, ever since he came to England, had abstained from all monastic observance. He was continually vexing his monks with reproaches and abuse, offending the landowners of the neighbourhood, and making himself universally unpopular.[4] In a letter to the cardinals Grandisson writes that his dear friend the Lord Abbot of Tavistock, from the moment of his arrival, has strayed from the monastic path. He treats his monks, "whom I consider for the most part good and satisfactory men," with contempt, brings frivolous lawsuits against influential neighbours, and wastes the property of the house. The bishop has tried to bring him to his senses, explaining English customs to him, and menacing him with the wrath of God. All in vain, however. While seeking absolution for his murderous assault, Bonus tried to throw the blame on Everard, a man of excellent character, who in consequence has now returned to the papal court empty-handed, to his no small loss.[5]

These denunciations might undermine the abbot's repute at

[1] *ibid.*, p. 182.
[2] *ibid.*, p. 190.
[3] *ibid.*, pp. 99, 193, 198, 223, 230.
[4] *ibid.*, p. 97.
[5] *ibid.*, p. 98.

Avignon; but meanwhile he was protected by the Canterbury rescript. One great irritant seemed likely to be removed when John de Courtenay received a papal nomination to the rich Cluniac priory of Lewes. Grandisson was delighted, for he and Courtenay were cousins.[1] In March 1330 Bonus received a favourable answer to a petition he had sent up, praying that he might be excused the payment of 500 marks with which he had purchased the royal consent to his appointment. It had been found on enquiry that there was no precedent for thus mulcting an ecclesiastic appointed by the Holy See.[2]

For a while it looked as if he might yet ride the storm; and perhaps he would have done so had he not been still heavily in debt. As it was, he found himself compelled to raise fresh loans in order to pacify his creditors. Two of these had recourse to Avignon, and there obtained judgement against him for £200.[3] It was reported that the abbey buildings were dilapidated, that some of the monks were wandering at large, and that the property of the house was daily being consumed in the most wasteful fashion.[4] In June of the following year the abbot was unable to meet the income-tax levied under papal authority to provide funds for a possible crusade. John de Courtenay's appointment to Lewes was resisted by the earl of Warenne and Surrey, who as patron of the priory claimed to exclude the Pope's nominee, and succeeded in driving Courtenay back to Tavistock.

In referring to lawsuits between Bonus and neighbouring landowners, the bishop doubtless had in mind the trouble that broke out over Whitchurch rectory. The abbot's predecessor had acquired the advowson in 1301 from Walter Labbé, who held Whitchurch manor in right of his niece Joan, then under age; and some years later the revenues of the parish church were appropriated to the abbot and convent in order that a chantry might be established at Whitchurch under an archpriest and three assistants. This plan was to be carried out after the death of the then rector, James Fraunceis. The appropriation was confirmed by the Crown, and the whole

---

[1] *Reg.*, p. 230.
[2] CCR 1330–33, p. 14.
[3] *ibid.*, 1327–30, p. 587; 1330–33, p. 127; *Reg. Grandisson*, p. 703.
[4] *ibid.*, p. 584.

scheme was formally approved by Bishop Stapeldon.[1] But on the death of Fraunceis in March 1331, Walter Labbé's son, who had married his cousin, the heiress, repudiated his father's grant of the advowson, and presented Master David Aliam to the vacant living. Naturally Bonus could not let this pass. He nominated a vicar of his own, but Grandisson, who seems to have made up his mind that this was merely one more proof of wrongheadedness on the abbot's part, brushed aside all remonstrances and directed the abbot of Buckland to institute Aliam. On proceeding to Whitchurch for this purpose, the abbot found the church doors closed against him and the approach barricaded. An armed guard was assembled under the leadership of four Tavistock monks, one of whom, it is of some interest to note, was the bishop's *protégé*, William de Inwoldesleghe. After much fruitless altercation, the abbot retired, uttering sentence of excommunication against the obstructors. Grandisson appealed to the government to intervene, and on the 8th of December 1332 ordered his decision to be proclaimed throughout the archdeaconry of Totnes. He admonished the abbot to let Aliam enter upon his benefice, on pain of excommunication and interdict, and directed that a copy of this notice should be affixed to the parish church of Whitchurch and the abbey church of Tavistock.[2]

Bonus replied by appealing once more to the court of Canterbury. This appeal was the signal for his final overthrow. By failing to pay an income-tax levied under papal authority, by failing also to satisfy the judgement given in favour of his creditors by the papal court of exchequer, and by his resistance in the affair of Whitchurch, he had rendered himself liable to excommunication. Sentence to this effect was now made public by order of the bishop. On the 8th of July 1333 the abbot was pronounced contumacious and suspended from the administration of his monastery. Finally, on the 24th of October, he was removed from office by episcopal decree. In explanation of this sentence Grandisson declared the abbey to be nearly bankrupt. It was feared that some of the monks would have to be sent out begging for their daily bread. The abbot was

[1] CPR 1292–1301, p. 616; DA lxxv, 1943, p. 199; *Reg. Stapeldon*, p. 402; CPR 1330–34, p. 111.
[2] *Reg. Grandisson*, pp. 675, 548, 951, 603, 677.

further accused of eating meat publicly in Lent without reasonable cause, and of other irregularities (*enormia*)—probably his addiction to the bottle—which "out of reverence for the monastic order and profession" the bishop could not bring himself to specify.[1]

At this point Bonus passes out of history, a beaten man. It is to be supposed that he went back to Avignon, and that something was done for him by his former friends. To these the bishop wrote protesting that he had nothing on his conscience in this matter. He had striven hard to bring the abbot to his senses, but in vain. The man was his own worst accuser.[2]

It is true enough that Bonus was out of place at Tavistock. The papal administration had done its best to smooth his path by posting Busse to Montacute and Courtenay to Lewes, but these sage measures had been thwarted in each case by vested interests on the spot. Judging, quite rightly, that Tavistock required new blood, the Pope's advisers conscientiously endeavoured to supply it. Their standpoint was that of an international authority not fully awake to the strength of national feeling, and they made the mistake of supposing that a subject of Edward III would be acceptable in any part of his dominions. Worse, they misjudged their candidate. In a situation demanding superhuman patience, modesty, and tact, Bonus failed to rise above a crudely human level. (One would give something to have heard him, back in Provence, enlarging postprandially on the theme of England and the English!)

If the system of direct appointment by the head of the Church failed to give Tavistock the right abbot, it did almost simultaneously provide Exeter with an outstandingly successful bishop. Throughout the forty-two years of his episcopate John de Grandisson devoted himself wholeheartedly to the care of his flock, preaching, writing, constantly visiting every corner of the diocese, and building on a magnificent scale. The nave of Exeter cathedral and the collegiate church of Ottery St Mary are his memorials. It would seem, however, that the advice Hugh de Courtenay gave him in the early days of his episcopate, not to judge rashly but to hear both sides, was nearer to the mark than its offended recipient thought. His

---

[1] *Reg.*, pp. 702, 716.
[2] *ibid.*, p. 109.

proceedings against Bonus were often hasty, and sometimes worse. Bonus, after all, had had some previous experience of abbatial office, and by no means all his difficulties were of his own making. Grandisson, however, gave him no chance to grapple with them in his own way. From the start he interfered in the administration of the abbey. By a series of contradictory mandates he goaded the abbot into insubordination. Then the other parties began to move against Bonus, knowing that they would have the bishop on their side. Thus it was that the affair of Whitchurch blew up, with all its discreditable consequences. Here Bonus should have taken warning from the fate of a previous abbot, John Chubb, deposed in 1269 by Bishop Bronescombe after he had begun an action at law, with every prospect of success, against the bishop's steward. Chubb, like Bonus, was in financial difficulties, and at odds with some of his monks; but Bronescombe's minions had been plundering the abbey right and left.[1] An abbot who put his bishop in the wrong could expect no quarter. This Chubb did, and this Bonus also did in the affair of Whitchurch. His duty bound him to uphold rights which Church and State had formally conferred upon the abbey; and when the bishop denied him justice he could do no less than appeal to a higher court. Ultimately the bishop found himself obliged to undo this particular wrong. Some time after Bonus had been struck down, Whitchurch was again appropriated to the abbey, this time with his full consent.[2] When Grandisson declared that he was acting in Christ's name and without ulterior motive,[3] he was not being hypocritical, but he deceived himself. At heart he wanted Bonus out of the way. Always devoted to the interests of his cousin John de Courtenay, he grasped the opportunity to make him abbot of Tavistock as soon as Bonus was removed. How ill-judged this appointment was appeared four years later, when he found himself obliged to suspend Courtenay for maladministration. Such episodes go far to explain and even justify the desire of monastic communities like Tavistock to shake off the jurisdiction of the local bishop.

[1] CCR 1268–72, p. 101; *Calendar of Miscellaneous Inquisitions*, I, p. 129.
[2] *Reg. Grandisson*, pp. 1107, 1432.
[3] *ibid.*, p. 717.

A SHEAF OF DOCUMENTS

A VICE-ARCHDEACON'S LEGACIES

THE document translated below was drawn up *c.* 1190. For three hundred and fifty years the original chirograph was preserved at Tavistock Abbey. It is now in the Devon County Record Office.[1]

"This is the agreement made between H[erbert], abbot of Tavistock, and the archdeacon of Cornwall, and between Jordan and William and Reginald, brothers of John, late vice-archdeacon of Cornwall, and the other kinsmen of the said John, touching the goods and chattels and debts of the said John, to wit: the said abbot shall have all the corn and tithes of Lamerton for the support of himself and of the monks of Tavistock. The abbot and monks shall also have all the said John's silver spoons. The archdeacon for his part shall have one palfrey belonging to the said John, with its harness. And William, brother of the said John, shall have one new cloak of burnet, to the use of a certain niece of his, for the portion which fell to him of the worn apparel and of such other of the said John's utensils as were not made of gold, silver, or mazer. All vessels of gold, silver, or mazer, with the said John's other goods and chattels and the debts that were due to him, shall be divided into three equal parts, whereof one part shall go to the abbot, one to the archdeacon, and the third to the brothers and kinsmen of the deceased. If the abbot and the archdeacon owed anything to the said John, they are and shall be quit of such debt for ever; but all the other debts are to be sought out and collected by the joint exertions, counsel, and expense of the parties and divided between them in three equal parts. If any measures have been taken by the abbot or by the archdeacon or by any of the said John's brothers for seeking out these chattels before the making of this agreement, each person shall render an account thereof. For the faithful observance of these

[1] Reproduced in DCNQ XXII, 1945, p. 285.

conditions the abbot and the archdeacon and Jordan and William and the other brethren of the aforesaid John have taken their corporal oath, in the presence of these witnesses: William, archdeacon of Dorset; Alard son of William, then sheriff; Richard Flammanc; Robert de Campellis; William de Cheinna; Hugh Cofin; Joel de Buchinton (knights); masters Peter Picot and Alured and Henry de Melewis, Richard son of Drogo (canons of Exeter); William de Spinevaus; John Walensis; Peter, brother of Walter the archdeacon of Cornwall; William de Burdevill; Guy de Daggevill; Ralph Gaue; and Gilbert, archdeacon of Totnes, whose seal, with the seal of H[erbert], abbot of Tavistock, is affixed to the present charter for the greater security of this agreement." [*Seals missing.*]

Apparently the vice-archdeacon's wishes concerning the disposal of his property had been expressed only in general terms, perhaps by word of mouth. This document shows how they were carried out in detail by agreement between his legatees. His life-interest in the Lamerton corn-tithe must have rested upon some arrangement with Tavistock, for the church of Lamerton, with its tithes and offerings, had been appropriated to the abbey by Bishop Bartholomew (1162–84), and the appropriation had been confirmed by Archbishop Richard (1174–84).[1] Bartholomew reserved one half of the tithes, offerings, legacies, burial fees, and produce of the glebe to the vicar of Lamerton for his portion, out of which the vicar was to maintain himself and to meet parochial expenses. The other moiety, free of all charge, was assigned to the abbot and convent; and from the document here reproduced it appears that they used it to subsidize a diocesan functionary who had no official income of his own. The vice-archdeacon being now dead, they were free to use their moiety for other purposes.[2] Hitherto they had been accustomed to provide food and drink for three poor men daily during Lent. They now resolved to do this every day throughout the year; and the Lamerton corn-tithe, "with the land of Thele belonging to the church of Lamerton, the buildings there, and the church-land called Eatgodeslond," were to provide the necessary funds. The

[1] ETC xxv, xxxi.
[2] A. Morey, *Bartholomew of Exeter*, p. 127, gives a list of the vice-archdeacons. Their office appears to have been short-lived.

vicar gave him consent, and John, bishop of Exeter, confirmed the new arrangement.[1]

These transactions illustrate a point which is often overlooked: namely, that tithe was not intended only for the support of the parish priest; it constituted a general fund, applicable at the discretion of the ecclesiastical authorities to such objects as the repair of the church fabric, the relief of destitution, hospitality to travellers, and indeed any recognized Church purpose.

Bishop John died on the 1st of June 1191. Gilbert had succeeded Bernard as archdeacon of Totnes some time after the 3rd of June in the preceding year.[2] The date given at the beginning of this note (*c.* 1190) is thus established within tolerably close limits.

The date is of particular interest since it falls within the period of approximately four years, beginning in December 1189, during which Devon, Cornwall, and five other counties lay outside the normal administration of the kingdom. They had been handed over to the king's brother John, who ruled them as a quasi-independent principality and appointed his own sheriffs. Hence the official list of sheriffs gives no name for Devon between 1189 and 1193. Our document partly fills the gap: it names Alard Fitz William, an early associate of John's,[3] as sheriff, and shows him surrounded by the leading personages of the Exeter shire-court and cathedral chapter.

It may be added that the earliest date given in the *Medieval Latin Word-List* for *mazerus*, meaning maple-wood, is 1245. Burnet, a dark brown wool-dyed cloth, is on record from 1188 onwards.

---

[1] ETC xlv, xlvi.

[2] Morey, *op. cit.*, p. 125.

[3] R. W. Eyton, *Court, Household, and Itinerary of King Henry II*, pp. 229, 249.

THE CUSTOMS OF STOKENHAM [1]

INQUEST holden at Stoke in Hamme, 6th August, 3
Edward II [1309], by the oath of William de Pyn, Geoffrey
de Bosco, Robert de Faleputte, William de Forde, John
Finamour, Reginald Pryce, Nicholas de Pole, Geoffrey de
Praulle, Robert de Coumbe, Nicholas de Praulle, Ralph
Wodye, and John le Fugh. They declare that Matthew Fitz
John held for the term of his life the manor of Stoke in Hamme.
The king has now committed it to Lord William de Monta-
cute.

There are two dovecotes, worth half a mark yearly; 150
acres of arable, worth, at 4d. the acre, 50s.; 7½ acres of meadow,
worth, at 2s. the acre, 15s.; 170 acres of pasture, worth, at
3d. the acre, 42s. 6d.; a wood called Haywode, 90 acres, of
which the underwood and pasture are worth 13s. 4d. yearly;
another wood called Colrigg Wood, 50 acres, value of underwood and pasture, 8s.; a lake with a fishery worth 10s.; a
watermill called Chedelington [Chillington] Mill, 10 marks
yearly; another mill called Langcoumb Mill, 9 marks.

There are also at Le Stert [Start], belonging to this manor,
60 acres of arable, worth, at 3d. the acre, 15s.; 2½ acres of meadow, worth, at 6d. the acre, 1s. 3d.; 200 acres of rough pasture
worth, at 1d. the acre, 16s. 8d.; and another water-mill, worth
8 marks a year.

Two free tenants pay 21s. 4d. It is the duty of one of them
to plough [on the lord's land] in winter with two ploughs for
one day. For this service he is to have 2d.; value of the service,
4d. He also pays 8s. at Michaelmas by way of 'aid'.

There are four free tenants called parson's men [*homines per-
sone*], who hold jointly two ferlings of land, paying 6s. 8d.
yearly, and 3s. 6d. as aid at Michaelmas. It is the duty of each
of them to do one day's winter ploughing with his own
plough; for this service he is to have 1d.; value of the service,
at 2d. each, 8d.

---

[1] Translated from PRO Inquisition post mortem, C 134, File 16, no. 9.
The bracketed interpolations are added by the translator.

There are 137 bondmen tenants (*nativi*], who pay £24 2s. 7d. yearly, and £12 2s. 10d. as aid at Michaelmas. It is the duty of each one of them to perform one service [for the lord] every week from Michaelmas to the Gule of August [August 1st], except Christmas, Easter, and Whitsun weeks: that is, 41 weeks. Value of these services, at ½d. per service, £11 14s. 0½d. Also to reap half an acre a week in autumn so long as the lord has corn to reap, and to gather, stack, and carry it home. Also to mow the stubble, thatch the farm buildings, or perform any other service at the will of the lord: namely, two services every week from the Gule of August to Michaelmas, the lord not supplying food; or to give the lord 1s. 4d. to waive these services. Value of the services, £9 2s. 8d. Also to join together in groups of four, each four to plough 1½ acres yearly with their own ploughs, the lord not supplying food. Value of this service, at 9d. the plough, £1 5s. 8¼d.

There are 36 [bond] tenants of another tenure, who pay £7 12s. 10¼d. yearly, and £3 16s. 9d. as aid at Michaelmas. It is their duty to plough like the other bondmen. Value of this service [at 9d. the plough], 6s. 9d.

Two other bond tenants pay 4s. 6d. yearly, and 2s. 4d. as aid at Michaelmas. It is their duty to get two pairs of coulters and shares made for the lord, the lord supplying iron and fuel; also to get the spindle of Chillington Mill repaired whenever it is broken, again with the lord's iron and fuel. Annual value of these services, 2s. Also to plough like the other bond tenants; value, 4½d.

A sheep-rent [*berbiagium*] of 56⅔ ewes is due at Hock-day from all the bond tenants; its annual value, at 1s. a head, is £2 16s. 8d.

There are also some cottagers, holding cottages with curtilages, and paying £2 4s. 3d. yearly.

Some of the bondmen are under obligation to transport three horseloads of fish from this manor to the manor of Stoke in Wiltshire, or to give the lord 20s. at the Gule of August for waiving this service. Also to station themselves, each day between Candlemas and Hock-day [February 2nd to the second Tuesday after Easter], by three rocks on the sea-shore, nine of them by each rock, with their own boats and tackle, and at their own charges, to take mullet; and the lord has the option of taking one-third of the mullet they net or a third of the price if it is sold; and meanwhile they are quit of other service.

In like manner the lord is entitled to have [i.e., to buy] every porpoise his men take, at 1s. apiece; and all salmon, giving nothing for this except a day's allowance of food to those who take it.

Every season if the lord buys fish in the manor he is to have eight plaice for a penny, eight bream for a penny, one skate for a penny, and twelve pennyworth of conger for elevenpence.

He is entitled to buy hens at a halfpenny each, geese for a penny each before the Birthday of St John Baptist [June 24th], or three halfpence each after that date, and a gallon of beer for a halfpenny.

These requisitions may be made by the lord at his own choice or need, or in his absence by the bailiff or warden [custos] of the manor. Annual value of the fishery with such requisitions, 40s.

It is the duty of all tenants who have boats to convey by water from Totnes, Kingsbridge, and Dartmouth, all wine required by the lord for consumption in the manor. For this service each boat is paid 4d. Value of such carriage, half a mark.

The pleas and profits of the manor court are worth £10 a year.

Total: £117 19s. 10½d.

There are also a number of burgesses at Chillington belonging to this manor, who pay for their burgage tenements £3 1s. 9d. in four equal quarterly payments. The pleas and profits of the borough court are worth £1. Total: £4 1s. 9d.

There is also an outland hundred of Coleridge belonging to this manor; it is worth £5 a year.

Total yearly value of the manor, with Start, the borough, and the hundred: £127 1s. 7½d.

WHAT IS A FARLEU?

IN EXPLANATION of the obscure word *farleu*, or *farley*, the Oxford English Dictionary quotes the following passage from Blout's *Law Dictionary* (1670):
"In the Mannor of West-slapton in Com. Devon, if any

Tenant die possessed of a Cottage, by custome he must pay
sixpence to the Lord for a farley which probably may be in
lieu of a Heriot; for in some Mannors Westward, they difference Farleu as the best good from Heriot the best Beast."

Then follows a quotation from *Notes & Queries*, 25 October,
1851. "Devonshire leases for lives often reserve a money payment on the death of each life as a *heriot* or *farlieu*." The etymology of the word is said to be unknown; and no examples
of its use are quoted outside Devonshire.

In going through the Tavistock records, I have kept an eye
open for anything which might throw light on the mysterious
term; with the result that several documents can now be cited
which help to explain its origin and meaning.

A lease of Troswell, in the manor of Werrington, granted
by the abbot of Tavistock in 1316, provides that the lessee may
withdraw, taking all his goods and chattels with him, at any
time during the currency of the lease, or alternatively when its
term of forty years shall have expired, on payment in either case
of sixpence *nomine farborgh*.[1] In a lease of Burnshall, in Milton
Abbot, drawn up twelve months later, and in two other leases
of the same period, the word is spelt *farburgh*.[2] It appears to
be a compound, the second element of which is *borh*, a pledge;
and it is invariably used in connection with the departure of a
tenant. In these leases it is not the annual rent that is the main
consideration, but the premium or entry fine paid on taking
up the lease. From the lord's point of view, therefore, a tenant
who surrendered his lease before it ran out was providing a
welcome opportunity for levying a new premium from his
successor at an earlier date than would otherwise have been
possible.

A Werrington lease dated 22 May 1334 permits the tenant
to throw up his lease on payment of sixpence, but does not

[1] "Et si predictus Henricus, heredes et assignati sui, in fine termini predicti,
vel infra, a predicta terra recedere voluerint, volumus et concedimus eisdem
quod quieti sint pro sex denariis nomine farborgh, et recedant cum omnibus
rebus et catallis suis absque omni calumpnia nostri et successorum nostrorum."
—W. D Bdle 73, no. 95.

[2] *ibid.*, Bdle 53, no. 223 (1s.); also, in the same bundle, nos. 122 (Taviton,
1319, 6d.) and 32 (Grendon, 1345, 1s.). In all three it is provided that the
outgoing tenant may take the year's crop.

refer to the payment by any distinctive name.[1] Henceforth, in Tavistock leases, the place of *farborgh* is taken by *farlevium*, or farleu, a distinct compound, which frequently occurs in association with a heriot.[2] The heriot, as is well known, was a death-duty; and it is clearly distinguished from a farleu in the lease of a fulling-mill at Parkwood, Tavistock, dated 1481. Here the tenant pays a rent of 11s. yearly, and is quit of all manorial dues, including heriot, but is bound to pay the landlord a farleu of 3s. 4d. at the expiry of his lease.[3] Similarly in 1447 and 1474 land at Nether Wilminstone in Tavistock is let subject to farleus of 10s. and 6s. 8d. at the end of the respective terms, and subject also to heriots of the same value, payable not only at death but—here confusion begins to appear—on surrender of the unexpired lease.[4] The fact that the same amount was always charged for both dues no doubt helped to blur the distinction between them. One lease, drawn up in 1486, stipulates that the best beast on the farm shall be given to the lord as heriot at the expiry of the term or as farleu on previous surrender.[5] But these documents are exceptional in seeking to maintain a distinction, however erroneously, between the two dues. In the great majority of fifteenth-century leases a mixed formula is used. The lessee, his heirs or assigns, will pay "a heriot or farleu" (*a*) after the death of any occupier while the lease is current; (*b*) on surrender of the unexpired lease; (*c*) at the expiry of the lease. The words have thus come to be used almost interchangeably of any payment, whether in money or in kind, made by a tenant to his landlord when a change of occupancy is brought about by circumstances envisaged in the lease.[6]

The fourteenth-century leases quoted above dispel all this

[1] Bdle 73, no. 96.

[2] Mr R. E. Latham has collected several examples of *farlevium* and *ferlevium*, all from Devon and Cornwall, of which the earliest is dated 1298. I have to thank him for this information, and also for a suggestion concerning the derivation of *farborgh*, which I have adopted in the text.

[3] W. D Bdle 53, no. 70.

[4] Tavistock Abbey White Book, fo. 21.

[5] *ibid.*, fo. 12 *b*.

[6] A typical formula is: "Et dabit . . . nomine herieti sive farleuii post decessum vel recessum cuiuslibet tenentis decedentis vel recedentis infra terminum predictum, ac etiam in fine termini."

confusion, and make it clear that a farleu, strictly speaking, is a payment due to the lessor on the determination of a lease, either when it expires in the normal course, or earlier at the discretion of the lessee. Legally it is rooted in the notion that every change of occupancy must be signalized by some public recognition of the lord's right: in this case, a small payment, tendered no doubt in open manor-court. And since the legalized withdrawal of a tenant from his holding has obvious affinities with the licensed departure of a soldier or official from his place of duty, one and the same term covers both. In other words, *farleu* is just a variant of the modern *furlough*.

In its military sense *furlough* seems to have been imported from the Netherlands during the seventeenth century: thus, Ben Jonson speaks of "a Low-Countrey vorloffe." We have seen that as a legal term it enjoyed a much earlier currency, albeit one localized in the south-west. Further research may ascertain whether, as seems likely, its original meaning was that of a payment made by a *gebur* or other dependent cultivator for licence to throw up his holding and to quit the manor.[1] Etymologically it is related to the Middle Low German *forlof*. Professor C. L. Wrenn, to whom I am indebted for some helpful observations, remarks that an unrecorded Old English word *farleaf* would regularly become *farleve* in Middle English. The latter, written *farleue*, would account for the Latinized spelling found in fifteenth-century documents. In any case, the basic meaning is *leave to fare*, or *to go forth*.

A FARMER'S LEASE

ON THE right bank of the Tavy, about half a mile above the confluence of that river and the Walkham, there stood, until the nineteenth century, a farm called Blackmoorham. Today no visible trace of it remains except a cow-shed; but the wood that clothes the river-bank is still

---

[1] Cf F. M. Stenton, *Anglo-Saxon England*, p. 309. Fines for entry and withdrawal were paid by free tenants on the Ely manors; they were called *onfare* and *offare* respectively.—N. Neilson, *Customary Rents*, Oxford, 1910, p. 89.

called Blackmoorham Wood. At the beginning of the fifteenth century Blackmoorham and Ramsham, a farm half a mile further up the Tavy, were held of the abbot of Tavistock by John Pasmere at a yearly rent of ten shillings. Pasmere, a burgess of Tavistock, and portreeve of that borough in 1404, did not work the farms himself. On the 3rd of May 1402 he underlet the whole of the premises, except a close already in separate occupation, to one Robert Weryng, senior, for twelve years, on terms which are of some interest.[1]

The agreement provides that the land shall be cultivated for the joint advantage of lessor and lessee, who will divide between them in equal shares the cost of seed-corn, repairs to ironwork, and repairs to the farm buildings, Pasmere being responsible for walls and main timbers, Weryng for roofs and fences. The purchase and carriage of sea-sand is to be paid for by whichever of them shall wish to apply that form of manure to the soil.

Pasmere, as lessor, is to pay the rent due to the chief lord. He agrees to stock the farm with 8 plough-oxen, 6 cows, 1 horse, 30 ewes, 1 gander with 3 geese, and 1 cock with 6 hens; and he is to make good any losses of stock from year to year until the lease expires, when all this livestock will revert to him. Further, he provides one plough, complete with the necessary ironwork, a wooden saddle and crook for the pack-horse, and shoeing for the eight plough-oxen.

The lessor, in short, supplies the capital, Weryng the labour. Weryng also makes his own small contribution to the live-stock, namely, one cow and a mare. Repairs will cost him nothing but his labour, since he is entitled to housebote, hay-bote, faldbote, and firebote from the surrounding woods.

The corn-crops are to be divided equally between lessor and lessee, the division being made by weight except in the last year, when the sheaves are to be counted on the ground. Weryng keeps all the produce of his own cow. All other produce—milk, butter, cheese, calves, lambs, poultry, and wool—are to be shared equally between the parties, subject to the customary allowance of butter, cheese, and milk for labourers employed at harvest. Lambs and calves are to be

[1] W. D Bdle 3, no. 5.

accounted for annually on the 3rd of May, but are not to be removed until they are three years old, except at the expiry of the lease, or earlier if both parties consent.

A penalty of 40s. is provided against any infringement of these terms on either side.

It will be seen that although the agreement has some features in common with the stock-and-land lease which, according to Thorold Rogers, became usual towards the end of the fourteenth century, it differs therefrom in that the tenant pays no rent. Weryng is rather in the position of a *métayer*. His tenancy is a virtual partnership under which lessor and farmer share the profits of the farm, capital and labour receiving approximately equal dividends. It seems unlikely that Weryng's case was unique; and it would be interesting to know just how widespread such agreements were in fifteenth-century Devon. The great defect of *métayage*, from the lessor's point of view, is that it provides the tenant with so many opportunities for cheating. In the case of Blackmoorham this risk was minimized, since Pasmere was on the spot, or near enough to exercise a fairly constant supervision.

A CELLARER'S ACCOUNT-BOOK

AMONG the surviving records of Tavistock Abbey is an account-book detailing the cellarer's expenditure during the forty-three weeks from 15 July 1536 to 11 May 1537. It is an oblong book (12½ by 4¼ inches), written on paper, and consisting of 56 pages sewn into three pieces of old parchment. These last had evidently been thrown out from the muniment room as worthless, but they contain records of the borough court of Hatherleigh for 2 October, 8 November, 14 December, 1391, and 16 September 1392, besides a precentor's undated account of the same period.

From what is known about the population of the abbey—monks, household servants, visitors, and pensioners—on the eve of the Dissolution, it can be said that the number of mouths for whom the cellarer catered day by day was seldom less than fifty, and may often have been more. The account-book shows an average expenditure of 32s. 4d. weekly. Not all of this was spent on victuals. There were purchases of odds and ends for the kitchen: spigots, tallow, ladles, a strainer, and a frying-pan, the latter an expensive item, costing 1s. 1d. There were also, on occasions, such miscellaneous expenses as the following:

For makyng of candelles & makyng clene of ye checkyn
cortt .. .. vjd.
For j horssemanys exp's & rewarde to Mr Wyse ys
man .. .. xd.
For mendyng of ye hagge [hedge] at ye Scelerys [Cel-
larer's] Close for ij days .. .. iiijd.
For delvyng of ye gardyn .. .. iiijd.

On the other hand, some of the provisions consumed make no appearance in the account because, as will be noted presently, they were supplied from other sources.

Readers acquainted with the history of English diet will know beforehand that vegetables make very little showing on the bill of fare. Peas, beans, and parsnips occur, but seldom. A good deal of coarse oatmeal was consumed; it was called *gert* (i.e., grit), and cost 8d. a peck. There are rare purchases of rice, at 1½d. and 2d. a pound. Bread, again, makes only one appearance; there was no need to buy it, for wheat and rye were grown on the demesne-lands, and 79 quarters of wheat came in every year from tenants at Plymstock who paid their rent in kind. Butter is purchased very often; milk and cream occasionally; but for cheese the abbey relied upon its home-farms. In 1537 the dairy at Hurdwick, near Tavistock, one of the main sources of supply, produced 52 stone of cheese, of which 17 stone were delivered to the abbey, 1 to the vicar of Tavistock, 2 to the prior of Scilly, 1 each to the auditor and the dairymaid, 11 to the farm hands and harvest workers, and the remainder sold at 8d. a stone, the stone being reckoned as 16 pounds.

The reference to the "chicken court," already quoted, implies that hens were kept on the premises; but eggs were frequently purchased. "For eggs, ixd." is a typical entry, leaving the price indeterminate.

Fish are called sayn-fish (from *seine*) if they are netted, hoke- (i.e., hook-) fish if caught by rod and line. Those mentioned by name are codling, cod, hake (a very frequent purchase), bass, ling, herring, mackerel, and pilchards, besides, of course, salmon, which as a rule is fresh, but once, in February, salted. Half a salmon usually costs 7d. or 8d. The "chunger," or conger, a rare visitant, costs 5d. Oysters arrive in mid-November, at 4d. a hundred, and are in constant request until March, by which time the price has come down to 2d.

During Lent no meat is purchased; but on Easter eve the end of abstinence is heralded by the following items:

For a vele	iijs. iiijd.
For a vele	ijs.
For a muttyn	xxijd.
Half a muttyn	xiiijd.
Half a muttyn	xijd.
For a lamme w^t ye p't	xiijd.
ij velys de Herdwyck	—

Those who have tasted real mutton, as distinguished from the elderly lamb which is passed off as mutton nowadays, are said to relish it far above any lamb, however young and tender; and the Tavistock monks clearly shared that preference. On the other hand, they consumed far more veal than beef. When the cellarer bought a "pygge," as he did very often, the price varied between 5½d. and 8d.

Chickens (1d. each) and capons (at 6d., 7d., or 8d. apiece) appear frequently; ducks and geese more seldom; the plover only once. From October to February woodcock is constantly in demand. There are no other game birds. Pigeons would be supplied from the manorial dovecotes, and rabbits from the warren in Dolvin Wood, but sometimes "ij copyl of conys" are bought for 1s. 4d. An item "for ij trusse of venison, vijd," occurs only once, the monastery having its own deer-park on the edge of Whitchurch Down. From other documents it appears that a few swans and peacocks were kept about the place, to be roasted for the lord abbot's table at Pentecost.

Salt, at 9d. or 10d. the bushel, pepper (11d. for half a pound), mustard (10d. for half a peck), oil, vinegar, nutmeg, ginger (2d. an ounce), cloves (5½d. an ounce), mace (do.), and cinnamon (1s. 2d. an ounce) make up the account for condiments and spices.

It may be assumed that the orchards were not unproductive; yet apples are bought very frequently, and pears on occasion, as are also figs at 1d. a pound, raisins at 1½d., and almonds at 3d. Prunes are seen only once.

The cellarer was not responsible for drinks. On each anniversary of the five principal benefactors of the abbey the almoner laid out 2s. 2d. on wine for the brethren, and 6s. 8d. on bread for distribution to the poor. Cider was brewed at Plymstock, and shipped up the Tamar to Morwellham. The fact that one of the officials bore the title of *medarius* would seem to imply that mead was brewed or at any rate drunk; but I have found no particulars of this. Ale, of course, was consumed at Tavistock, as elsewhere throughout England, on an oceanic scale.

At Easter, the Assumption, Christmas, and Epiphany, the purchases of meat are noticeably heavy. At Michaelmas a goose costs 6d. On the 21st of March, feast of St Benedict, the patriarch of Black Monks, a rather unusually long bill for raisins, almonds, and spices indicates that the community of Tavistock, without breaking the rule of Lenten abstinence, indulged in what the author of *The Rites of Durham* termed "a scholastical and moderate congratulation amongst themselves."

A CHAPTER OF RELIGIOUS HISTORY

I

A CYNIC might find some amusement in comparing the manifesto put out in 1549 by "the Commoners of Devonshyre and Cornwall in diuers Campes by East and West of Excettor" with the petitions forwarded from Plymouth and Tavistock nearly a hundred years later. At the earlier date the populace had risen in spontaneous revolt against the religious changes. They demanded the re-establishment of the chief monasteries, and utterly rejected the new English prayer-book, which they irreverently likened to "a Christmas game."[1] This determined loyalty to the old faith outlived the suppression of the revolt, and persisted into the early decades of Elizabeth's reign. Cuthbert Mayne, the first missionary priest to be executed under the penal statutes, was a Devonshire man. Strype, describing the visitation of Oxford in 1579, says: "in Exeter College, of eighty were found but four obedient subjects; all the rest secret or open Roman affectionaries . . . These were chiefly such as came out of the western parts, where popery greatly prevailed."[2] Yet by 1641 the townsmen of Plymouth were dividing the blame for all their troubles impartially between Turkish pirates, Irish rebels, and "popish lords and bishops."[3] Within three generations a county which had given the most convincing proof of its attachment to catholicism had become one of the most firmly Protestant in England.

The crucial question in this, as in all revolutions, was: how much, if any, of the old system shall be preserved? Once the Latin mass and papal jurisdiction had been suppressed, had not innovation gone far enough? There were many, including the queen herself, who thought it had. But to the puritan or low-church party this was merely the first instalment of true

[1] F. Rose-Troup, *The Western Rebellion of 1549*, 1913, p. 221.
[2] Quoted by H. N. Birt, *The Elizabethan Religious Settlement*, 1907, p. 294.
[3] HMC Fourth Report, 1874, p. 114.

reformation. And, as it happened, the men who took in hand the work of protestantizing Devonshire were wholly puritan in sympathy. That unprepossessing nobleman Francis, earl of Bedford, had spent some time at Geneva and still corresponded with Pietro Vermigli ("Peter Martyr"). He and Cecil, so the Spanish ambassador reported, were the two members of Elizabeth's council who busied themselves most to destroy the old faith.[1] Appointed lord lieutenant of Devon, Cornwall, and Dorset in 1558, he threw all his influence into the puritan scale. A visitation in which the Devonshire-born Jewel, bishop of Salisbury, took the most active part, carried out a thorough purge of the cathedral chapter.[2] The dean, sub-dean, and treasurer were all deposed. James Turberville, last catholic bishop of Exeter, and "an honest gentleman" as even Cecil admitted, was removed from his see and spent the remainder of his days a prisoner.[3] His place was taken by William Alley, a man after Bedford's heart; and other key positions were filled by radicals like Richard Tremayne, who as proctor for the Exeter clergy in the convocation of 1562 pressed for the abolition of surplices, copes, and saints' days,

[1] Birt, *op. cit.*, p. 47.

[2] Jewel to Peter Martyr, 2 November 1559: "If inveterate obstinacy was found anywhere, it was altogether among the priests . . . But let them make what disturbance they please; we have in the meantime disturbed them from their rank and office."—*ibid.*, p. 177.

[3] In his propaganda Cecil stated that Bishop Turberville "lived at his own liberty to the end of his life." The known facts are that he was deposed in August 1559 and committed to the Tower 18 June 1560. In September 1563 he was handed over to Grindal, the Elizabethan bishop of London, in whose custody he remained until January 1565, when the Privy Council permitted him to be released on condition that he gave bonds to remain at some fixed address in London and to present himself before Grindal whenever summoned. In June of the same year he was re-arrested and sent again to the Tower. There is no record of his death or burial. Two contemporary writers, Rishton and Bridgewater, state that he died in prison, and G. E. Phillips conjectures 1 November 1570 as the date of his decease (*The Extinction of the Ancient Hierarchy*, 1905, pp. 198, 245, 247, 349, 358). There are indications, however, that he spent his last years in seclusion at a house named Gaulden, or Golden, in the remote parish of Tolland, Somerset: see *Proc. Somerset Arch. and Nat. Hist. Soc.*, XXIII, 1877, pp. 70–87. According to the calendar of the Prerogative Court of Canterbury administration of his estate was granted so long afterwards as April 1667, but there is no entry in the act-book of that year.

of "all curious singing and playing of the organs," and of the use of the cross in baptism.[1] One by one the parsonages were occupied by men who shared this outlook. Bishop Jewel in his last years receded from the puritan extreme. He still professed a desire to see all vestiges of popery swept out of the Church, but when a candidate for a benefice obstinately declined to wear a surplice, the bishop refused to institute him. His *protégé* Hooker, like himself a Devonian by birth, was destined to write the classic defence of the anglican compromise. But by the time Hooker published his *Laws of Ecclesiasticall Politie*, Devon had become a puritan stronghold.

In the conference between the high- and low-church factions which took place at Hampton Court in 1604, the leading spokesman on the puritan side was John Rainolds, or Reynolds, a native of Pinhoe, near Exeter. Rainolds had been scolded by Queen Elizabeth for his "obstinate preciseness." At Hampton Court, when he objected to the phrase in the marriage service, "With my body I thee worship," King James told him that if he had a good wife of his own he would see the matter in a different light.[2] The conference having failed to reconcile the disputants, all the clergy were ordered to subscribe a series of new canons enforcing anglican discipline. At first the stalwarts of Devon showed a bold front. They employed one Melanchthon Jewel, a former basket-maker and an itinerant preacher, to consult the lawyers and to stir up sympathizers in other districts. But Jewel was arrested, and in a very short time the opposition collapsed, only five clergymen

---

[1] J. Strype, *Annals of the Reformation*, Oxford, 1824, I, p. 500. The dean of Exeter, Gregory Dodds, associated himself with these demands. Tremayne had been in Germany during Mary's reign. Installed as treasurer of the cathedral in 1560, rector of Doddiscombsleigh 1561–64, and of Combe Martin from 1569, he was the earl of Bedford's candidate for the bishopric in succession to William Alley, but not being appointed, remained treasurer until his death in 1584.

[2] *Dictionary of National Biography*. The most enduring result of the conference was the Authorized Version of the Bible (1611), said to have been initiated by Rainolds himself. He took charge of the group which translated the Hebrew prophets. In the work of biblical translation he was forestalled by his catholic brother William, professor of divinity and Hebrew in the English College at Rheims, who had a hand in Gregory Martin's version of the New Testament (1582).

forfeiting their benefices in the whole diocese of Exeter.[1]

The cathedral city furnished a type of the puritan hero in the person of a well-to-do shopkeeper, Ignatius Jourdain, who became mayor in 1617. During the great epidemic of 1625, which put all the magistrates to flight, he won general admiration by remaining in the city and taking care of the poor. This worthy's nightly custom of patrolling the ale-houses made him the scourge of late tipplers. In the morning he always rose from bed at three o'clock, "and that in the coldest season of the year, to meditate and pray in secret" until six, when he conducted family prayers. Between these activities he found leisure to beget seventeen children. As M.P. for Exeter he promoted a bill to punish adultery with death; but this measure did not become law until ten years after his own decease, when it was largely nullified by the reluctance of juries to convict.[2]

A climate of opinion which nourished men like Jourdain was naturally unfavourable to Laudian high-churchmanship. The Stuart policy, "no bishop, no king," ranged Devonshire on the opposition side in politics. In this connection it is only necessary to recall that two of the five members charged with treason in 1642 sat for Devonshire constituencies: Pym for Tavistock and Strode for Bere Alston.

On the clerical side the prevailing temper is well illustrated in the career of Thomas Ford (1598–1674). Born at Brixton, near Plymouth, and educated at Magdalen Hall, Oxford, Ford distinguished himself, as a graduate of thirty-three, by thundering from the pulpit of the university church against the president of Magdalen, who had changed the communion-table into an altar. Expelled from the university in consequence, he was invited by the corporation of Plymouth to become their preacher; but the king and Laud intervened, and the offer had to be withdrawn. Ford then went to Germany as chaplain to an English regiment commanded by George Fleetwood, which whom he was connected by marriage. He stayed abroad nearly six years. Then the Fleetwoods presented him to a family living in Northamptonshire, which he held until the outbreak of the civil war. An active adherent of the

[1] W. H. Frere, *The English Church in the Reigns of Elizabeth and James 1*, 1904, pp. 316–21.
[2] DA xxix, 1897, pp. 350 sqq.

party now denominated presbyterian, he became a member of the Westminster Assembly, and preached before both houses of parliament. Early in 1647 he came down to Exeter; and there can be little doubt that he came on a mission from the party headquarters.

Having a majority in parliament, the presbyterians were now endeavouring to build up their own system on the ruins of the anglican church. Two new catechisms were drawn up, expounding the body of doctrine set forth in their famous Westminster Confession. As a substitute for episcopal government they formulated a scheme of provincial assemblies meeting half-yearly. Ministers were to be elected by their congregations, and were to meet once a month in district assemblies, or 'classes', which in turn were subordinate to the provincial and national assemblies, and these, in the last resort, to parliament. But the presbyterians were hampered by the growing influence of a party still further to the left, the congregationalists, otherwise called independents, recruited mainly from the artisan class, whereas the presbyterians were for the most part men of property. Hence the presbyterian scheme ordained by parliament was never put into full operation. But Devon was one of the counties where the soil was most congenial, and Ford was at hand to sow and water it. There is evidence that the county was divided into seven 'classes', and that from 1649 onwards these district gatherings controlled the ordination of new ministers.[1] Meanwhile numbers of anglican clergy were ejected from their parishes. Between 1643 and 1660 142 benefices in Devon and 88 in Cornwall were put under sequestration.[2]

The further step of setting up a provincial assembly for Devon as a whole was taken in October 1655. According to Calamy, it was George Hughes, formerly vicar of Tavistock, and now of St Andrew's, Plymouth, who took the initiative on this occasion, acting in concert with Ford.[3] They called a

[1] W. A. Shaw, *History of the English Church, 1640–1660*, 1900, II, pp. 374, 447, point out that the ministers of the First Division are on record as performing the work of ordination in 1654, nearly eighteen months before the establishment of the Exeter Assembly.

[2] A. G. Matthews, *Walker Revised*, 1934, p. xiv.

[3] E. Calamy, *The Nonconformist's Memorial*, 1802, II, p. 60.

meeting at Exeter, which was attended by twenty-two other ministers representing the seven divisions of the county, and drew up an elaborate constitution, providing for subdivisional meetings to be held every six weeks, divisional meetings once a quarter, and a general meeting yearly. Ordinations would be the business of the divisions, but the general assembly would control the local associations and seek to promote uniformity in doctrine, worship, and discipline. A moderator would be elected to take the chair, and a scribe to keep the minutes. All questions should be decided by majority vote.[1]

At a second meeting, held in May 1656, these articles were signed by 108 ministers, and also by two leading congregationalists, Lewis Stucley and Thomas Mall, who at this time shared with Ford the use of the cathedral, preaching in the nave while Ford did so in the choir.[2] With a clear-cut scheme of organization, the Assembly deliberately avoided nailing its colours to any doctrinal mast. All it asked of members was "that none shall wilfully contradict" the Westminster Confession "in his preaching;" and to this the congregationalists were allowed to add a rider: "in any of the fundamentall doctrines therein contained." To compensate for this dilution of an already somewhat tasteless brew, they undertook to refrain from sarcasm in the pulpit.[3] During the next three years debates between the left and right wings occupied the Assembly to the exclusion of most other business. In 1658 the machinery of divisional or 'classical' meetings began to creak, but meetings continued to be held down to the fall of the Commonwealth. The minutes of the Assembly break off in 1659; and then or soon afterwards the whole organization was overwhelmed by a tidal wave of anglican reaction.

---

[1] The minutes of the Assembly from 18 October 1655 to 5 May 1659 were printed by R. N. Worth in DA IX, 1877, pp. 279–88. Shaw, *op. cit.*, II, p. 448, is obviously right in holding that the first list of twenty-three subscribers printed by Worth (*loc. cit.*, p. 281) gives the names of those who attended the preliminary meeting in October.

[2] According to Bishop Ward, there were "no greater enemies in the world" than Ford and Stucley. They attacked each other in books and sermons, despite their "sweet concurrence" in "the principles of rebellion" (DCNQ XXI, 1941, p. 359).

[3] DA *loc. cit.*, pp. 280 (article 10), 284 (articles 5 and 6).

On the 24th of August 1662, when the Act of Uniformity came into force, seventy-three Devonshire ministers forfeited their livings.[1] The leaders went into retirement, Ford living very privately in the earl of Bedford's house and afterwards at Exmouth, while Hughes, after nine months' internment on Drake's Island, settled quietly at Kingsbridge. But though the attempt to suppress anglicanism and to capture the endowments which the anglicans had taken over from their catholic predecessors thus ended in failure, the defeated party could still muster powerful support. Bishop Ward declared that at least fourteen justices of the peace in Devon were "arrant presbyterians." Sir John Davie headed the list; his mansion at Creedy was their "chief place of resort." Sir Walter Young and Sir Edmund Fowell were "great favourers" of the party, as were also Thomas Reynell, "a very dangerous Comon wealthsman," John Hale, "a great Oliverian," and John Arscott and his wife, both "very bad."[2] Twenty-two of the ejected ministers were living in the episcopal city. Three of them, including Stucley himself, were reported in 1665 to be "holding conventicles."[3]

The Declaration of Indulgence called forth an address of thanks signed by seventy-two ministers, and prompted Stucley's adherents to inform Charles II that they could not but regard his majesty as "the Breath of their Nostrills" and "the Repairer of their Breaches."[4] In the twelve months during which the Declaration held good, the number of licences taken out for dissenting preachers and meeting-houses in Devonshire was higher than in any other county. Classified under the several denominations, these licences are a good index of their relative strength.

Presbyterian	119
Congregationalist	32

[1] Matthews, *Calamy Revised*, p. xii. The total numbers of those ejected in 1660–62 were: 121 in Devon and 42 in Cornwall (*ibid.*).

[2] J. Simmons in DCNQ xxi, 1941, pp. 226 (from Bodleian MS. Add. c. 305), 284.

[3] *ibid.*, p. 287; G. Lyon Turner, *Original Records of Early Nonconformity*, 1911, I, p. 184.

[4] Lyon Turner, *op. cit.*, I, p. 204.

Baptist 7

Quaker 2

——

160[1]

The Declaration was cancelled on the 7th of March 1673, and before the end of the same month the Test Act obliged all office-holders to take the oath of supremacy and to communicate according to the anglican rite. For the next sixteen years dissenters had to face intermittent bouts of persecution. Every loophole that Stuart policy tried to open for them was blocked by their own intolerance. Drugged with no-popery propaganda, they told the house of commons they would sooner forgo their liberty than consent to share it with their fellow-Christians of the Roman fold. (Their mouthpiece on this occasion was an alderman named Love!)[2] A blaze of publicity attended their sufferings, which however were considerably mitigated by the attentions of their friends. One of them, locked up in Exeter castle, was said to be "in a fair way to become rich," and George Trosse relates that when he and four of his brethren were imprisoned there, fourteen wealthy citizens took turns in sending them a plentiful dinner every day.[3] Finally, the downfall of James II removed any danger of a relief they might have had to share with catholics. The Toleration Act of 1689 allowed them, on certain conditions, to have their own teachers, preachers, and places of worship. Henceforth Protestant nonconformity enjoyed legal recognition. The heirs of the Elizabethan settlement, renouncing the ideal of a united national Church for which they had contended so long, ranged themselves on one side or the other of the dividing line between 'church' and 'chapel'.

The nonconformist clergy of Devon hastened to avail themselves of the new freedom. On the 17th of March 1691 fifteen ministers and one candidate for ordination held a meeting at Tiverton, which was also attended by delegates from the western division of Somerset. At least three of the ministers were survivors from the old Exeter Assembly. This

[1] *ibid.*, II, pp. 1144–85.

[2] D. Neal, *History of the Puritans*, 1822, IV, p. 418.

[3] DCNQ *loc. cit.*, p. 227; J. Murch, *History of the Presbyterian and General Baptist Churches in the West of England*, 1835, p. 382.

body they proceeded to reconstitute. All of those present were presbyterians, and the eleven articles of agreement to which they put their signatures were modelled on those of 1655. But at the next meeting, held at Topsham (23–24 June 1691), and described as a General Meeting of the United Brethren of the City and County of Exeter and County of Devon, the veteran John Flavell of Dartmouth, who took the chair as moderator, persuaded them to admit congregationalists into membership, in accordance with a scheme which had just been accepted by their brethren in London. It was proposed to hold a general assembly of the two denominations in the western counties once a year at Bristol, Taunton, or Exeter; and meetings were held accordingly at Taunton in 1691 and Bristol in 1694. (Faithful to the spirit which had called forth Milton's *Areopagitica*, the Bristol meeting decreed "that no controversial Book or Sermon be printed without the approbation of the Provincial Association, or such select numbers of Ministers as shalbe appointed in each Division for that end.") But the organization struck less vigorous roots in the other counties, and after 1694 the scheme of joint meetings was tacitly abandoned. The Devonshire Assembly made one excursion to Plymouth in 1695. Thenceforth it regularly met at Exeter in the spring and autumn of each year. The proceedings opened with a sermon; in 1699, when the preacher spoke for more than two hours, it was agreed "that all future Preachers have warning given them to keep to their hour: And that the Clark turn the Glass when the Text is nam'd and take it away as soon as 'tis run out." (Appropriately enough, this preacher's name was Toogood.) Then another minister extemporized a prayer; and finally the gathering turned its attention to the business of the day.[1]

Although the Assembly exercised some functions of a quasi-episcopal character, it would be an error to regard it as the governing body of the nonconformist churches. It was rather a professional guild of clergy. Its principal objects were to

[1] The minutes of the Assembly from 17 March 1691 to 4 September 1717 and from 1721 to 1753 are preserved in the Dr Williams Library, Gordon Square, Bloomsbury. They have not been printed; and many of them are in cipher. Those of the intervening years, the period of the great trinitarian controversy, have probably been destroyed.

assist the training of candidates, to regulate admissions to the clerical body, and to maintain a high standard of professional decorum. At the very first meeting it took steps to raise a "Fund for pious Uses," that is to say, for subsidizing poor congregations and educating likely aspirants to the ministry. In the first five years it spent £663 12s. 2d. on these objects, out of a total income of £770 13s. 7½d. In 1694 it resolved that "no candidate should be ordained by any of the United Brethren of this County but by order of the Assembly." Three years later a protest was received from Dorset: one of the members, John Ashwood, had been ordaining a minister at Bridport *motu proprio*. He was asked to "forbear such practices," and a motion authorizing private ordinations was rejected "after much debate." The normal procedure was for a young man who had completed his training in philosophy and theology at some recognized academy to apply to the Assembly for a preaching licence. He then preached by invitation in one pulpit after another, until a particular congregation proposed that he should settle with them. There ensued a period of trial, during which a highly critical audience formed their own estimate of his oratorical powers. (Two delegates from South Molton inform the Assembly that Mr Rutter "doth not give Satisfaction; That they cannot profit by him; that He is not Popular, nor Lively, that he doth not rouze them." The Assembly is of opinion that these are trivial objections; but Mr Rutter, "forseeing some difficulties that may probably ensue on his going there, voluntarily quits his interest in the people of South Molton,"[1]) During his probation the sacraments would be administered by visiting clergy. If his preaching gave satisfaction he became a settled pastor and was expected to present himself to the Assembly for ordination. This was a new and formidable trial. On the evening before the ceremony the candidate was examined by a committee of ministers, to whom he read a Latin thesis on some theological question set beforehand, and answered any objections they might put forward. Next he read out a profession of faith, composed by himself for the occasion; and he might be asked

[1] The critical faculty appears to have been highly developed at South Molton. An earlier preacher complained that some of his flock there "chose rather to ly at home on the Lords day than to attend on his preaching."

to translate a verse or two from the Greek Testament into Latin and English. If he satisfied the examiners, the public ordination took place next day. It began and ended with hymns and prayers. After a sermon the candidate was required to give an account of his beliefs, standing opposite the pulpit, and to answer any questions the preacher might think fit to propound. Then the senior minister present recommended him to God and "set him apart for the pastoral office." It is hardly surprising that some young preachers fought shy of such an ordeal. In 1709, "upon complaint that some Candidates who are settled and constant Preachers . . . defer their Ordination, whence several inconveniences proceed, viz: Some Children dy un-baptiz'd, Dissenters are forc'd to carry their children to the Publick Churches to have them baptiz'd, etc.," the Assembly resolved that in future a promise should be exacted from all applicants for preaching licences that they would offer themselves for ordination soon after receiving a call to some particular congregation.

Sometimes a new 'meeting' would be set up, and supplied by direct nomination from the Assembly. Thus, in 1700 Plympton applied for a minister, reporting that there were about 200 'hearers', who would raise £25 a year themselves in addition to the £6 already granted from the London Presbyterian Fund. In 1709 Hatherleigh, with about 150 hearers, made a similar application. Sometimes requests came from very far afield. In 1707 the people of Carolina asked for a minister to be sent out there. Six years later "Mr Bishop informed the Assembly from Sir John Davie that a new Colledge being erected in Connecticut Colony in New England, their Agent Mr Dummer desires Encouragement from this Assembly for a Library." Sir John responded with a subscription of ten pounds, and thirty ministers with gifts of books.

While formally disclaiming any intention of meddling with politics, the Assembly carried a resolution in May 1696 assuring William III that they would all give up the ghost if he should "miscarry"; and ten years later they decided to pray for the house of Hanover. From time to time cases of conscience were brought up for debate. ("May a man marry his deceased wife's niece?" "In case a person can't drink Wine, may not beer or cyder be receiv'd by such a one in the Lord's Supper?") The Assembly also controlled the forms of worship. (1707: "Resolv'd that 'tis convenient for us ordinarily to administer the Lords Supper at least once in Two Months in our respective Congregations. Upon inquiry it appeared that the Lords Supper was administered once a month in Exeter, Plymouth, and Bideford." 1709: "Agreed That 'tis expedient that only Davids Psalms, and Scriptural Hymns, be ordinarily us'd in our Publick Assemblies for Religious Worship." 1710: "It is generally expedient that Children be baptiz'd in publick.")

Occasions for rebuking sin were happily infrequent. "One of the Brethren, Mr Ball, spake with much warmth against Ministers wearing *Long Light Powder'd Wigs*, as that which gives great offence to serious people, and is a great hinderance to the success of our Ministry." The worst case with which the Assembly had to deal was that of John Edwards. This unruly member first gave trouble by causing a local schism at Honiton. Scarcely had this been put to rights when he "fell into a notorious scandal." "The Assembly was informed that Mr John Edwards of Honiton's wife was deliver'd of a Child in twenty weeks after they were married; that he did at first for a considerable time deny that he ever lay with her before Marriage, offering to call God to wittness, and take the Sacrament upon it. But now owns it and endeavours to justify it, behaving himself proudly and impudently, discovering no Signs of Repentance for his foul miscarriage and the great Scandal he hath brought upon the United Brethren." For such a hardened wretch there could be no place in the Assembly. He was cast out; and from another source we learn that he rounded off his infamous career by joining the established Church.[1]

The minutes of 1701 give a list of forty-four ordained ministers and twenty preachers. In 1715, according to a report sent to Daniel Neal, the historian of puritanism, there were seventy-six meeting-houses in Devonshire, of which fifty-two were presbyterian.[2] They were staffed, as we have

[1] He finished up as a preacher at Northleigh (Murch, *op. cit.*, p. 316).
[2] BM Add. MS. 9428, ff. 180, 181 (letter from Joseph Hunter to Lysons, giving a transcript of Neal's return).

seen, by a highly educated and professionally trained body of
men, whose corporate authority was upheld and fostered by
the Exeter Assembly. The clergy, being financially dependent
on their congregations, needed a counterpoise to the element
of lay control, and this the Assembly gave them; it was a sort
of clerical trade union. Its authority rested chiefly on the
control of ordinations. But the power of the laity, and especially of the well-to-do who subscribed most largely to the funds,
could not be safely challenged. The plutocratic class which had
so effectually asserted itself against the Stuarts formed the
backbone of the presbyterian body; and presbyterianism appealed to them for this reason above all, that it gave them a
degree of control they could never enjoy under the Roman or
the anglican systems. Even the humbler members of the
congregation, possessing as they did the right of objecting to a
preacher who did not "rouze" them, could look with pity on
their anglican neighbours, condemned perhaps to listen Sunday
after Sunday to some interminable bore in whose appointment
they had had no say.

It might have been expected that questions of theology
would be left to the Assembly; but in fact it was a theological
crisis that moved the laymen to assert their supremacy, and
that in the most downright fashion. A leading baptist, Matthew
Caffyn, had lately reopened the great debate which had con-
vulsed the Church of the third and fourth centuries. The
doctrine which identified Christ with the second Person of
the divine Trinity was now again called in question. In 1700
the national assembly of baptist churches passed a resolution
tolerating heterodox opinions on this subject. Twelve years
later the anglican writer Samuel Clarke published a disquiet-
ing book on *The Scripture Doctrine of the Trinity*, which was
eagerly read by dissenters, and in particular by the students
of Joseph Hallett's presbyterian academy at Exeter. The
academy itself was orthodox, but these ardent young spirits
found a ready welcome at the house of the baptist minister,
where they were free to talk as much heresy as they pleased.
Gradually the infection spread. Several of the older ministers
ranged themselves in secret on the heretical side. One of them,
James Peirce, a man of wide reading and an able pamphleteer,
was very generally suspected, and not unjustly, of cherishing

heterodox opinions which he did not mean to avow if he could help it. Peirce in fact concealed his doubts under a mask of the grossest bibliolatry, declaring that without scriptural warrant he would not commit himself to the proposition that two and three make five. The Assembly evaded the issue for as long as possible; but in 1718, at the September meeting, after pro- longed discussion, it adopted a trinitarian formula as express- ing the "general sense" of its members. By this time the affair was being hotly canvassed by the citizens at large, and the Exeter presses teemed with anonymous unitarian pamphlets. Excitement mounted still further when Sir Robert Price, the judge of assize, attributed the increase of crime in Devonshire to the decay of orthodox religion. It was at this point that the leading laymen decided to intervene.

A committee had been established in 1687 to look after the temporal business of the three presbyterian congregations in the city.[1] It consisted of thirteen laymen, who co-opted new members whenever a vacancy occurred. The Thirteen had entire control of the finances; they apportioned stipends be- tween the ministers, and were responsible for the upkeep of the meeting-houses. Earlier in the year this body had sent a deputation to the Exeter ministers, urging them to preach "in defence of the Eternal Deity of Jesus Christ," a doctrine which had been solemnly affirmed in the Westminster Con- fession and which presbyterians, no less than catholics and anglicans, had hitherto regarded as a fundamental tenet of their faith. In their capacity of trustees the Thirteen were bound to consider the legal aspect. They had reason to fear that unitarianism would jeopardize the whole structure built up since the Toleration Act, for the benefits of the act were expressly withheld from "any person that shall deny in his preaching or writing the doctrine of the blessed Trinity" as declared in the Thirty-Nine Articles. Accordingly they now approached the three chief suspects, Peirce, Hallett, and Withers, and asked them for an unequivocal statement of their personal beliefs. Receiving no satisfaction, they wrote up to Salters' Hall, the presbyterian headquarters in London, for

[1] These were: James's Meeting, named after James II, Bow Meeting, and the Little Meeting nearly opposite Friars Gate. There was also a congrega- tionalist meeting, founded by Lewis Stucley, in Castle Lane.

advice. The advice they got was to consult a panel of local ministers. They then appealed to seven members of the Exeter Assembly,[1] who replied that denial of the divinity of Christ was a disqualifying error which would justify congregations in withdrawing from their ministers. The lay trustees thereupon decided that Peirce and Hallett should preach no more in any of the three chapels, and orders were given not to admit them for the future.[2]

It will be useful to glance at the composition of the body which laid its ban on the two heretics. A vacancy at this juncture had reduced the Thirteen to twelve. Their names are admirably representative of the class which formed the mainstay of the presbyterian cause. Henry Walrond, member of an old landed family, squires of Bradfield near Uffculme, was a freeman of the city, resident in the cathedral close. Thomas Jeffery and Edmond Cock were prominent serge manufacturers, masters of the company of Weavers, Fullers, and Shearmen in 1707 and 1709 respectively. It was to the last-named that John Baring, ancestor of the great banking family, apprenticed himself when he settled in Exeter, a Lutheran immigrant from Bremen. Baring subsequently married the daughter of another member of the committee, John Vowler. Vowler and four of his colleagues are described as grocers: that is, wholesale dealers.[3] The rest of the twelve were merchants, James White being one of the richest in the city. His stock was valued at £500, and Samuel Munckley's at £400, in the assessment of 1690. John Pym was a freeman of the city, as was also Francis Lydston, a neighbour of Vicary and Vowler in the rich central parish of St Petrock. The Vicarys and Munckleys were connected by marriage. Though debarred from municipal office by the Test Act, all these worthies took an active part in the commercial life of Exeter. They formed a prosperous com-

---

[1] John Ball of Honiton, William Horsham of Topsham, Samuel Hall and John Moore of Tiverton, John Walrond of Ottery, Josiah Eveleigh of Crediton, and Joseph Manston of Lympstone.

[2] Murch, *op. cit.*, pp. 388–98; A. Gordon, *Addresses Biographical and Historical*, 1922, pp. 123–35.

[3] The others were Benjamin Brinley (assessed in 1690 on stock valued at £400), Anthony Vicary (stock £200), John Stephens, and Mark Burridge. I am indebted to Dr W. G. Hoskins for these particulars of the Thirteen.

munity, cemented by frequent intermarriage as well as by religious sympathy.

Peirce and Hallett, after their ignominious dismissal, formed a schismatic congregation, and their adherents, to the number of about three hundred, built them a chapel at the Mint.[1] This was not the only local schism. John Fox, who had signed a manifesto drawn up by Peirce and his friends, relates that in consequence "there was scarce any for me to preach to, besides the poor remains of a few broken congregations."[2] Nor was the disruptive effect confined to Devonshire. The appeal of the Thirteen to Salters' Hall gave rise to the most acrimonious debates at headquarters, which divided the adherents of both denominations throughout the kingdom. Perhaps the most damaging consequence of the Exeter dispute was that it threw a searchlight on the evasive tactics by which Peirce and his friends tried to mask their heterodox opinions. It is impossible to acquit the presbyterian clergy of a fundamental lack of candour. Many of them were sailing under false colours. They were supposed by their flocks and by the public at large to hold the belief set forth in the Westminster Confession, and their orthodoxy was further guaranteed by the subscription to the Thirty-Nine Articles required of them under the Toleration Act.[3] Yet the Exeter Assembly deliberately framed its constitution in terms which left its members free to cherish any number of private reservations concerning the Westminster creed; and many of the most eminent presbyterian divines, including the great Calamy himself, never signed the Articles at all, though they allowed it to be supposed that they had done so.[4] The strong measures taken by what Peirce called "the

[1] This chapel, opened about a year after the schism, was sold to the Wesleyan Methodists in 1810.

[2] DA xxviii, 1896, p. 147. Fox also tells us that his father-in-law Isaac Gilling, minister of Newton Abbot, stood by Peirce, "so that above one half of his hearers fell from him."—ibid., p. 157.

[3] Articles xxxiv, xxxv, and xxxvi, and the opening clause of Article xx, were excepted from this requirement.

[4] John Fox relates that Calamy "took the first opportunity when I was alone with him to tell me that I need not trouble myself" about subscribing the Articles, "for if I could keep myself to myself (that was his expression) there was no occasion of subscribing to them at all, none would ever suspect an omission in such a case as this, or think of examining about it. He said it was

western Inquisition" did not suppress heterodoxy, but in the long run merely drove it underground. During the next three generations unitarian opinions, though seldom openly avowed, gained ground among the clergy; and ultimately the entire theological structure of presbyterianism fell to pieces, eaten away by this insidious dry rot.

II

Thus far we have traced in outline the history of Devonshire presbyterianism as a whole. Turning now from the general to the particular, let us see if the record of a single congregation will furnish us with rather more precise and vivid impressions of nonconformist men and manners in the heyday of presbyterianism and in its period of subsequent decline.

In this field, as in so many others, the town of Tavistock provides a truly representative sample of the national experience. Dominated by the puritan earls of Bedford, it lay exposed from 1558 onwards to all the symptoms and tendencies that characterized the advance of left-wing protestantism throughout England. The court rolls of Elizabeth's reign show the machinery of seignorial control being set in motion to propel the earl's tenants onwards and upwards towards heights of godliness undreamed of in the bad old days of popery. Dancing, profanity, and bowl-playing all came under the ban. Recalcitrance on the tenants' part, though rare, was not unknown. Interrupted in the middle of a game of bowls, a certain Francis Stitteston exclaimed: "Tushe, I have played at bowls this daye, and I will playe agayne, in spyte of all my lordes officers. Where is there a man thatt dare to saye mee naye?"[1]

---

his own case, he had never taken them, and was never suspected" (DA *loc. cit.*, p. 137). Most nonconformist writers have condemned these subterfuges. Thus, Murch (*op. cit.*, p. 399) remarks on the "unworthy compromises" to which the heterodox resorted in concealing their opinions on important topics; and A. H. Drysdale says "the aspect of dishonesty and cowardice it seemed to wear" was the worst feature of the movement.—*History of the Presbyterians in England*, 1889, p. 512.

[1] Hurdwick court roll, 28 March 1573. He was fined 4d. at the next lawday.

Absence from church was punishable with a fine, and worse might befall if the culprit stayed away "on account of religion," or in other words because he preferred some other form of worship.

In 1638 the puritan George Hughes, a preacher of considerable reputation, became vicar of Tavistock. The titles of his published works are characteristic, and in their way endearing. They include: *The Art of Embalming Dead Saints*, a funeral sermon; *A Dry Rod Blooming and Fruit-bearing, or, a treatise of the Pain, Gain, and use of Chastenings*; and *Væ-Euge-Tuba, or, The Wo-Ioy-Trumpet, Sounding the third and greatest woe to the Antichristian world, but the first and last joy to the Church of the Saints*. The occupation of the town by royalist troops towards the close of 1642 drove Hughes from Tavistock, and in March 1644 he was appointed vicar of St Andrew's, Plymouth. We have seen that under the Commonwealth he shared with Thomas Ford the leadership of the presbyterian party in Devon. Calamy says "no minister in the West had a greater influence among his brethren."[1] His departure left Tavistock to the ministrations of a successor whose name is unrecorded. Towards the end of 1649, the vicarage being again vacant, the earl of Bedford announced that he would leave the inhabitants to make their own choice; and they, little suspecting what they were in for, chose the reverend Thomas Larkham.[2]

Born at Lyme Regis, and educated at Trinity Hall, Cambridge, Larkham, at the age of twenty-four, was instituted vicar of Northam, near Bideford. There he remained fourteen years, until his habit of vituperation made the place too hot for him. With suits pending against him in three or four different courts, he finally absconded from his parish and fled to New England, explaining afterwards that "episcopal tyranny, and tenderness of conscience" had forced him into exile. The settlers on the Pascataqua chose him for their pastor, and soon the whole colony was in an uproar, for, as Governor Winthrop

[1] *The Nonconformist's Memorial*, II, p. 60.
[2] For an excellent and fully documented account of Larkham by Mrs G. H. (afterwards Lady) Radford, see DA XXIV, 1892, pp. 96-146. In 1871 the Rev. W. Lewis published extracts from Larkham's diary, carefully removing all references to tobacco and strong drink. A second edition was printed in 1888.

observed, "he would take upon him to rule all, even the magistrates." After two stormy years, Larkham suddenly took ship for England, leaving his wife and three younger children behind him.[1] He is next heard of in Kent, where he created a disturbance by invading another minister's pulpit. Lord Lisle took him as his chaplain to Ireland, whence, early in 1648, he returned with Sir Hardress Waller's regiment. For a short time in April the regiment was stationed at Tavistock; afterwards it moved to Plymouth. In November of the following year a court martial dismissed him from his post of regimental chaplain for defaming several of the officers. It was this born trouble-maker whom the parishioners of Tavistock now invited to become their shepherd.

Larkham was no presbyterian. His fondness for tobacco, drink, and bowls showed that he was no puritan either; and in church matters he was an Independent *sui generis*, always on the worst of terms with his fellow clergy. He called the disciples of his predecessor Hugonites, and refused to let Hughes preach at Tavistock. When his people failed to keep pace with his frequent remodellings of the ecclesiastical system, he reviled them as grunting swine, serpents, vipers, scabs, ninnihammers, purguinions, squint-eyed fools, sons of witches, and the devil's dishclouts. (To someone who enquired what ninnihammer meant, he explained that it was something nine times worse than a cuckold.[2]) A deputation of seventeen parishioners waited on him at his house and asked him to forbear these "horrid imprecations"; they were excommunicated for their pains. In a pamphlet called *Naboth* he endeavoured to justify his conduct. A group of leading parishioners retaliated with *The Tavistock Naboth proved Nabal*.[3] Then Larkham brought out a reply entitled *Judas Hanging Himself*; but

---

[1] "It was time for him to be gone," says Winthrop, "for not long after, a widow which kept in his house, being a very handsome woman and about fifty years old, proved to be with child, and being examined, at first refused to confess the father, but in the end she laid it to Mr Larkham."—*Journal History of New England*, 1908, II, p. 89. There are several references in Larkham's diary to his departure from New England, but he never says why he left.

[2] *A Strange Metamorphosis*, p. 8.

[3] London, 1658. The only known copy of this tract is in the Bodleian Library.

his opponents had the last word, and delivered it at some length, with *A Strange Metamorphosis in Tavistock, or the Nabal-Naboth improved A Judas, set forth in reply to a Scurrilous Pamphlet called Judas etc., whose attestations are invalidated, contradictions cleared, and lyes put up again into his own Bag.*[1]

By the time Charles II returned to England, Tavistock had had enough of Larkham. The earl of Bedford demanded his resignation, and presented an anglican in his place. For nearly three months the ejected preacher lay in gaol at Exeter. Then he came back to Tavistock, and after an interval went into business as an apothecary. Besides inheriting money through his wife, he had made a good deal by sermons preached at a distance from Tavistock before his ejection, and had boasted that "he could live if he never received Parish Maintenance more."[2] The parish register records his burial on the 23rd of December 1669.

Each of the three contending systems, anglican, presbyterian, and independent-congregational, had now had free play at Tavistock; and the majority of the inhabitants were clearly of opinion that two were enough. Some of Larkham's adherents, unaware perhaps how far removed he was from poverty, continued to make him gifts of money after his ejection; thus, he notes in his diary, 16 September 1662, "Mrs Brownsdon, in acknowledgement of her duty, though I could not do the office of a pastor, gave me 10s.; the first present I received since August 18th last past." Similar offerings were brought from time to time by his former deacons; but with the Clarendon Code in force it would have been highly dangerous for him to "do the office of a pastor," and although the contrary is still sometimes asserted locally, there is no evidence that he braved the law to this extent after his imprisonment at Exeter. All the indications are that Larkham's cause died with him.[3]

---

[1] There is a copy in the British Museum. Neither of Larkham's tracts is known to exist.

[2] He also said he had five hundred books in his study. An inventory drawn up after his death showed chattels valued at £78 3s. 4d., including books to the value of £20 (Matthews, *op. cit.*, p. 315).

[3] The statement that Larkham continued to officiate in premises lent by the earl of Bedford seems to have been first made in print by Murch (*op. cit.*, p. 483) on information supplied by the Rev. W. Evans a hundred and

Under the Declaration of Indulgence a licence was taken out for a congregationalist meeting in the house of David Condy at Tavistock, but a few months later this was amended to "presbyterian."[1] With Larkham out of the way, the Tavistock dissenters rallied again round the "Hugonite" banner. They were encouraged by occasional visits from William Pearse, a minister in presbyterian orders who had been vicar of Dunsford under the Commonwealth and after his ejection took up farming at Strashleigh in the South Hams.[2] By 1687 they were numerous enough to require the services of a resident pastor. Taking advantage of the new Declaration of Indulgence issued by James II in that year, they invited an elderly Cornish minister, Henry Flamank, to settle in the town. Flamank was a presbyterian of the sternest and most orthodox type, one who would sooner remain under proscription than accept 'liberty of conscience' from a popish king. Not that he ran any serious risk. He had been turned out of the rectory of Lanivet, which, having never received anglican orders, he was no longer qualified to hold, but after that he had been left in peace to exercise his ministry in the family mansion at St Enoder.[3] At Tavistock he could rely on the protection of the duke of Bedford, whose personal sympathies were wholly presbyterian. The duke indeed soon gave a signal proof of his good will. About a year after the passing of the Toleration Act the lease of the abbey site expired with the death of Sir John

---

fifty years after the event. It is contradicted by the silence of Calamy, of Larkham's own diary, and of the Bedford estate records. Cf. DA xxiv, 1892, p. 143.

[1] Lyon Turner, *op. cit.*, ii, pp. 540, 566.

[2] The statement in *Calamy Revised*, p. 384, that Pearse "preached at Tavistock for nineteen years to a congregation meeting in the great hall of Tavistock Abbey by permission of the earl of Bedford," must be understood in the light of facts mentioned in the same article: viz., that after his ejection Pearse farmed at Strashleigh for some years, returned to Dunsford and was licensed as a preacher there in 1672, then went to London, where in 1683 he was arrested and imprisoned. Calamy's own statement (*Continuation*, i, p. 340) that Pearse "preach'd privately in *Tavistock* as he had Opportunity," is probably true to fact. The earl of Bedford was not in a position to lend the abbey buildings, for down to 1690 the premises were held on life-lease by Sir John Maynard.

[3] Matthews, *op. cit.*, p. 200; cf. Calamy's *Continuation*, i, p. 212.

Maynard, and a new lease was granted to Thomas Willesford; but from this the duke excepted one large building, the misericord, or dining hall of the monastic infirmary, which he placed at the disposal of Flamank's congregation. In 1701 the second duke gave a formal lease of the hall, thenceforth called the Abbey Chapel, to the local presbyterian trustees, who thus acquired a place of worship in the heart of Tavistock, venerable for its antiquity, and capable of seating more than two hundred people.[1]

Flamank died on the 8th of May 1692, from his deathbed recommending the congregation to elect Jacob Sandercock as his successor. The new minister, a Cornishman of humble origin, had been trained by Matthew Warren, and preached for some time at Tiverton, where he acquired a wife with a fortune of seven hundred pounds.[2] According to his cousin John Fox, "he had in him very much of the wisdom of the serpent, and so thoroughly understood the temper of his people that he knew how to govern them absolutely and to please them at the same time . . . He was one of those Dissenting Ministers who believ'd the cause of separation to be the cause of God, and this made him sit the easier with his people, who were of the true old stamp." A pillar of the Exeter Assembly, "he had many presents and many sums of money given both from private people and the fund, to both which he was constantly recommended by Mr Walrond and some other leading ministers . . . He was very often employ'd in reconciling family differences, in which he had very good success, for great deference was paid to his judgement by people of all denominations in the town."[3]

[1] It is highly improbable that Maynard, a cautious octogenarian lawyer, would have connived at this use of the hall before the passing of the Toleration Act. On the other hand, Prince, who published his *Worthies of Devon* in 1701, refers to what he misnames "The Refectory or Common Hall of the Abbey" as "lately converted into a nonconformist meeting-house" (*op. cit.*, p. 619), so the conversion evidently took place several years before the granting of a formal lease. We may safely date it 1691. The register of baptisms begins in the following year.

[2] The statement in Murch, *op. cit.*, p. 490, that he served as Flamank's assistant at Tavistock from 1688, is not borne out by Fox (DA xxviii, 1896, p. 151), or by Sandercock's own "List of those baptized since my coming to Tavistock," the first entry in which is dated 19 September 1692.

[3] DA xxviii, 1896, pp. 151, 152.

Sandercock's career is altogether typical. A successful ministry, an advantageous marriage, and the backing of well-to-do adherents lifted many of his colleagues from obscure beginnings to positions of respectability and political influence. Under Sandercock the congregation of the Abbey Chapel is said to have included forty-one borough and twenty-two county electors.[1] "He was very often consulted in politics, for he was able to direct the votes of most of his hearers in time of an election, and therefore was in high esteem with the old Sir Francis Drake, by whom he hath often provided for such of his friends as wanted places."[2] He died on the 24th of December 1729, having "maintain'd his power and reputation to the end."

The most conspicuous member of his congregation was a purse-proud *parvenu* named Jacob Saunders, who by marriage had acquired some property in the town. In 1716, on the death of Thomas Willesford, Saunders took over the lease of the abbey site, and proceeded to destroy the frater, chapter-house, and cloisters. On the foundations of the frater he built himself what his friends called a "neat house" and his enemies a "pompous dwelling," which cost upwards of £3000 and was still unfinished at his death. It seems to have been felt that in converting one monument of popery to nonconformist use and destroying the others, presbyterianism was in some obscure fashion scoring a point over the established Church. By his will Saunders left an annuity of four pounds to Jacob Saundercock.[3] His only son, baptized in the Abbey Chapel in 1717, died without issue in 1762, when the house and site reverted to the duke.[4]

In a letter to the duke's agent the next minister, Peter Jillard says: "His Grace's long and continu'd Services to the Town, and the Great unmerited Favours I have personaly receiv'd, engage me to use all that little Influence I may have,

[1] DA XXI, 1889, p. 158.
[2] Fox, *loc. cit.* On the political transactions of Sir Francis Drake, third baronet, of Buckland Monachorum near Tavistock, see Lady E. F. Eliott-Drake, *Family and Heirs of Sir Francis Drake*, 1911, II, pp. 34, 48, 52, 142, 144, 187, 197.
[3] P.C.C. Romney 220.
[4] Mellowed by time, and gothicized by the subsequent addition of battlements, the house is now the Bedford Hotel.

to persuade People to Gratitude, to be Friends to themselves, and not displease so Great a Man, so well able and forward to serve his Friends." The writer goes on to ask that his brother may be given a job at thirty or forty pounds a year. He deplores the behaviour of the inhabitants: "so much Rudeness, with no more Deference paid to Superiors."[1] Writing to his other friends, Mr Jillard frequently dilated on the immorality of Tavistock. "Whoever laments the wickedness of the age would look with an eye of peculiar pity and compassion on this town... Vice bears such an head there, no place I imagine more corrupt. The poor very numerous and wicked, and the rich [what did he expect?] far from being exemplary christians." (The parish register bears out this denunciation. It shows that the proportion of bastard to legitimate births, which had been as 1 to 68 in the seventeenth century, was 1 to 34 between 1687 and 1736, and in the succeeding fifty years 1 to 18.[2]) In the face of so much vice there was little that the minister could do; but against illiteracy he did make some headway. In the teeth of Bishop Trelawny his predecessor had opened a charity school; this Jillard now revived, with Sandercock's daughter for schoolmistress. Presently twenty children were being instructed by means of the *New London Method of Teaching*, Janeway's *Token for Children*, and Isaac Watts's *Songs for Children*—these last "universally relished among the people of the church and meeting." "Most of the parents belong to the established Church," but they "are only desired to carry their children to public worship, chusing what mode they please." In addition to the schoolchildren, companies of boys and girls "come alternately every week to my house. I endeavour to make my discourses from the scripture more acceptable by giving now and then a Bible."[3]

In 1741 this zealous minister resigned and betook himself to a new post at Bristol. For a year and more his place remained vacant; then the leaders of the congregation applied to Dr Doddridge, who recommended a former pupil of his,

[1] Bedford Office, Bloomsbury, Devon Letters 1738–63 (P. Jillard to Robert Butcher, 19 September 1738).

[2] Barham, 'Remarks on the Abstract of the Parish Registers of Tavistock', in *Journal of the Statistical Society of London*, IV, 1841, p. 41.

[3] T. Gibbons, *Memoirs of the Rev. Isaac Watts, D.D.*, 1780, pp. 450–59.

Samuel Merivale, at that time minister of Sleaford in Lincoln-shire, though not as yet ordained. Merivale, having just been crossed in love, welcomed the opportunity of removing to a new and distant scene. The stipend offered him was £45 a year. It sounds little enough, but as one of his colleagues after-wards wrote: "A single man with that income could, even so lately as 1772, make a decent appearance and be able to spare something for charitable purposes. There was hardly any Dis-senting congregation without some one or more families ready to board a minister, not desiring to gain, aiming only at a fair recompence. Many ministers, at that time, in the West of England, were boarded by respectable persons for less than £20 per annum; and in good farm houses, a much smaller sum was accepted for being found every thing like other members of the family. A gratis horse was frequently at the service of ministers."[1] This was the case with Merivale: "I have already," he writes not long after his arrival, "received presents to the amount of £5 or £6; viz: cloth for a coat, a great coat, new shirts, a pair of handsome silver buckles, half a hogshead of cider, horses for every journey I have undertaken, and the promise of a watch."[2] The real difficulty was not financial, but intellectual and moral. For, as he confessed in a private letter, his notions concerning the Trinity were not as settled as he could wish. He would have to satisfy the Exeter Assembly before he could be ordained, and in uttering a trinitarian pro-fession of faith, "perhaps I should not understand the words just in the same sense with those who require this declaration from me." However, once past that ordeal, "I would en-deavour to behave in such a manner as might give as little offence as possible, and not expose me to suspicion with regard to my orthodoxy."[3] In the upshot all went well. He arrived in Tavistock at the beginning of March 1743, and when he had preached for four or five Sundays, received a formal invitation, signed by about sixty people, to remain as their minister. Having contrived to satisfy the Assembly, he was ordained in August 1744 and began to administer the sacraments. He men-tions 140 as the number of his first communicants.

[1] Murch, *op. cit.*, p. 337.
[2] Anna W. Merivale, *Family Memorials*, Exeter, 1884, p. 12.
[3] Merivale, *op. cit.*, pp. 10, 11.

Lodging in the house of James Hillow, whom he describes as "a rich old humorist" and "the most substantial tradesman in the town," he presently began courting Hillow's niece, a young woman of "Disposition strictly virtuous and pious," with a fortune of eight hundred pounds and a face "pretty much disfigured with the Small Pox." For four years the lovers corresponded, styling themselves Fidelio and Charissa. After their marriage Charissa bore him three children, then inherited from her cousin, a Bideford attorney, an unexpected additional fortune of something like £10,000 and herself died shortly afterwards.

Samuel Merivale is a representative figure, alike in his matrimonial prosperity and in his cautious heterodoxy. Informed that some of the Plymouth dissenters required a minister to preach the doctrine of the Westminster catechism, he exclaimed: "A fine Time I should have of it indeed, to be called upon to satisfy them of my Belief of those Doctrines. I would as soon subscribe the Articles of Pope Pius' creed as the answers in that Catechism relating to the Trinity, Original Sin, Justification etc."[1] To Priestley he wrote: "I have been generally cautious enough to avoid engaging in disputes on the subject of the Trinity, and to keep my freest thoughts pretty much to myself."[2] But such reticence was becoming less and less necessary, for unitarianism was rapidly gaining ground. In 1753 Micaiah Towgood induced the Exeter Assembly to relax its insistence on orthodox Christology. Seven years later a plan was formulated for establishing a new academy at Exeter, to be conducted "on liberal principles" by Towgood and other like-minded divines, and in 1762 Merivale quitted Tavistock to join the staff of this institution.

The register of baptisms begun by Sandercock enables us to compare the numerical strength of the presbyterian and anglican bodies in Tavistock. The following table gives the decennial totals of baptisms at the Abbey Chapel under Sandercock, Jillard, Merivale, and Merivale's two successors,

---

[1] *ibid.*, p. 36.

[2] *ibid.*, p. 44n. In worldly transactions Merivale displayed the strictest probity. At the least prosperous stage of his career he voluntarily accepted responsibility for his mother's business debts. It may be added that his *Daily Devotions for the Closet* have been many times reprinted.

Bernard Dowdell (1762–72) and Theophilus Edwards (1772–94), and also the totals of those registered at the parish church.[1]

Date	Church	Chapel	Date	Church	Chapel
1697–1706	859	158	1747–1756	731	144
1707–1716	672	123	1757–1766	754	129
1717–1726	692	131	1767–1776	758	180
1727–1736	742	126	1777–1786	851	201
1737–1746	737	105	1787–1796	976	117

Theophilus Edwards, a Welshman trained at Carmarthen, left in 1794 to succeed an avowed unitarian at the Mint, Exeter.[2] It will be noticed that the figures show a marked decline towards the close of his ministry. The contagion of doctrinal uncertainty had now spread from the ministers to their congregations, and when Edwards left, a schism took place between the adherents of his successor, William Evans, and the more orthodox minority. The latter withdrew from the Abbey Chapel, and on the 3rd of July 1796 formed themselves into a new society, denominated congregationalist, with William Rooker as their pastor.[3] The baptismal statistics, compared with previous decades, illustrate the effect of the schism on the body that still worshipped in the Abbey Chapel.

Date	Church	Chapel
1797–1806	1150	58
1807–1816	1602	53
1817–1826	1534	54
1827–1836	1477	51

[1] The figures for the parish church were published by Barham, *loc. cit.* Those from the chapel are compiled from the register, which is now at Somerset House (Non-Parochial Registers, Devon, 94).

[2] Murch, *op. cit.*, p. 403.

[3] DA LXXIX, 1947, p. 169; DCNQ XXIII, 1948, p. 251.

According to James Manning, Evans was one of those ministers who "preferred the old name of Presbyterian," though
teaching a qualified unitarianism; he believed that Christ was
something more than man and less than God.[1] Some of his
flock considered that he might have been more strenuous in
his endeavours "to gain proselytes to the doctrine of the Divine
Unity."[2] After his retirement in 1840 a meeting of subscribers
decided that "the Society as it at present exists had better be
dissolved." In the following year it was reconstituted as
"The Tavistock Unitarian Church."[3] This body, holding a
creed which men like Hughes, Flamank, and Sandercock
would have abhorred, continued to meet in the Abbey Chapel
until 1949, but from 1840 onwards the presbyterian name has
been extinct in Tavistock.[4]

In this local disintegration we behold the symptom of a
general decline. By putting the episcopal office into commission the clergy had staved off disaster for a while, but as soon
as their provincial Assembly relaxed the doctrinal tests with
which it had safeguarded ordinations, all the dykes went down.
There was no liturgical bond of union, for the presbyterians
had always valued extemporary above liturgical prayer. The
original objection to articles of belief imposed by an anglican-
minded State widened into an objection to fixed beliefs of any
kind. Boundless freedom of speculation became the watch-
word.[5] Merivale's academy at Exeter was little more than a
theological debating society; it had to be closed down as soon
as he was in his grave. In 1792 a "Society of Unitarian Christians" was founded at Exeter. Nine years later the old Exeter
Assembly decided to meet only once a year instead of twice as
formerly. With a greatly reduced membership, it now had
little business to transact.[6] The prosperous class which had
been its mainstay began to see in ecclesiastical dissent the germ
of social disruption. When the unitarian minister at Exeter

---

[1] BM Add. MS. 9429, fo. 24(James Manning to Lysons, 15 March 1819).
[2] DCNQ XXIII, 1948, p. 290.
[3] *ibid.*, pp. 315, 316.
[4] Since 1962 the chapel has been used by a congregation known as the
Christian Brethren.
[5] This phase is well discussed by Drysdale, *op. cit.*, pp. 509–20.
[6] Murch, *op. cit.*, p. 555.

celebrated the execution of Louis XVI with a Jacobin sermon, Merivale's son indignantly withdrew and set up a private conventicle in his own house. His grandson finally conformed to the established Church.[1] Many other families took the same road. For those who were not minded to do so, there was a choice of exits. Quakers made their appearance at Tavistock in 1702, and in 1746 the brothers Wesley preached there. The minutes of the Methodist Annual Conference held in London two years later reveal the existence of Methodist societies at Tavistock and Devonport, as well as at seven Cornish centres. Among the Wesleyan Methodists of Tavistock in the nineteenth century it is interesting to come upon the name of Flamank.[2] The old cause lay stone-dead, its mantle torn to shreds by a disparate multitude of legatees.

[1] Merivale, *op. cit.*, pp. 133, 190.
[2] DA LXXVIII, 1946, pp. 239–41; LXXIX, 1947, p. 169.

INDEX

P

225

Fox, John, 211, 217
Fraunceis, James, 178
Frithestan, bishop of Winchester, 29
Fromund, John, 169, 173
Fugh, John le, 185
Furnellis, Geoffrey de, 93

Gara Bridge, 18, 25
Garvo, cardinal de, 173, 177
Gaue, Ralph, 183
Geoffrey, abbot of Tavistock, 95, 96
Geoffrey Fitz Baldwin, 102
Giffard, Robert, 99, 102; Walter I, 98, 102; Walter II, 99; Walter III, 99; William, 99
Gilbert, archdeacon of Totnes, 183, 184
Gildas, 87
Glastonbury Abbey, 63n., 70–88
Godfrey, abbot of Tavistock, 96, 97
Godric, 42, 43
Gorges, Eleanor and Ralph de, 131
Grandisson, John de, bishop of Exeter, 172, 174–81
Gray, H. L., 129, 130, 134, 136, 147, 150
Gulworthy, 154, 155, 160, 161, 162
Gytha, mother of Harold, 98

Halberton, 144
Hale, John, 202
Hallet, Joseph, 208, 209–11
Halsinger (Braunton), 142
Hanslope, Michael de, 91
Harbourne, River, 17, 18
Harding, son of Eadnoth, 92, 106
Hartland, 98
Hatherleigh, 97, 114n., 118, 124, 192, 206
Haverfield, F., 13
Hean, patricius, 84
Hemyock, 148
Henry I, 90, 91, 92, 99, 106, 107, 155
Henry II, 94
Henstill, 33, 40
Herbert, abbot of Tavistock, 96, 102, 161, 182
Herbert Fitz Herbert, 99
Higden, R., 85
Hillow, James, 221
Hittisleigh, 49, 52
Holcombe Rogus, 59

Honiton, 104n., 207
Hooker, Richard, 198
Hoskins, W. G., 46, 56, 210n.
Hospitallers, 109, 110, 111, 116, 118
Hughes, George, 200–2, 213, 214, 223
Huish, North, 23, 25
Huish, South, 15, 23, 24
Hulham, 137
Hurdwick, 106, 108, 111, 118, 142, 160, 163n., 193
Hutton, Matthew, 89

Ideford, 136
Ilchester, Richard of, 97, 98
Indract, St, 73, 84, 85
Indulgence, Declaration of, 202, 216
Ine, king of Wessex, 62, 73, 84
Inwoldesleghe, William de, 175, 176, 179
Irish colony at Glastonbury, 74–84

Jackson, Prof. Kenneth, 15
James I, 198
James II, 203, 209n., 216
Jeffery, Thomas, 210
Jerrold, D., 129
Jewel, John, bishop of Salisbury, 197, 198
Jewel, Melanchthon, 198
Jillard, Peter, 218, 219
John XXII, Pope, 169
John, King, 120, 156, 184
John, bishop of Exeter, 184
John, vice-archdeacon of Cornwall, 182–84
John, Eric, 19, 36
Joseph of Arimathea, 87, 88
Jourdain, Ignatius, 199

Kemble, J. M., 11–13
Kenn, 137
Kennerleigh, 43, 51
Kent, Nathaniel, 142
Kentisbeare, 144
Kenton, 104n., 143, 144
Ker, N. R., 57n., 67
Kernet, William de, abbot of Tavistock, 116
Kingsbridge, 16, 22, 24, 25, 27, 104n., 187, 202
Kingsteignton, 137
Kingston, 13, 14, 15, 23, 143